LESSONS LEARNED FROM LEADING ENTREPRENEURS

Case Studies in Business & Entrepreneurship

TODD A. FINKLE, PH.D.

For information:

Dr. Todd A. Finkle

Pigott Professor of Entrepreneurship

Gonzaga University

502 E Boone Avenue

Spokane, WA 99235-009

e-mail: finklet2000@yahoo.com

Printed in the United States of America

ISBN-13: 978-0-615-52277-7

1. Entrepreneurs: Case Studies; 2. New Ventures: Case Studies; 3. Entrepreneurship: Case Studies; 4. Family Business: Case Studies; 5. Franchising: Case Studies. 6. Entrepreneurial Financing: Case Studies. 7. Small Business Acquisitions and Valuations: Case Studies. 8. Business Strategy: Case Studies. 9. Entrepreneurial Personality: Case Studies. 10. Corporate Entrepreneurship and Innovation: Case Studies. 11. Small Business Management: Case Studies.

I would like to dedicate this book to my family, especially my wife Patti who has been extremely supportive of me through the process of writing the book.

Acknowledgements

This book would not have been possible without the support and guidance from a number of people. First, my co-authors on some of the cases: Drs. Michael Mallin, Andrew Thomas, Tim Wilkinson, Bob Figler, Ken Dunning, and Phil Greenwood.

I am very grateful for the support of the faculty, staff and donors of Gonzaga University. Mr. Mark Pigott endowed the position I currently hold at Gonzaga entitled the "Pigott Professorship in Entrepreneurship." I would also like to thank the following individuals who played a role in the assistance in the production of this book: Drs. Bud Barnes, Ken Anderson, Kent Hickman, Dan Lawson, Vivek Patil and Dan Stewart.

I would be remiss if I did not mention Dr. Robert Pricer (retired from the University of Wisconsin at Madison) my entrepreneurship professor and mentor. Dr. Don Kuratko (Indiana University) has also played a vital role in my professional development. My entry into the academic field of entrepreneurship in the 1980's was an early stage in the development of the field and they both helped me navigate the land mines of academia throughout the years.

I would also like to thank Drs. Ray Bagby, William Sandberg, J. Kay Keels, and James Chrisman who have all been affiliated with the journal *Entrepreneurship Theory & Practice* at some point in my career. They all played an important role in helping me develop quality cases that are located in this book. I would also like to thank Trey Carland for his assistance in allowing me to reproduce a few cases that I wrote for his journal, the *Journal of the International Academy for Case Studies*. I would also like to thank Rajah Bose for allowing me to use the picture myself.

Finally, I want to sincerely thank Dr. Paul Buller from Gonzaga University for his collegiality, guidance, support, and resources to help me finish this book. He was kind enough to allow me extra resources (Richard Scoresby), our joint graduate assistant, to finish the book. Thank you, Richard, for your hard work and dedication to the project.

CONTENTS

Preface

Case studies have historically been a very effective way to teach people about the various principals of business and entrepreneurship. This case book integrates theory with practice by taking over 15 years of research on a variety of large and small companies including Apple, Berkshire Hathaway, Google, Waste Management, Inc., Blockbuster, Republic Industries and many others. The reader will learn not only about the companies, but also about the founding entrepreneurs of these companies. The cases serve as an excellent benchmark for people wanting to learn about the various facets of business with an emphasis on entrepreneurship and business strategy.

This case book can be used by both practitioners and educators. All of the cases in the book have been through a rigorous peer review process in leading academic journals except for one.

This case book integrates theory with practice by examining the success stories of some of the most successful entrepreneurs of our generation: Steve Jobs & Apple, Inc.; Warren E. Buffett & Berkshire Hathaway, Inc.; Sergey Brin & Larry Page of Google, Inc.; and Wayne Huizenga's Waste Management, Inc., Blockbuster, Inc. & Republic Industries.

Steve Jobs and Apple, Inc. start your journey by investigating the life and passion of entrepreneur, Steve Jobs. Jobs and his friend, Steve Wozniak founded and built Apple, Inc. into a multi-billion billion dollar company. The case illustrates the rise, fall, and current state of Apple, Inc. The case illustrates how individual passion, determination, and innovation are critical elements in the start up and growth of a business. Apple, Inc. is arguably one of the most innovative technology companies to emerge in the last three decades. Apple, Inc. is responsible for bringing to market such products as the Macintosh computer and laptop, iPod and iTunes, iPhone and iPad.

Warren E. Buffett & Berkshire Hathaway, Inc. discusses the history and background of one of the most successful entrepreneurs, Warren E. Buffett, and the company that he built, Berkshire Hathaway, Inc. The investment genius of Buffett who is affectionately called the "Oracle of Omaha" is examined. The progressions of Buffett's entrepreneurial endeavors are followed from his youth, college, Wall Street, investment partnership, and Berkshire Hathaway. The case discusses Buffett's keys to success, including his value system, and investment philosophy. The case creates an investment philosophy that Buffett uses when he performs due diligence on potential investments. Readers are also exposed to the entrepreneurial personality of Buffett as well as the current investments that Buffett has made. The case also gives an in-depth analysis of the background, personality, and history of Warren E. Buffett. Buffett's childhood and psychological makeup are discussed as well as the various influences in his life.

Corporate Entrepreneurship & Innovation in Silicon Valley: The Case of Google, Inc. examines one of the most successful technology companies of all time. The Google case documents the background and education of the founders, Sergey Brin and Larry Page. The case takes the reader through each of the steps leading up to the start-up and growth of Google, Inc. The case also looks at the background and infrastructure of Silicon Valley, philanthropic endeavors of Google, past and current business strategies utilized by the company, and keys to success.

Wayne Huizenga: The Tale of a Classic Entrepreneur examines the childhood, background, and education of Wayne Huizenga. Huizenga's career started with a single garbage truck in 1962, from which he was the only person in history to build three Fortune 1000 companies and six NYSE-listed companies. H. Wayne Huizenga had become one of the richest men in the world with a net worth of $2.3 billion. The case documents Huizenga's life as a self-made entrepreneur who made his fortune in garbage hauling (Waste Management, Inc.), video rentals (Blockbuster, Inc.), automobile sales and rentals, security alarms, professional sports franchises, hotels, portable toilets, lawn care, bottled water, pest control, billboards, and machine parts washing service (Republic Industries, Inc.). He is also the only person to ever own three professional sports teams in a single market.

Beano's Ice Cream Shop is a classic case study that has appeared in several leading textbooks all over the world. This case study involves the following in regards to the acquisition of a franchise: franchise selection process, negotiations with a potential investor, and valuation. The case acquaints the reader with: (1) the difficulty of starting new ventures, (2) the sources of advice for acquiring a franchise, (3) the opportunity costs of becoming self-employed, and (4) the complexities of finding and negotiating with a financial partner.

The Crowne Inn: The Case of a Family Business in Turmoil is a case that focuses on valuation and succession issues. The owner of the family business passed away and the stock of the company moved into the wife's name. The son was attempting to purchase the family business from the mother. The family's attorney, Bobby Free, devised three possible solutions to the problem: (1) have the son pay a lump sum, (2) have the son pay a smaller lump sum and a set amount per month, or (3) sell the business outright to an outside party.

Timko Export Management Company: The Dynamics of International Entrepreneurship focuses on the dynamics related to small-to-medium sized manufacturing enterprises going global. The case examines the economic risk. Specifically, the case follows how a global manufacturer grew, competed, and managed the risks involved with operating an international business and the preventative measures it may have taken to protect itself in the event of a currency crisis.

West Point Market: Managing a Challenge from the EEOC illustrates how an independent family business dealt with a charge of racial discrimination from a federal agency. Issues of race, politics, and finance complicate this challenge. The case provides an example of a real-life potentially devastating decision-making situation. The case is unique in the sense that it was initiated with a commissioner's charge from the EEOC in Washington, DC. Commissioner's charges rarely attack small businesses. They almost always target larger organizations like Toyota, Procter and Gamble, and PepsiCo. Russell Vernon, a second-generation owner and manager of a successful upscale specialty store, West Point Market, must decide whether to go to court, settle or reconcile with the Equal Employment Opportunity Commission. He firmly believes that he is innocent. If he chooses to settle the case out of court, he could be construed as a racist. If he chooses to go to court and loses, his business may not survive. The future of his family business depends on the outcome of his decision. This emotionally charged situation is presented as a management decision that must be based on an analysis of the facts. The case discussion will be greatly enhanced if the students who, no doubt, will already have positions on "the role of governmental agencies" and "the use of racial-based quotas in the workforce" are taught to take a cost/benefit approach to a matter that they may have strong feelings about.

Should I Buy the Jerry's Famous Frozen Desserts Chain? focuses on the acquisition of a very successful frozen dessert retail chain. The purpose of the case study is to acquaint the reader with the flow of events that occur during the initial stages of a small business acquisition. The case evaluates the various forms of debt and equity financing that are available and how to structure a deal to purchase the chain.

About the Author

Dr. Todd A. Finkle is the inaugural Pigott Professor of Entrepreneurship at Gonzaga University, which is ranked in the top 25 of all entrepreneurship programs by *U.S. News and World Report*. Dr. Finkle is a noted business professor, consultant, and speaker. Dr. Finkle comes to Gonzaga after playing a leadership role in the creation and development of an entrepreneurship program, which was ranked by *Entrepreneur* magazine three times.

Dr. Finkle has founded four businesses, a non-profit, and grew up in a family-owned business. He has consulted worldwide with businesses, universities, and organizations in the development of their organizations.

Dr. Finkle was recently invited for a second time to visit billionaire Warren Buffett for a day at his Corporate Headquarters in Omaha. Both times Finkle was extremely innovative in his approach to get invited with his respective universities and students. The first time he wrote an in-depth case study on Buffett and Berkshire Hathaway over two years and received a letter from Buffett within 10 days. The second time he assigned a class project to his students to come up with creative products that would entice Buffett to invite Gonzaga University to Omaha. Finkle sent three of the products to Buffett and he responded within five days and invited Gonzaga to Omaha.

Dr. Finkle recently finished in 1st Place for the "Most Innovative Pedagogy for Entrepreneurship Education Award" at the United States Association for Small Business and Entrepreneurship (USASBE) annual conference. The awards were based upon a non-profit organization called the Entrepreneurship Education Consortium, which Dr. Finkle and six other universities co-founded. Finkle was also a former runner-up for the most innovative entrepreneurship educator in the world by the Academy of Management and a MOOT CORP® Fellow through the IC² Institute at the University of Texas at Austin.

Dr. Finkle has produced more than 185 books, papers, presentations, and grants related to entrepreneurship. His research has been recognized nationally and internationally in the top entrepreneurship and strategic management journals and books. His research has been recognized internationally in leading journals such as the *Journal of Business Venturing, Entrepreneurship Theory and Practice, Journal of Small Business Management,* and *Psychology and Marketing*. He received his BS degree in Life Sciences from the University of Nebraska-Lincoln, an MBA from the University of Wisconsin at Madison and a Ph.D. in Entrepreneurship/Strategic Management. Dr. Finkle has visited top entrepreneurship programs throughout the U.S. to enhance his entrepreneurial skills.

STEVE JOBS AND APPLE, INC.

Todd A. Finkle, Gonzaga University
Michael L. Mallin, The University of Toledo

Finkle, Todd A. & Mallin, Michael (2011). Steve Jobs and Apple, Inc. *Journal of the International Academy for Case Studies*, 16, 7, 31-40.

CASE DESCRIPTION

The primary issues in this case involve business startup and management, and are appropriate for entrepreneurship and management courses. A secondary issue demonstrates how personal drive and motivation are critical components of successfully managing and growing a business, thereby making this case appropriate for discussion on the topic of strategic management. The case chronicles the life and passion of entrepreneur, Steve Jobs – illustrating the rise, fall, and current state of the Apple Computer Company. The case has a difficulty level 2 and is designed to be covered within one (75 minute) class period. The required preparation time is about 2 hours. It is appropriate for small business, entrepreneurship, or management classes. The purpose of this case is to illustrate to students how individual passion, determination, and innovation is a critical element in business start up success and also to stimulate critical thinking in terms of future direction for a company in a struggling economy.

CASE SYNOPSIS

The Apple Computer Company is arguably one of the most innovative technology companies to emerge in the last three decades. Apple, Inc. is responsible for bringing to market such products as the Macintosh computer and laptop, iPod and iTunes, and most recently, the iPhone. The success of the company can be traced primarily to a single individual - founder, Steven Jobs. Jobs and his friend, Steve Wozniak founded and built Apple into a 32 billion dollar company. The company enjoyed much success during the past decade with its stock price hitting a high of $200 in 2007. More recently, the stock has retreated to around $90 causing a massive decline in shareholder wealth. Today, Apple CEO Steve Jobs is faced with the challenge of resurrecting his once dominant company in light of weak economic conditions and sub-par personal health. The case chronicles the life of Steve Jobs, the rise of Apple, Inc. and his personal challenges as CEO of the company to continue to provide innovative products to a marketplace of technology avid consumers.

INTRODUCTION

In late 2008, amid the swirling news reports and rumors of his failing health, Steve Jobs, the co-founder, Chairman, and CEO of Apple, Inc. issued the following statement to his employees at Apple's international corporate headquarters in Cupertino, California. "We are in the worst economic environment since the Great Depression. However, we are determined to continue to make Apple the most innovative company in the world while increasing shareholder wealth. While hundreds of companies are firing employees, we have no intention of doing so. We will overcome this challenging economic environment and remain a strong innovative company. While others will decrease spending we will increase spending on R&D and come out way ahead of our competition in the long run."

Jobs co-founded Apple Computer with Steve Wozniak in 1976. After founding Apple, Jobs was fired by the company's board of directors 10 years later at age 30. After his termination, he went on to create two more companies. During this period Apple went through three different CEOs and their stock price dropped to $2 a share. As a result, Jobs was invited back to join the company as CEO. Not only did Jobs rejuvenate Apple, but it flourished. Jobs led the company to the forefront with cutting edge products and their stock price grew to around $200 a share by 2007. However, in 2008 Apple's stock price had dropped to around $90 due to the recession around the world. Fortunately, Apple had an abundance of cash (approximately $9 billion) on hand with no debt. The company was one of the few companies, large or small, that was able to operate with virtually no debt.

After his speech, Jobs walked into his office and sat down. Based on current economic conditions around the world, he wondered what his next steps should be to increase shareholder's wealth. Apple never issued dividends and this policy worked well for them over the years. However, Jobs wondered what he should do next to increase the firm's profitability.

STEVEN PAUL JOBS

Steven Paul Jobs was born on February 24, 1955, in San Francisco, California. Growing up in Mountain View, the heart of Silicon Valley, he exhibited behavior problems while in elementary school. During fourth grade, Job's teacher would bribe him with candy and money in order to curb his behavior. Reflecting back on these years, Jobs recounts that if such behavior continued, it would "absolutely have landed me in jail" (Leander, 2008). He found school to be so easy that he was able to skip 5th grade and move directly into Middle School. He found middle school chaotic and persuaded his parents to move to Los Altos in 1967 where he could attend the much nicer Cupertino Junior High School. This area (Los Altos, Cupertino, and Sunnyvale), was full of engineers and with this emerged many young startup companies (e.g., Hewlett-Packard).

Job's introduction to the world of electronics came during High School with the discovery of electronic hobby kits, Jobs realized that the electric world was not as complicated as it first seemed and that electronics was an interesting field. It quickly became his passion. He began attending lectures conducted by the Hewlett Packard Company (HP). This further fueled his appetite for the field and eventually he found summer employment at HP. It was here that he met future co-founder and co-adventurer Steve Wozniak.

Jobs graduated Homestead High in 1972 and eventually attended Reed College, a small regional liberal arts school in Portland, Oregon. He lasted a semester before dropping out. Though no longer enrolled, he still attended classes that interested him. Not having a place of his own, he frequently slept at the home of friends. Collecting and recycling cans provided him with money and free meals were obtained by walking across town to the Hare Krishna temple.

Jobs eventually returned home and got a technician job at the Atari Company, which paid him a mere $5 hourly wage. He was viewed by his fellow workers as arrogant and this caused problems with several employees. As a result, he was scheduled to work the night shift when there were fewer people. This enabled him to sneak his friend, Steve Wozniak into the building so that they could play favorite video games. In exchange for this kind gesture, Wozniak assisted Jobs with the technical side of his job. Unbeknownst to either of them, this was the beginning of a partnership that would form the beginnings of Apple Computer Company.

STEVE WOZNIAK AND STEVE JOBS

Steve Wozniak's passion for electronics stemmed from his father's career as an engineer at Lockheed Martin (Wozniak, 2006). Wozniak formally studied electrical engineering at the University of Colorado at Boulder and De Anza College near his hometown in the bay area of California. Ironically however, he did not earn a degree from either college. Instead, he withdrew from college and began building computers with a friend. To help fund his interest in building computers, Wozniak learned how to construct a "blue box" from an article he read in Esquire Magazine. Blue boxes were handheld devices used to make free, illegal phone calls. Steve Jobs contributed to this partnership by providing the component parts. These parts cost Jobs $40 and the blue boxes were mainly sold to students in dorms and door-to-door for $150. Jobs and Wozniak shared the profits from the sale of the blue boxes. Though this venture was profitable, they ceased operations for fear of a police crackdown.

Around this same time, Atari had been gaining popularity through the sales of their video games and was looking to advance their success even further. Jobs, who was still working for the company, was approached by Atari founder, Nolan Kay Bushnell. Bushnell invited Jobs to develop the circuitry that would transform the popular game, Pong into something more innovative. Jobs was given four days to create this new game called Breakout. Knowing that this project was beyond his capabilities, he contacted his friend, Steve Wozniak to help him accomplish the task. Wozniak was excited to take on the challenge. Four days was not a lot of time to accomplish what needed to be done given that Wozniak was now working full time at HP. To accomplish the task, Wozniak worked at HP during the day and then worked with Jobs during the evenings and nights. In four days time, they accomplished what they sat out to do. They were both very proud of their work. They created a viable game that took a high level of technical skill and did it under relatively intense time pressure. The two split the $700 compensation paid by Atari, however to Wozniak the real compensation was the sense of accomplishment and excitement realized by completing the task. Looking back on this experience Wozniak claims, "I would have done it for a quarter" (Linzmayer, 2004).

After the success of creating the Breakout circuitry, Wozniak and Jobs began to attend meetings of the Homebrew Computer Club together. The club consisted of other electronics enthuiasts. The meetings consisted of members presenting news of new innovations in the electronics world and discussed updates of the progressions made by members in creating their own computers. During one of these meetings Wozniak presented an apparent working model of a computer that could be viewed on a television set, as opposed to a costly monitor. Immediately, Jobs had a vision and plan for this innovation which was to sell the blue prints to a company that would manufacture the computer.

The two decided to pitch the idea to their employers at HP and Atari. Both companies were impressed, but neither had the desire to take on the project. Jobs' business-savvy took over as he persuaded Wozniak that this creation was good enough that they should try to produce and market the computer on their own. The main problem was that they lacked the capital to get the operation started. Both made sacrifices. Jobs provided $1500 by selling his Volkswagen van and Wozniak contributed $250 by selling his HP financial calculator. While driving along a strip of highway the two began to discuss what they would call their new company. Jobs, who still owned part of a 220 acre, farm in Oregon, said, "We should call the company Apple Computer."(Young and Simon, 2005).

APPLE COMPUTER

Apple Computer was incorporated in 1977 and went public in 1980. The atmosphere and the excitement surrounding the public offering was immense as it turned out to be the largest public offering in the last 24 years. Jobs' share of the company was worth around $82 million at the stock's lowest point in 1982 and far surpassed this mark as the stock price rose throughout the life of the company.

Jobs was more than just an aggressive businessman. His approach to marketing was intellectual and methodical. This approach was exemplified by the details that went into packaging of the original Macintosh (Mac) Personal Computer (PC). He gave the final approval on all software that ran on the machines and provided much input on how television ads were presented and the message that they were meant to convey.

Jobs' attention to detail, confidence, and controlling personality were his strongest assets (although some also felt these characteristics were his biggest flaws). His propensity to dictate decisions and manipulate people was noticed by other executives of the company. This persona and mentality led to occasional differences of opinion and ironically, eventually led to a divorce from the company he co-founded.

Job's had an erratic temper due to his drive for perfection. According to some, the inventor and innovator was a "control freak, egomaniac, and fearsome tyrant" (Deutschman, 2000). Others described him as transforming from a charismatic leader to an ego-maniac and tyrant with a "wicked tongue" (Kahney, 2008). In addition, Jobs thought of most people as "bozos" (which ironically led to the user-friendliness of Apple's products). All of this fueled Apple's Board of Directors decision to ask Jobs to resign from the company. Jobs was essentially forced out due to a clash of egos and a dispute about the power structure of the company between himself and CEO John Sculley. Steve Wozniak also chose to leave the company citing reasons that he felt that his efforts were being wasted in favor of new directions that upper management wanted the company to pursue.

LIFE AFTER APPLE

Jobs did not leave without a plan. He founded a new computer company to compete with Apple. The NeXT Company, marketed computer systems to schools and other teaching organizations. He began by touring campuses across the country and surveying school stakeholders to understand their needs. Jobs inquired about the pros and cons of currently used computers and learned what the ideal computer should offer to create efficiency and harmony among its users. Five key employees from Apple joined Jobs in his new venture. Apple threatened a lawsuit against Jobs for stealing employees but it was eventually settled out of court.

However, through eight years of its existence the company was only able to sell 50,000 computers. NeXT was relegated to downsizing and was solely involved in distribution of its software packages.

In 1986, Jobs bought the majority share of a puttering computer graphics company, called Pixar, for $10 million from George Lucas. Lucas, the famed creator of the Star Wars movies, was looking to sell of some of his assets to fund his divorce. Jobs saw a lot of promise in Pixar. At the time Pixar specialized in systems that enabled and enhanced computer graphic imaging. One of their strategies for marketing the systems was creating short movies featuring computer animation capabilities. The short films became popular in the industry and at least one of the short films won an Academy award for Best Animated Short Film in 1988 (Tin Toy). Though the short animations received attention and recognition, the company still had trouble selling their systems. So, in 1988 Jobs and Pixar decided to focus on developing imaging software capabilities and market them to companies to produce animated commercials (Tropicana, Life Savers and Listerine were some of the first brands to contract Pixar to produce commercials).

Pixar's big break came after approaching Disney to distribute an hour long animated film written and created by Pixar. Disney surprisingly responded with an offer for Pixar to create a screenplay for a feature length film. Disney put up a modest budget and retained most interests in the revenue earned through a three-film deal. After the release and success of Toy Story, Jobs took the company public and offered 6.9 million shares at its IPO. This move provided the bargaining power for Jobs to negotiate a bigger piece of the profits from Disney. In exchange for Pixar's co-financing of additional movies, Disney agreed to a new five film agreement which gave Pixar a much bigger share of revenues. Such titles such as *Toy Story* (I & II), *A Bug's Life*, *Cars*, and *The Incredibles* highlight the impressive resume of Pixar Animation Studios under Jobs' leadership. Toy Story alone brought in $358 million in worldwide theatre revenue (Linzmayer, 2004).

People in the industry knew that the deal was made possible because of the charisma, confidence and negotiating talents of Jobs. Pixar executive Ed Catmull said "It took somebody of Job's stature to get us a parity deal with Disney" (Linzmayer, 2004). Former Pixar Marketing Director Pamela Kerwin said "He had the brains, energy, and chutzpah to protect Pixar's interest. He enabled us to negotiate as equals" (Linzmayer, 2004). Jobs investment and financing of Pixar was rewarded handsomely. Through his investment he was awarded 30 million shares of Pixar worth around $1 billion.

JOBS RETURN TO APPLE

Although Jobs had left Apple years ago and had no official title or duties he still retained substantial amounts of stock in the company and served as part time advisor. Since his departure in 1985, there were three permanent CEOs and the stock price reached a low of $2. Subsequently, all of those CEOs were forced to resign. By 1997 and desperate for a new leader that could revitalize Apple, the board of directors approached Jobs with an offer to rejoin the company as their CEO. Reluctantly, he decided to take on some temporary leadership roles while a search for a new CEO was conducted. The position eventually became more permanent.

To bring fresh ideas and perspectives, Jobs immediately replaced almost all the board members with hand-picked people. He then embarked on entering into an agreement with arch rival Microsoft. This involved a commitment by Microsoft to produce Microsoft Office and Internet Explorer versions that were compatible with Apple's Mac. Also as part of the agreement Apple agreed to create its Mac OS with Internet Explorer as its default browser. This was seen as taboo by many Apple loyalists, however Job's view was - "If you can't beat them, join them." To this point Microsoft had outsold, outperformed and outmaneuvered Apple at almost every stage of the recent PC movement. Instead of an obstacle, he viewed Microsoft as an opportunity.

Another strategic move initiated by Jobs was the "store within a store" concept. Apple partnered with CompUSA to create an entire department in each of Comp USA's 148 stores that offered only Apple products. Upon the opening of these "stores" the new Apple Power Mac computer line was offered. These computers contained new G3 processors created by IBM and Motorola. Next, the new Apple Store were introduced an online market place where customers could customize and purchase Apple computer systems. Both of these new initiatives were immediately successful. Since the implementation of the agreement with CompUSA, Mac sales at CompUSA stores had more than quadrupled and sales from the Apple stores topped $12 million within the first 30 days of its existence.

In an effort to reduce costs, Jobs decided to outsource manufacturing of some of the component parts used in making their hardware. In addition, in an effort to reconfigure the product distribution strategy, Apple expanded the number of outlets that it sold its computers and accessories. This move provided Apple more exposure to a larger audience. In the years to come, Apple enjoyed success with innovative products including the iMAC, iPod, and iPhone.

iMAC, iPOD, and iPhone

One of the most popular releases by Apple after Jobs took over was the iMac Personal Computer (Kahney, 2004). It introduced a stylish design that caught consumers' attention and was difficult for stores to keep in stock. This innovative product combined the tower within the monitor. The system was not only attractive (available in a variety of colors), but it was known for its high level of performance at a competitive price (Linzmayer, 2004). However, despite the success of iMac, Jobs knew that Apple could not become complacent. Apple continued to update and introduce improvements to this computer system line and began offering new versions of their lap tops. After just one year of Job's return to Apple, the company announced a profit of $106 million - a vast improvement compared to the $1.6 billion in losses suffered over the previous 17 months (Kahney, 2004).

Although Apple flourished in the next few years under the leadership of Jobs, they lagged in the emerging MP3 market. They entered this market in 2001 with their own brand of music purchasing. Apple's iTunes was the first to introduce an online store for selling music downloads and quickly gained market share as consumers quickly took to this new and innovative way of obtaining music (Boddie, 2005). For as little as 99 cents per song, consumers could choose music from the major record labels and thousands of independent ones (Yoffie and Slind, 2008). To further enhance its popularity, Apple created its own Mac line of computers with CD burning capabilities. This laid the ground work for Apple's introduction of the iPod - one of the most popular and adapted products worldwide.

The iPod was released to compete with traditional MP3 players. The major advantages over MP3 players were its compact size, large storage capacity, and speed of uploading music. The original iPod was sleek and small, weighing only 6 ½ ounces. It had the ability to hold up to a thousand songs in its huge five gigabyte hard drive and could load one thousand songs in as little as ten minutes. Its battery could hold a charge for up to 10 hours and it simply integrated with its popular iTunes online store.

The original iPod was compatible only with Apple systems and software, but in 2002 the decision was made to release a version that also worked with the Windows operating system. This decision increased iPod sales worldwide. Within the first nine months of its release over one million units had been sold and through 2007, this number has since increased to 100 million. Industry prognosticators predict that by the end of 2009, an additional 200 million units will have been sold. Given these projections, Apple's iPod could is on track to become the largest selling consumer electronic product of all time (Mark and Crossan, 2005).

In 2007 Apple joined with AT&T and introduced the iPhone. The iPhone was marketed as the most sophisticated "smart phone". The iPhone had built in iPod music playing capabilities, a 3.5 inch high quality interactive touch screen, a 2 mega-pixel camera, GPS capability, and access to the Internet. Alliances with Yahoo!, You Tube and Google also enabled the phone to provide customized services and video enabled capabilities. Owners of the phone could choose between using AT&T's own web network or any other publicly offered internet access (e.g., web "hot spots"). Originally a 16 gigabyte iPhone sold for $499 and a smaller 8 gigabyte model was offered for $399. Despite the initial price, sales of the iPhone far exceeded predictions. Apple sold 270,000 iPhones in the first 30 hours of its U.S. debut. The iPhone was a big hit! Through its introduction, Jobs was able to negotiate very favorable agreements between Apple and AT&T. Branding, pricing and development of the iPhone were almost exclusively under the control of Apple. Also included in the partnership was a profit sharing agreement that gave Apple 10% of the revenue from iPhone internet subscriptions. Such an agreement was ground breaking in the cellular industry.

However, the introduction of the iPhone was not without its challenges. One problem was that AT&T's edge network was relatively slow. Another issue was that the iPhone came equipped with a battery that was not replaceable and users were not able to increase the memory capacity. In response to customer unhappiness Apple released a new version in 2008 that ran on a faster 3G network, however the short battery life and storage capacity issues still remained unresolved. The iPhone shortcomings have allowed competitors to gain some ground in the smart phone industry. For example, Japan's cellular phone market already is inundated with high performance smart phones that rival the iPhone. Though the iPhone continued to be a huge success, competitors were beginning to catch up. To maintain and grow their share, Apple must continue to be an innovator in the smart phone industry.

THE KEYS TO JOB'S SUCCESS AND FUTURE CHALLENGES

According to Steve Jobs, the reason why his companies have become so successful is because they hire the very best people in the world to work for them (Morrow, 1995). While this strategy is definitely a huge part of the success of Jobs and Apple, it definitely is not the only reason. Jobs, from a very young age, had a tireless work ethic, particularly toward his passion, electrical engineering. His work ethic was the motivation that led him to learn about the advanced technical knowledge of the computers that Apple has been building for decades. Jobs' vision to see the potential in the opportunities allowed him to take full advantage of these ventures. Jobs envisioned a revolutionary process to bring together the world of computers and the need of consumers. His innate ability to understand human behavior helped him to predict what people desired even before they knew it themselves. His business savvy, negotiation skills, and propensity to take risks enabled him to transform technology into companies that flourished.

Steve Jobs has undoubtedly brought success and riches to Apple and Apple's shareholders. This past decade has catapulted Apple to the position of being able to compete and possibly overtake perennial industry leader Microsoft. Company revenues have seen annual revenue increases progressively since 2003 (see Exhibit 1). However, the recent economic downturn has hurt Apple. The stock price has been on a steady decline. From August of 2008 to March 2009 Apple's stock price went from trading around $200 to trading around $90 (www.apple.com). In 2008 many industries, along with the U.S. economy as a whole, experienced unprecedented declines. Record high unemployment rates, and near collapses of the housing and automobile industries contributed to the current recession. Consumer confidence dwindled and as a result retail sales dipped steeply throughout the year. Job's challenge now is how to once again increase shareholder wealth for the company.

Exhibit 1: Apple, Inc. Financials Fiscal Year Ended Sep. 30, 2008

	9/30/2008	9/30/2007	9/30/2006	9/30/2005	9/30/2004	9/30/2003
Income Statement Analysis (Million $)						
Revenue	32,479	24,006	19,315	13,931	8,279	6,207
Operating Income	6,748	4,726	2,645	1,829	499	138
Depreciation	473	317	225	179	150	113
Interest Expense	Nil	Nil	Nil	Nil	3	8
Pretax income	6,895	5,008	2,818	1,815	383	92
Effective Tax Rate	29.90%	30.20%	29.40%	26.40%	27.90%	26.10%
Net Income	4,834	3,496	1,335	1,335	276	68
S&P Core Earnings	4,834	3,496	1,259	1,259	164	-119
Balance Sheet and Other Financial Data (Million $)						
Cash	24,490	9,352	6,392	3,491	2,969	3,396
Current Assets	34,690	21,956	14,509	10,300	7,055	5,887
Total Assets	39,572	25,347	17,205	11,551	8,050	6,815
Current Liabilities	14,092	9,299	6,471	3,484	2,680	2,357
Long Term Debt	Nil	Nil	Nil	Nil	Nil	Nil
Common Equity	21,030	14,532	9,984	7,466	5,076	4,223
Total Capital	21,705	15,151	10,365	7,466	5,076	4,223
Capital Expenditures	1,091	735	657	260	176	164
Cash Flow	5,307	3,813	2,214	1,514	426	181
Current Ratio	2.5	2.4	2.2	3.0	2.6	2.5
% Long Term Debt of Capitalization	Nil	Nil	Nil	Nil	Nil	Nil
% Net Income of Revenue	14.9	14.6	10.3	9.6	3.3	1.1
% Return on Assets	14.9	16.4	13.9	13.6	3.7	1.0
% Return on Equity	27.2	28.5	22.8	21.3	5.9	1.6

*Per Share Data, Income Statement Analysis, and Balance Sheet & Other Financial Date attained from https://research.scottrade.com/research/common/pdf.asp?sym=AAPL&reportType =SNPReport.

DISCUSSION QUESTIONS

1) Discuss the attributes that contribute to the success of Steve Jobs.

2) Discuss the attributes that contribute to the success of Steve Wozniak.

3) Is Steve Jobs an entrepreneur? Is Steve Wozniak an entrepreneur? If not, what are they?

4) What did Steve Jobs do to make Apple Inc. so successful? What grade would you give Jobs as an entrepreneur?

5) How do you as a consumer of Apple Inc. products view the company? How do you view the products that they sell? How are these views the same or different relative to how you perceive other technology companies (like Microsoft for example)?

6) What were the major problems and/or opportunities facing Apple, Inc. in 2008 and what recommendations would you make to Steve Jobs? Why?

REFERENCES

1. Angelelli, L. (2008). Steve Paul Jobs. *Computer Science Department NSF-Supported Education Infrastructure Project*, http://ei.cs.vt.edu/~history/Jobs.html (last viewed June 22, 2008).

2. Boddie, J. (2005). Has Apple Hit the Right Disruptive Notes? *Strategy & Innovation*, (July – August), 3-4.

3. Deutschman, A. (2000). *The Second Coming of Steve Jobs*. Broadway Books, New York.

4. Apple Company Profile, retreived from https://research.scottrade.com/research/com mon/pdf.asp?sym=AAPL&reportType=SNPReport.

5. Kahney, L. (2004). *The Cult of Mac*. No Starch Press Inc., San Francisco, CA.

6. Kahney, L. (2008). *Inside Steve's Brain*. Penguin Books Ltd., New York, 5.

7. Linzmayer, O. W. (2004). *Apple Confidential, The Real Story of Apple Computer*, Inc. New York, 4.

8. Mark, K. and M. Crossan (2005). Apple Computer, Inc.: iPods and iTunes. *Ivey Case Studies*, Richard Ivey School of Business, Ivey Publishing, 1-14.

9. Morrow, D. (1995). Oral History Interview With Jobs, April 20, 1995.

10. Moisescot, R. (2008). *Steve Jobs: A Biography by Romain Moisescot. All About Steve Jobs*, http://www.romain-moisescot.com/steve/home/home.html (last viewed June 22, 2008).

11. Young, J. S. and W. L. Simon (2005). *iCon Steve Jobs: The Greatest Second Act in the History of Business*. John Wiley and Sons, New Jersey, 35.

12. Wozniak, S. and G. Smith (2006). *iWoz: Computer Geek to Cult Icon: How I Invented the Personal Computer, Co-Founded Apple, and Had Fun Doing It*. W.W. Norton & Co., New York.

13. www.apple.com. Apple, Inc. Investor Relations, access 6-6-09.

14. Yoffie, D. B. and M. Slind (2008). Apple Inc., 2008. *Harvard Business School Case Studies*, February (708-480), 2-32.

WARREN E. BUFFETT AND BERKSHIRE HATHAWAY, INC.

Todd A. Finkle, Gonzaga University

Finkle, Todd A. (2010). Warren E. Buffett & Berkshire Hathaway, Inc. *Journal of the International Academy for Case Studies*, 16, 5, 61-88.

ABSTRACT

The case discusses the history and background of one of the most successful entrepreneurs, Warren E. Buffett, and the company that he built, Berkshire Hathaway, Inc. The investment genius of Buffett who is affectionately called the "Oracle of Omaha" is examined. The progressions of Buffett's entrepreneurial endeavors are followed from his youth, college, Wall Street, investment partnership, and Berkshire Hathaway. The case discusses Buffett's keys to success, including his value system and investment philosophy. Students are required to analyze the entrepreneurial personality of Buffett as well as perform a financial analysis on the company. Students are required to make recommendations on what Berkshire should do next in this fragile economy, which Buffett characterized as a recession.

The case gives an in-depth analysis of the background, personality, and history of Warren E. Buffett. Buffett's childhood and psychological makeup are discussed as well as the various influences in his life. The case is especially interesting because it follows the path of one of the most successful entrepreneurs of all time. Students have the ability to follow the life of one of the richest people in the world. The case also gives an overview of the stages that Berkshire Hathaway goes through leading up to 2008. Financial statements are provided so the students can perform financial ratio analysis and evaluate the company's financial disposition. The current economic crisis facing the U.S. is evaluated. Students are required to evaluate Buffett's investment philosophy and make recommendations as to what moves the company should make.

INTRODUCTION

It was Thursday, November 20, 2008 and Warren E. Buffett, 77 years old, was about to bite into his favorite meal at his favorite restaurant, a New York strip steak at Gorat's Steakhouse in Omaha, Nebraska. As he chomped down on the steak, he gleefully sloshed down the food with a cool, refreshing cherry coke. Buffett, fondly called the "Oracle from Omaha", had accomplished what few people on earth had done. He built one of the most successful companies of all time with a market capitalization of over $227 billion. As Chairman and Chief Executive Officer of Berkshire Hathaway, Inc. he had become the richest man in the world with a net worth of over $62 billion (Forbes, 2008).

From his humble beginnings in Omaha, Nebraska, Buffett had built a dynasty over four decades by buying out-of-favor stocks and businesses whose management he deemed superior (Hamilton 2008).

If you were an investor in 1956 and gave Buffett $10,000 to invest, today it would be worth more than $500 million. Exhibits 1-5 show Berkshire Hathaway's portfolio of businesses (Kilpatrick 2008, p. 13).

Exhibit 1 – List of Companies that Warren Buffett owned as of 9/30/2008

No	Company	No	Company
1	Acme Brick Company	27	International Dairy Queen, Inc.
2	Applied Underwriters	28	Iscar Metalworking Companies
3	Ben Bridge Jeweler	29	Johns Manville
4	Benjamin Moore & Co.	30	Jordan's Furniture
5	Berkshire Hathaway Group	31	Justin Brands
6	Berkshire Hathaway Homestates Companies	32	Larson-Juhl
7	BoatU.S.	33	Marmon Holdings, Inc.
8	Borsheims Fine Jewelry	34	McLane Company
9	Buffalo NEWS, Buffalo NY	35	Medical Protective
10	Business Wire	36	MidAmerican Energy Holdings Company
11	Central States Indemnity Company	37	MiTek Inc.
12	Clayton Homes	38	National Indemnity Company
13	CORT Business Services	39	Nebraska Furniture Mart
14	CTB Inc.	40	NetJets®
15	Fechheimer Brothers Company	41	The Pampered Chef®
16	FlightSafety	42	Precision Steel Warehouse, Inc.
17	Forest River	43	RC Willey Home Furnishings
18	Fruit of the Loom®	44	Scott Fetzer Companies
19	Garan Incorporated	45	See's Candies
20	Gateway Underwriters Agency	46	Shaw Industries
21	GEICO Auto Insurance	47	Star Furniture
22	General Re	48	TTI, Inc.
23	Helzberg Diamonds	49	United States Liability Insurance Group
24	H.H. Brown Shoe Group	50	Wesco Financial Corporation
25	HomeServices of America, a subsidiary of	51	XTRA Corporation
26	MidAmerican Energy Holdings Company		

Source: Links to Berkshire Hathaway Subsidiaries: http://www.berkshirehathaway.com/subs/ sublinks.html, Accessed December 3, 2008

Exhibit 2 – Companies in which Warren Buffett has a stock position, the amount of stock and its current value 9/30/2008

No	Ticker	Company	Industry	Shares	Value ($1000)	Weighting Percent
1	WFC	Wells Fargo & Company	Banks	290,407,668	10,899,000	15.59%
2	KO	Coca-Cola Company	Food & Beverage	200,000,000	10,576,000	15.13%
3	AXP	American Express Company	Financial Services	151,610,700	5,371,570	7.69%
4	KFT	Kraft Foods Inc.	Food & Beverage	138,272,500	4,528,420	6.48%
5	PG	The Procter & Gamble Company	Personal & Household Goods	105,847,000	7,376,480	10.55%
6	COP	ConocoPhillips	Oil & Gas Producers	83,955,800	6,149,760	8.80%
7	USB	U.S. Bancorp	Banks	72,937,126	2,627,190	3.76%
8	BNI	Burlington Northern Santa Fe Corp.	Industrial Goods & Services	63,785,418	5,895,690	8.44%
9	JNJ	Johnson & Johnson	Pharmaceuticals & Biotechnology	61,754,448	4,278,350	6.12%
10	MCO	Moody's Corp.	Industrial Goods & Services	48,000,000	1,632,000	2.34%
11	WMT	Wal-Mart Stores Inc.	Retail	19,944,300	1,194,460	1.71%
12	KMX	CarMax Inc.	Retail	18,444,100	258,217	0.37%
13	USG	USG Corp.	Construction & Materials	17,072,192	437,043	0.63%
14	BUD	Anheuser-Busch Companies Inc.	Food & Beverage	13,845,000	898,264	1.29%
15	CMCSK	Comcast Corp. Special	Media	12,000,000	236,640	0.34%
16	UNP	Union Pacific Corp.	Industrial Goods & Services	8,906,000	633,751	0.91%
17	GE	General Electric Company.	Industrial Goods & Services	7,777,900	198,336	0.28%
18	NKE	NIKE Inc.	Personal & Household Goods	7,641,000	511,183	0.73%
19	MTB	M&T Bank Corp.	Banks	6,715,060	599,319	0.86%
20	LOW	Lowe's Companies Inc.	Retail	6,500,000	153,985	0.22%
21	UNH	United Heal Group Inc.	Health Care Equipment & Services	6,379,900	161,986	0.23%
22	WSC	Wesco Financial Corp	Insurance	5,703,087	2,036,000	2.91%
23	IR	Ingersoll-Rand Company Ltd.	Industrial Goods & Services	5,636,600	175,674	0.25%
24	COST	Costco Wholesale Corp.	Retail	5,254,000	341,142	0.49%
25	NRG	NRG Energy Inc.	Electricity	5,000,000	123,750	0.18%
26	BAC	Bank of America Corp.	Banks	5,000,000	175,030	0.25%
27	WLP	WellPoint Inc.	Health Care Equipment & Services	4,777,300	223,424	0.32%
28	SNY	SanofiAventis	Pharmaceuticals & Biotechnology	3,903,933	128,323	0.18%
29	HD	The Home Depot Inc.	Retail	3,700,000	95,793	0.14%
30	GCI	Gannett Co. Inc.	Media	3,447,600	58,299	0.08%
31	IRM	Iron Mountain Inc.	Industrial Goods & Services	3,372,200	82,215	0.12%
32	STI	SunTrust Bank Inc.	Banks	3,204,600	144,175	0.21%
33	ETN	Eaton Corp.	Industrial Goods & Services	2,908,700	163,411	0.23%
34	TMK	Torchmark Corp.	Insurance	2,823,879	168,869	0.24%
35	WBC	WABCO Holding Inc.	Automobiles & Parts	2,700,000	95,958	0.14%
36	NSC	Norfolk Southern Corp.	Industrial Goods & Services	1,933,000	127,984	0.18%
37	WPO	The Washington Post Company	Media	1,727,765	961,351	1.38%
38	CDCO.OB	Comdisco Holding Co. Inc.	Industrial Goods & Services	1,538,377	14,530	0.02%
39	GSK	GlaxoSmithKline Plc.	Pharmaceuticals & Biotechnology	1,510,500	65,546	0.09%
40	UPS	United Parcel Services Inc	Industrial Goods & Services	1,429,200	89,882	0.13%

Source: Gurufocus.com: http://www.gurufocus.com/holdings.php?GuruName=Warren+Buffett

Exhibit 3 – Berkshire Hathaway's Portfolio: Numbers of Shares 9/30/2008

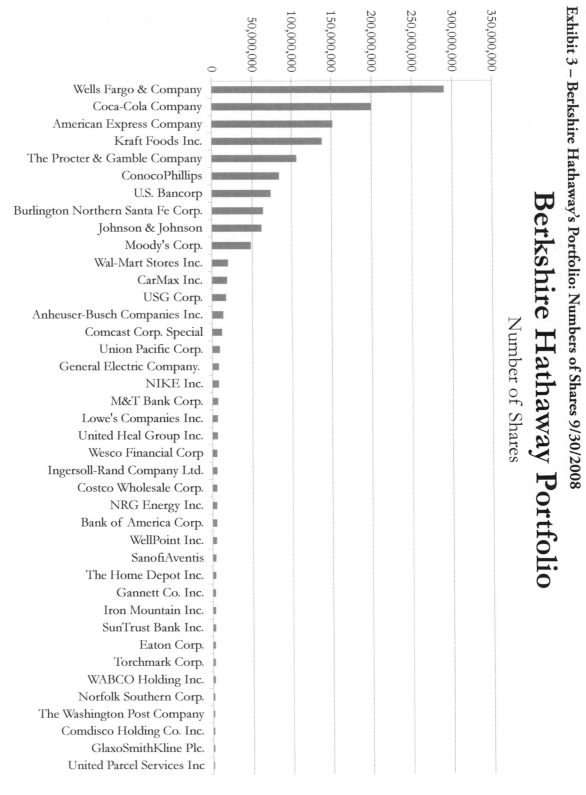

Berkshire Hathaway Portfolio

Number of Shares

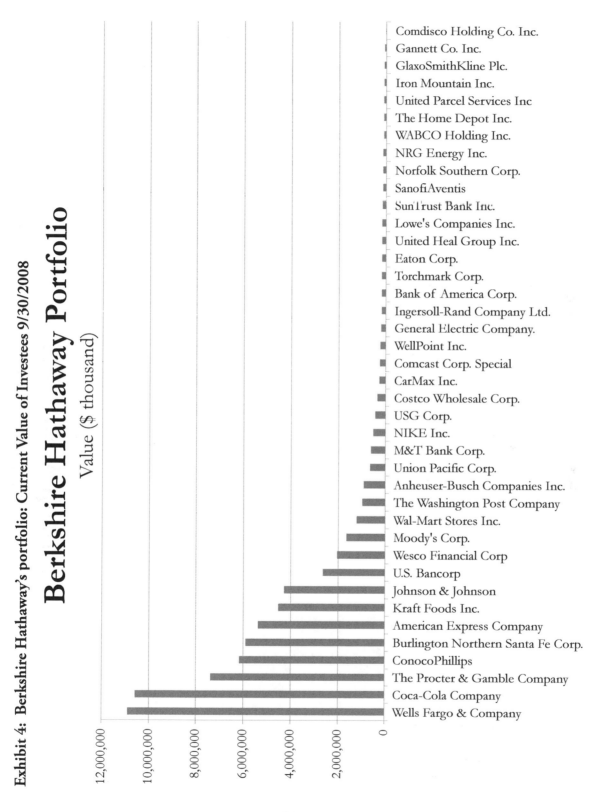

Berkshire Hathaway Portfolio

Value ($ thousand)

31

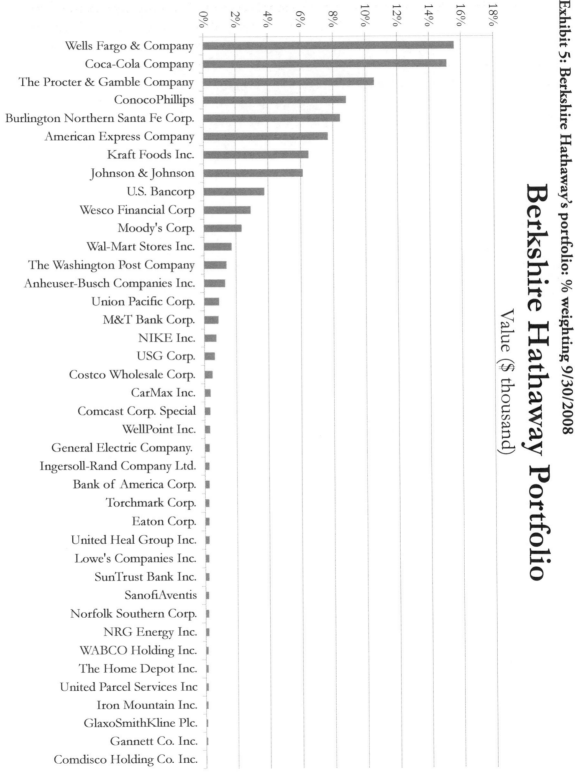

Berkshire Hathaway Portfolio

Value ($ thousand)

Wells Fargo & Company	
Coca-Cola Company	
The Procter & Gamble Company	
ConocoPhillips	
Burlington Northern Santa Fe Corp.	
American Express Company	
Kraft Foods Inc.	
Johnson & Johnson	
U.S. Bancorp	
Wesco Financial Corp	
Moody's Corp.	
Wal-Mart Stores Inc.	
The Washington Post Company	
Anheuser-Busch Companies Inc.	
Union Pacific Corp.	
M&T Bank Corp.	
NIKE Inc.	
USG Corp.	
Costco Wholesale Corp.	
CarMax Inc.	
Comcast Corp. Special	
WellPoint Inc.	
General Electric Company.	
Ingersoll-Rand Company Ltd.	
Bank of America Corp.	
Torchmark Corp.	
Eaton Corp.	
United Heal Group Inc.	
Lowe's Companies Inc.	
SunTrust Bank Inc.	
SanofiAventis	
Norfolk Southern Corp.	
NRG Energy Inc.	
WABCO Holding Inc.	
The Home Depot Inc.	
United Parcel Services Inc	
Iron Mountain Inc.	
GlaxoSmithKline Plc.	
Gannett Co. Inc.	
Comdisco Holding Co. Inc.	

0% 2% 4% 6% 8% 10% 12% 14% 16% 18%

32

Despite Buffett's personal and professional successes, his company was still faced with one of the toughest economic environments since World War II. The stock market was currently in a bear market. On November 20, 2008 Berkshire's stock price was down 48% from its high of $148,300 on December 6, 2007. This was surprising given that Berkshire Hathaway had advanced 17 out of the past 20 years and Buffett's stock had beaten the S&P 500 index on average 21% versus 10% since 1965. Exhibits 6-11 show the performance of Berkshire's stock price through the years.

Exhibit 6: Comparison of the Performance of Berkshire Hathaway's stock versus the S&P 500: 1965-2007

Year	In per-share book value of Berkshire Hathaway(1)	In S&P 500 with dividends included (2)	Relative results (1)-(2)
1965	23.8	10.0	13.8
1966	20.3	-11.7	32.0
1967	11.0	30.9	-19.9
1968	19.0	11.0	8.0
1969	16.2	-8.4	24.6
1970	12.0	3.9	8.1
1971	16.4	14.6	1.8
1972	21.7	18.9	2.8
1973	4.7	-14.8	19.5
1974	5.5	-26.4	31.9
1975	21.9	37.2	-15.3
1976	59.3	23.6	35.7
1977	31.9	-7.4	39.3
1978	24.0	6.4	17.6
1979	35.7	18.2	17.5
1980	19.3	32.3	-13.0
1981	31.4	-5.0	36.4
1982	40.0	21.4	18.6
1983	32.3	22.4	9.9
1984	13.6	6.1	7.5
1985	48.2	31.6	16.6
1986	26.1	18.6	7.5
1987	19.5	5.1	14.4
1988	20.1	16.6	3.5
1989	44.4	31.7	12.7
1990	7.4	-3.1	10.5
1991	39.6	30.5	9.1
1992	20.3	7.6	12.7
1993	14.3	10.1	4.2
1994	13.9	1.3	12.6
1995	43.1	37.6	5.5
1996	31.8	23.0	8.8
1997	34.1	33.4	0.7
1998	48.3	28.6	19.7
1999	0.5	21.0	-20.5
2000	6.5	-9.1	15.6
2001	-6.2	-11.9	5.7
2002	10.0	-21.1	31.1
2003	21.0	28.7	-7.7
2004	10.5	10.9	-0.4
2005	6.4	4.9	1.5
2006	18.4	15.8	2.6
2007	11.0	5.5	5.5
Compounded Annual Gain 1965-2007	**21.1**	**10.3**	**10.8**
Overall Gain 1964-2007	**400,863**	**6,840**	

Source: Berkshire Hathaway's 2007 Annual Report: http://www.Berkshirehathaway.com/ letters/2007ltr.pdf Accessed June 30, 2008.

Exhibit 7: Berkshire Hathaway, Inc. Class A Stock Price 1990-December 12, 2008

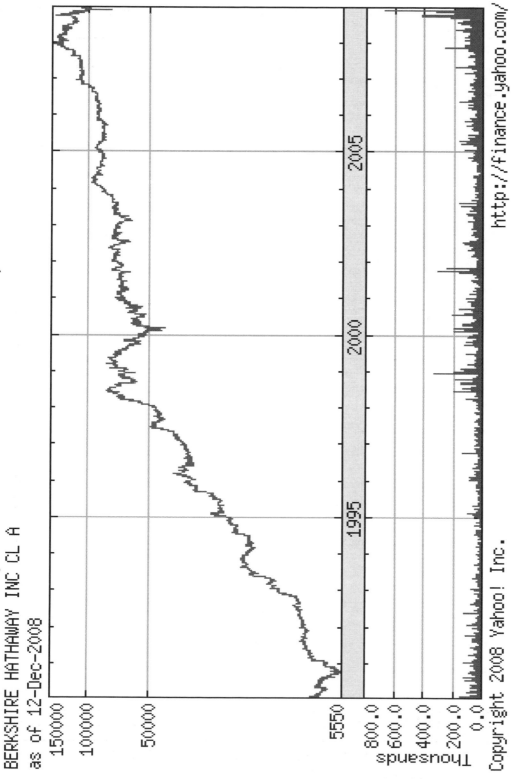

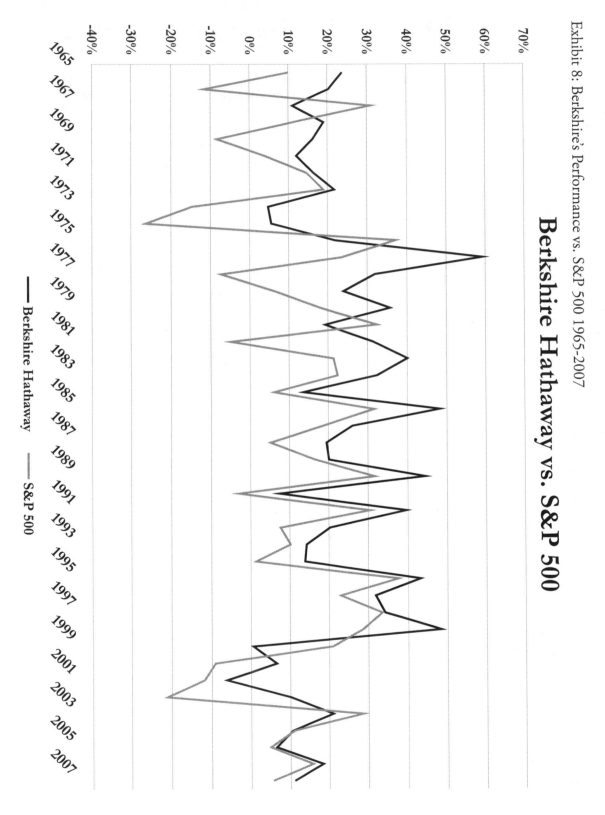

Shows how big of effect BH has on S&P 500

Exhibit 8: Berkshire's Performance vs. S&P 500 1965-2007

Berkshire Hathaway vs. S&P 500

—— Berkshire Hathaway   —— S&P 500

Exhibit 9: Berkshire's Performance vs. S&P 500 1965-2007

Relative Result: Berkshire Hathaway vs. S&P 500

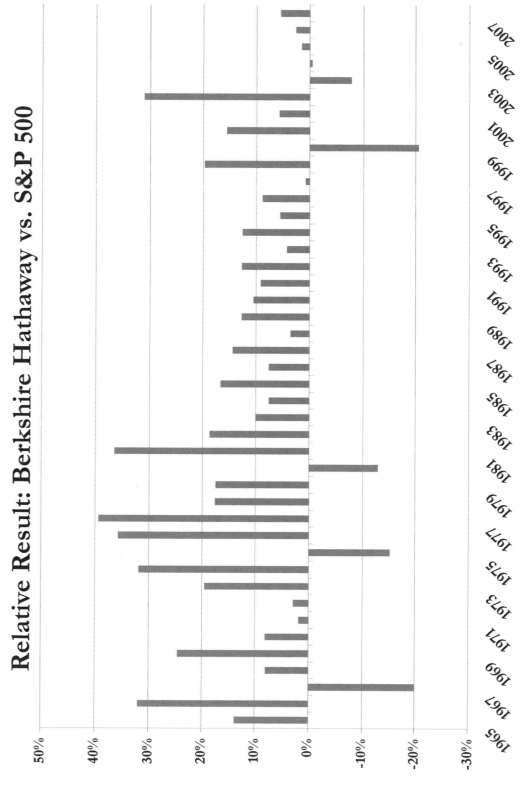

Exhibit 10: Compounded Annual Gain of Berkshire's Stock from 1969-2007

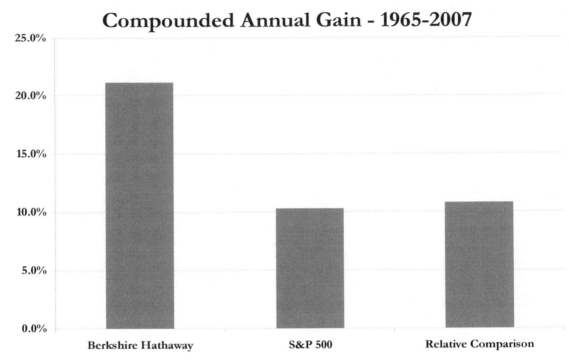

Compounded Annual Gain - 1965-2007

Exhibit 11: Overall Gain Berkshire's Stock versus the S&P 500 Index 1965-2007

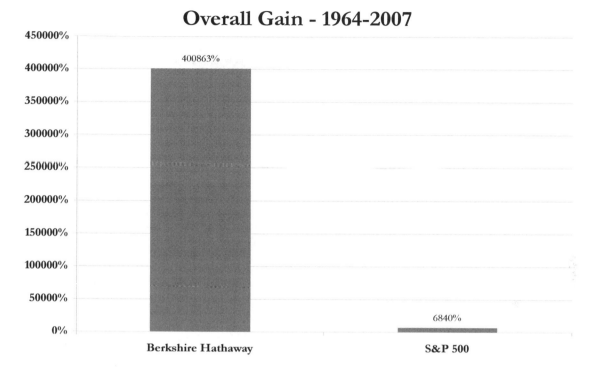

Buffett stated that even though the numbers do not state it, the U.S. is in a deep long-lasting recession (*USA Today*, 2008). The economy was dealing with a triple whammy; a drop off in consumer spending, the housing bust, and the subprime financial disaster (over leveraged firms, which eventually lead to the collapse of Bear Stearns, the first Wall Street investment bank since the Great Depression). These crises, combined with higher gas and food prices, fewer jobs, and personal income not keeping pace with inflation, all had Buffett concerned. Despite this, Buffett was optimistic. In a recent interview he stated, "We may not be better in five months, but I know we will be better off in five years" (Crippen, 2008).

Buffett typically excelled during downturns in the economy. His investment philosophy of value investing entailed buying undervalued assets when others were selling. Buffett used his entrepreneurial mindset and skills to seek out undervalued companies. Buffett wondered how Berkshire would handle this recession.

WARREN E. BUFFETT

Warren Buffett was one of three children born to Howard and Leila Buffett in the heart of the Midwest in Omaha, Nebraska in 1930 during the Great Depression. His family had roots in the United States dating back to the 1600's. Buffett's great grandfather started a grocery store in 1869 in downtown Omaha. Buffett and the future Vice Chairman of Berkshire Hathaway, Charlie Munger, would later go on to work in the grocery store.

Entrepreneurship flourished in the Buffett household. Not only did Buffett's father own his own stock brokerage called Buffett-Falk & Company, but he also sold diamonds on the side to hedge for inflation (Kilpatrick, 2008, p. 38). Buffett's youth was also influenced by his mother's family who owned their own print shop. But it was Buffett's great grandfather's grocery store that had a major impact on Buffett's future. He was paid $2.00 a day for 12 hours of work doing manual labor, which included sweeping floors and unloading trucks. It was here that Buffett decided that he did not want to do manual labor for the rest of his life.

This exposure to entrepreneurship from all of these family members rubbed off on Buffett at a young age. The first few cents Buffett earned came from selling chewing gum. And from the day he started selling, at age six, he showed an unyielding attitude toward his customers that revealed his later style. Buffett stated, "I remember a woman saying, I will take one stick of Juicy Fruit. I said, we do not break up packs of gum, I mean, I have got my principles." Making a sale was tempting, but not tempting enough. If he sold one stick to her, he would have four sticks left to sell, not worth the work or the risk. He made two cents profit per pack (Schroeder, 2008, parade.com).

After this venture, Buffett began purchasing six packs of coke from his grandfather's store for 25 cents and sold individual bottles for 5 cents (Miles, 2004). He also began to learn about investments from his father's library and had a paper route.

For Buffett's 10th birthday, his father took him to New York. A scene from the stock exchange dining room captured his imagination. According to Buffett, "We had lunch with At Mol, a member of the stock exchange. After lunch, a guy came along with a tray that had all these different kinds of tobacco leaves on it. He made up a cigar for Mr. Mol, who picked out the leaves that he wanted. I thought: It does not get any better than this." Buffett had zero interest in smoking a cigar, but he saw what hiring a man for such a frivolous purpose implied. It meant that, even while most of the country was still mired in the Depression, the cigar man's employer, the stock exchange, was making a great deal of money. That day, a vision of his future was planted. He wanted money. Buffett stated, "It could make me independent. Then I could do what I wanted to do with my life. And the biggest thing I wanted to do was work for myself" (Schroeder, 2008, *The Snowball*).

At age 11, he purchased three shares of Cities Service for $38. He later sold it for $40, only to watch it increase in value to $200 (Kilpatrick, 2008, p. 62). This was one of the first lessons that Buffett learned about patience in investing.

By age 13, Buffett filed his first tax form with the Internal Revenue Service (IRS). On the tax form he deducted his bicycle as a $35 expense. At age 14, he purchased 40 acres of land from his father for $1,200, which he rented out.

By the time Buffett was in junior high school his father moved the family to Washington D.C. because he was elected to Congress. While in Washington, Buffett continued his serial entrepreneurial endeavors. He started a pinball and peanut vending machine business called the Wilson-Coin-Operated Machine Company. At age 15, Buffett and a partner named Don Daly, purchased a pinball machine for $25 and placed it in a barber shop. They split the proceeds 50/50 with the owner. They were so successful that they purchased five more machines and eventually had sales of $200 a month (Steele, 1999, p. 28). Buffett also made $175 a month from his two paper routes. Additionally, he made money by going to golf courses and gathering lost golf balls, cleaning them, and then reselling them to golfers.

Another entrepreneurial venture in high school was with Don Daly, a high school friend. It involved purchasing a 1928 Rolls Royce for $350, fixing it up, and renting it out for $35 a day (Vick, 2000, p. 10). At age 16, Buffett graduated from high school 16th in his class of 350 at Woodrow Wilson High School (Steele, 1999, p. 29). After high school, Buffett sold the Wilson-Coin-Operated Machine Company for $1,200 and had savings of $6,000, which he used for college.

Buffett was not keen on going to college, but his father pushed him to attend the Wharton School of Business at the University of Pennsylvania. He spent two years there and complained that he was bored and more interested in the practical applications of the business world. So Buffett transferred to the University of Nebraska at Lincoln. He graduated with a Bachelor of Science degree from the University of Nebraska at Lincoln in 1950 at the age of 19 while working full-time.

Buffett then applied to the Harvard Business School, but was rejected because they thought he was too young. After reading the *Intelligent Investor* (1949) by Benjamin Graham, he decided that he wanted to study under Graham at Columbia Business School. He applied, was accepted, and studied under Graham and another famous investor, David Dodd, for one year. He earned a Master of Science degree and was one of Graham's prized students.

It was under Graham that Buffett learned his investment philosophy. He was exposed to Graham's two famous books, *Security Analysis* (1934) and *The Intelligent Investor* (1949). After graduation, Buffett told Graham that he would work for his firm for no pay. Unfortunately, Graham turned him down saying that he undervalued himself.

As a result, Buffett moved back to Omaha and worked as a stockbroker for his father's investment firm Buffett-Faulk and Company from 1951-1954. During this period, he was keeping in close contact with Graham and making investment recommendations to him.

Graham eventually hired Buffett at his firm called the Graham-Newman Corporation, from 1954-1956. At age 24, Buffet was making $12,000 a year at Graham's firm on Wall Street.

Over the next two years Buffett learned as much as possible from Graham. During those years, Buffett learned about arbitrage. In 1956, Graham retired and Buffett moved back to Omaha where he started his own investment partnership.

BUFFETT AND HIS PARTNERSHIPS

At age 26, Buffett made the decision that he wanted to be an entrepreneur again. Buffett knew that he was not a corporate man and envisioned working for himself. He had amassed savings of over $140,000 from his two years of working on Wall Street. Over the years, he had been approached by several family members for financial advice. As a result, he decided to create an investment partnership called Buffett Partnership, Limited.

According to Buffett, "I will run it like I run my own money. I will take part of the profits and losses but I will not tell you what I am doing". The partnership was created with Buffet as the general partner with seven limited partners. Buffett contributed only $100 and seven friends and family members contributed $105,000. His office was located in a three story Dutch colonial home that he purchased for $31,500 in 1957. The house was adjacent to a busy street and had a handball court inside. Buffett had no office and ran things from a tiny sitting-room off his bedroom with no secretary and no calculator (Kilpatrick, 2000, p. 88).

That summer Buffett garnered his first outside investor, Homer Dodge, a physics professor and president of Norwich University in Vermont. Dodge wanted to invest in the partnership because he heard of Buffett's talent from Benjamin Graham. Dodge drove 1,500 miles to give $120,000 of his family's savings to Buffett. In 1983, when Dodge died, his investment with Buffett was tens of millions of dollars (Kilpatrick, 2000, p. 89).

At age 27, Buffett had three partnerships. At 28, he had five partnerships. By the time Buffett was 30 years old he had seven partnerships worth over $7 million of which $1 million was his. In 1962 Buffett also began buying shares of a textile manufacturer named Berkshire Hathaway, Inc. located in New Bedford, Massachusetts.

In 1965, Buffett's Partnership received a check for $300,000 from one of the great businessmen of his times, Laurence Tisch, with a very simple note "include me in". Tisch described Buffett as one of the greatest investors of his generation (Mazzocco, 1999, p. 94). By 1965, Buffett controlled Berkshire Hathaway, Inc. which had a stock price of $18.00 (Fridson, 1999, p. 179). In 1966, Buffett became chairman of the company.

In 1969, Buffett decided to liquidate his partnership. He transferred all of the assets from his partnership into shares of Berkshire Hathaway, Inc. and gave the partners their shares. Buffett was now going to use Berkshire as a holding company to purchase other companies and investments. At the end of its life of 13 years, the partnership was worth $100 million. The Partnership returned an average annual return of 30% (Kilpatrick, 2000, p. 16).

BERKSHIRE HATHAWAY, INC.

In 1970, Buffett was now the Chairman of Berkshire Hathaway, a public company. This was when he began to write his famous annual letter to shareholders. The annual shareholder letters would be his signature as he discussed the firm's strategies, entrepreneurial pursuits, investment decisions and philosophies, state of the industry and economy, and more importantly the mistakes the firm made. Shareholders were always excited about the letters as they used this literature as vital learning tools. To this day, shareholders and investors use Buffett's shareholder letters as learning tools about business and investments.

In the early years, Berkshire Hathaway, Inc. entered into the insurance industry acquiring such companies like Geico and National Indemnity Insurance Company. The main business activity for Berkshire was the property and casualty insurance conducted on both a direct and reinsurance basis. Buffett liked the insurance industry because it gave Berkshire free cash flow to invest in the advance of the payout of any claims.

From 1965 to 1985 the company purchased companies like See's Candies, The Washington Post, and Nebraska Furniture Mart. By 1985, the stock price of Berkshire had grown to $1,000 a share. In the 1990s the company began purchasing investments in Coca-Cola, Gillette, Anheuser-Busch, ConocoPhillips, General Electric, Johnson & Johnson, Kraft Foods, Wal-Mart, etc.

Unfortunately, things were not as good for Berkshire Hathaway, the textile manufacturer. The company was shut down in 1985 due to increased competition. However, Buffett continued to keep the name of the company, Berkshire Hathaway, Inc.

More recently, the company has been expanding internationally. In 2006 it purchased 80% of Iscar Metalworking Companies based out of Israel that does business in 60 different countries.

In 2008, Berkshire was a conglomerate holding company located in Omaha, Nebraska that owned companies and subsidiaries, engaged in a number of diverse business activities. The company had over 223,000 employees however its corporate headquarters in Omaha had only 12 employees and office space of 3,500 square feet. Berkshire's Vice-Chairman was Charlie Munger, a childhood friend who attended the same grade school as Buffett. The company owned over 70 companies and had shares in great companies like American Express, Wells-Fargo, Coca-Cola, Kraft, Burlington Northern Santa Fe, Dairy Queen International, Wal-Mart Stores, Inc., Procter & Gamble, Washington Post Company, Wells Fargo & Company, and other public companies.

Berkshire had two classes of stock; Class A, which was the highest priced stock listed on the New York Stock Exchange. The company also released a class B share. Berkshire's stocks never split as Buffett's investment philosophy was to reinvest the dividends. Berkshire's financial statements can be seen in Exhibits 12-15.

Exhibit 12: Berkshire Hathaway Balance Sheet 2004 – 2008 (2nd qtr)

(in million dollars)

	2008 Q2	2007	2006	2005	2004
Assets					
Cash and Short Term Investments	31,159	44,329	43,743	44,660	43,427
Total Receivables, Net	0	0	0	0	0
Prepaid Expenses	0	0	0	0	0
Property/Plant/Equipment, Total – Net	43,708	36,190	33,342	7,500	6,516
Goodwill, Net	33,524	32,862	32,238	23,644	23,012
Intangibles, Net	0	0	0	0	0
Long Term Investments	109,408	106,570	89,845	83,505	79,569
Insurance Receivables	30,008	13,157	12,881	12,397	11,291
Note Receivable - Long Term	0	12359	11498	11087	9175
Other Long Term Assets, Total	3,739	3,987	1,964	2,875	4,376
Other Assets, Total	26,246	23,706	22,926	12,657	11,508
Total Assets	**277,792**	**273,160**	**248,437**	**198,325**	**188,874**
Liabilities and Shareholders' Equity					
Accounts Payable	0	0	0	0	0
Payable/Accrued	21,236	19,646	19,890	8,699	7,500
Accrued Expenses	0	0	0	0	0
Policy Liabilities	72,844	70,575	62,208	62,371	64,384
Notes Payable/Short Term Debt	0	0	0	0	0
Current Port. of LT Debt/Capital Leases	0	0	0	0	0
Other Current Liabilities, Total	16,821	18,825	19,170	12,252	12,247
Total Long Term Debt	36,235	33,826	32,605	14,451	8,837
Deferred Income Tax	0	0	0	0	0
Minority Interest	4,230	2,668	2,262	816	758
Other Liabilities, Total	8,432	6,887	3,883	8,252	9,248
Total Liabilities	**159,798**	**152,427**	**140,018**	**106,841**	**102,974**
Redeemable Preferred Stock	0	0	0	0	0
Preferred Stock - Non Redeemable, Net	0	0	0	0	0
Common Stock	8	8	8	8	8
Additional Paid-In Capital	27,132	26,952	26,522	26,399	26,268
Retained Earnings (Accumulated Deficit)	75,973	72,153	58,912	47,717	39,189
Other Equity, Total	14,881	21,620	22,977	17,360	20,435
Total Equity	**117,994**	**120,733**	**108,419**	**91,484**	**85,900**
Total Liabilities & Shareholders' Equity	**277,792**	**273,160**	**248,437**	**198,325**	**188,874**
Total Common Shares Outstanding	1.55	1.55	1.54	1.54	1.54
Total Preferred Shares Outstanding	0	0	0	0	0

—*Source: http://moneycentral.msn.com/investor/invsub/results/statemnt.aspx?Symbol=US:BR K.A&lstStatement=Balance&stmtView=Ann. Accessed December 3, 2008.*

Exhibit 13: Berkshire Hathaway Income Statement 2004 – 2008 (2nd qtr)

	2008 Q2	2007	2006	
Total Premiums Earned	6,231	31,783	23,964	
Net Investment Income	246	5,598	1,811	
Realized Gains (Losses)	-	-	-	
Other Revenue, Total	23,616	80,864	72,764	
Total Revenue	30,093	118,245	98,539	
Losses, Benefits, and Adjustments, Total	5,671	28,409	20,126	
Amortization Of Policy Acquisition Costs	-	-	-	
Gross Profit	24,422	89,836	78,413	
Selling/General/Administrative Expenses, Total	2,049	7,098	5,932	
Depreciation/Amortization	-	-	-	
Interest Expense (Income), Net Operating	493	1,910	1,724	
Unusual Expense (Income)	-	-	-	
Other Operating Expenses, Total	17,409	60,667	53,979	
Operating Income	4,471	20,161	16,778	
Interest Income (Expense), Net Non-Operating	-	-	-	
Gain (Loss) on Sale of Assets	-	-	-	
Other, Net	-	-	-	
Income Before Tax	4,471	20,161	16,778	
Income Tax – Total	1,443	6,594	5,505	
Income After Tax	3,028	13,567	11,273	
Minority Interest	(148)	(354)	(258)	

Source: http://moneycentral.msn.com/investor/invsub/results/statemnt. aspx?Symbol=US%3aBRK.A. Accessed December 3, 2008.

Exhibit 14: Berkshire Hathaway Cash Flow 2004 – 2008 (2nd qtr)

(in million dollars)

	2008 Q2	2007	2006	2005	2004
Net Income/Starting Line	–	13,213	11,015	8,528	7,308
Depreciation/Depletion	–	2,407	2,066	982	941
Amortization	–	–	–	–	–
Non-Cash Items	–	354	258	104	–
Changes in Working Capital	4,991	(3,424)	(3,144)	(168)	(938)
Cash from Operating Activities	4,991	12,550	10,195	9,446	7,311
Capital Expenditures	(2,538)	(5,373)	(4,571)	(2,195)	(1,278)
Other Investing Cash Flow Items, Total	(16,886)	(8,055)	(9,506)	(11,646)	1,593
Cash from Investing Activities	(19,424)	(13,428)	(14,077)	(13,841)	315
Financing Cash Flow Items	(31)	387	84	188	166
Total Cash Dividends Paid	–	–	–	–	–
Issuance (Retirement) of Stock, Net	–	–	–	–	–
Issuance (Retirement) of Debt, Net	1,287	979	2,406	5,563	(322)
Cash from Financing Activities	1,256	1,366	2,490	5,751	(156)
Foreign Exchange Effects	7	98	117	(123)	–
Net Change in Cash	(13)	586	(1,275)	1,233	7,470
Net Cash - Beginning Balance	44,329	43,743	45,018	43,427	35,957
Net Cash - Ending Balance	31,159	44,329	43,743	44,660	43,427
Cash Taxes Paid	2,921	5,895	4,959	2,695	2,674

Source: http://moneycentral.msn.com/investor/invsub/results/statemnt.aspx?Symbol=US:BRK. A&lstStatement=CashFlow&stmtView=Ann. Accessed December 3, 2008.

Exhibit 15: Berkshire Hathaway Income Statement & Balance Sheet 10 Year Summaries 12/1998-12/2007

Income Statement - 10 Year Summary (in Millions)

	EBIT	Depreciation	Total Net Income	EPS	Tax Rate
Dec-07	20,161	2,407	13,213	8,548	32.7%
Dec-06	16,778	2,066	11,015	7,144	32.8%
Dec-05	12,791	982	8,528	5,538	32.5%
Dec-04	10,936	941	7,308	4,752	32.6%
Dec-03	12,020	829	8,151	5,309	31.7%
Dec-02	6,359	679	4,286	2,795	32.4%
Dec-01	1,438	1,517	795	521	41.0%
Dec-00	5,587	1,712	3,328	2,185	36.1%
Dec-99	2,450	1,165	1,557	1,025	34.8%
Dec-98	4,314	376	2,830	2,262	33.8%

Balance Sheet - 10 Year Summary (in Millions)

	Current Assets	Current Liabilities	Long Term Debt	Shares Outstanding
Dec-07	273,160	152,427	33,826	1.5 Mil
Dec-06	248,437	140,018	32,605	1.5 Mil
Dec-05	198,325	106,841	14,451	1.5 Mil
Dec-04	188,874	102,974	8,837	1.5 Mil
Dec-03	180,559	102,963	9,119	1.5 Mil
Dec-02	169,544	105,507	9,288	1.5 Mil
Dec-01	162,752	104,802	12,504	1.5 Mil
Dec-00	135,792	74,068	2,663	1.5 Mil
Dec-99	131,416	73,655	2,465	1.5 Mil
Dec-98	122,237	64,834	2,385	1.5 Mil

Source: http://moneycentral.msn.com/investor/invsub/results/statemnt.aspx?Symbol=US:BRK.A &lstStatement=10YearSummary&stmtView=Ann. Accessed December 3, 2008.

BUFFETT'S INVESTMENT PHILOSOPHY

Warren Buffett followed a value investment strategy similar to Benjamin Graham. His investment strategy consisted of discipline, patience, and value that consistently outperformed the market. Buffett's moves were mirrored by thousands of investors throughout the world. It was not uncommon to see double digit increases in stock prices of companies after Buffett's investments were made public. Berkshire acquired great businesses that traded at a discount to their intrinsic value and he held them for a long time.

Buffett stated, "We want businesses to be ones (a) that we can understand; (b) with favorable long-term prospects; (c) operated by honest and competent people; and (d) available at a very attractive price" (Gurufocus.com). Buffett stated, "Success in investing does not correlate with I.Q. once you are above the level of 25. Once you have ordinary intelligence, what you need is the temperament to control the urges that get other people into trouble in investing" (Buffet, 2008). Buffett and Munger never hired any consultants to help them.

Buffett stated, "I do not want to buy into any business that I am sure of. It probably is not going to offer any credible returns. Why should something that is essentially a cinch offer you 40% a year? We do not have huge returns in mind, but what we do have in mind is never losing anything" (Buffet, 2006).

Buffett followed the value investing methodology where one purchased stocks that are undervalued by the marketplace. The problem with this methodology is that there is no one best universal way to value a company. Valuing companies is different depending on the industry and stage of growth. Valuing companies was a competitive advantage that Buffett brought to Berkshire. He seemed to have the magical touch when valuing companies. It was not uncommon for Buffett to follow a company's management team and performance over a number of years before he would invest in a company.

At the 2008 Berkshire Hathaway Shareholder's Meeting, Buffett stated that business education was highly overvalued. He stated that he did not believe in the Efficient Market Hypothesis, which was taught at most business schools. Buffett stated that these schools have you taking all of these different classes, when all you really need to know to become a successful investor is two courses: (1) A course on how to value companies and (2) A course on human behavior in the markets.

VALUE INVESTING

According to Buffett, "The two most important essays ever written on investments were written by Benjamin Graham in his book Intelligent Investor in Chapter 8 on the attitude towards stock market fluctuations and Chapter 20 on the margin of safety. I have no idea what the stock market is going to do. It is something that I never think about at all. But I am looking for the stock to go down so I can buy it on sale. I want the stocks to go down, way down so I can make better buys (Buffet, 2006).

Buffett only invested in businesses that he understood, and he always insisted on a margin of safety. The margin of safety was when an investor only purchased securities when the market price was significantly below its intrinsic value. In other words, when the market price was significantly below your estimation of the intrinsic value, the difference was the margin of safety. This difference allowed an investment to be made with minimal downside risk (Investopedia.com).

Buffett combined Graham's investment philosophy with his own by answering the following issues related to a potential investment:

- Is the business easy to understand and analyze? Buffett only liked businesses that he could understand. Buffett stated that if he was teaching a course on valuation, his final exam to the students would be to value an Internet company. If the student answered the question, he or she would receive an F.

- Is the company in an industry with good economics, i.e., not an industry competing on price? Does the company have a consumer monopoly within their industry (e.g., Gillette, Coke, Dairy Queen, etc.)? Coca-Cola and Gillette have what Buffett calls a moat, where the resources necessary to overcome the brands are enormous.

- How old is the company? Buffett liked to look at a 10 year track record of financial statements. He also liked to compare the company with other firms within their industry.

- Buffett preferred firms that did not require a great deal of capital. The business should not have high maintenance cost of operations, high capital expenditure or investment cash outflow. This was not the same as investing to expand capacity. For example, in 1972, Berkshire bought See's Candies, who had a $4 million pre-tax profit for $25 million. Buffett stated that Berkshire never hired a consultant; their idea was to go out and buy a box of candy and see if they like it. Buffett purchased the company with the idea that Berkshire could raise the prices of the candy without investing a great deal in capital. That formula has worked and today the company has a net profit of $60 million a year.

- Does the company have a high Return on Equity (ROE)? Buffett preferred 15%, but was willing to go lower depending on the economic conditions.

- Was the company's debt-to-equity ratio low enough so the company can pay its debt obligations? Can the company repay debt even in years when earnings are lower than average?

- Does the company have a quality, ethical management team that had passion? For example, in 1983 Buffett purchased the Nebraska Furniture Mart. At the time it was the largest furniture store in the U.S. Buffett purchased the company from the founder, Rose Blumkin (also called Mrs. B), with a handshake and $55 million. Blumkin came to the U.S. from Russia in 1917 with $66 and no knowledge of English. She learned English from her five year old daughter and in 1937 she started her store in the basement of her husband's pawn shop in Omaha. After the acquisition, Blumkin had enough money to retire, but she continued to work because of the passion she had for her business. Blumkin's motto was to be honest and sell cheap.

- Is the company free to adjust prices for inflation and still maintain profitability?

- Will the value added by retaining earnings lead to an increase in the stock market value of the company?

- Did the company have consistent strong free cash flow to maintain its current operations? Did the company retain earnings for growth and what is management's track record on those investments? (Investmentu.com 2008, Buffet & Clark 2001)

- Is the stock undervalued by at least 25%? Is the intrinsic value of the company 25% less than the market value of the company?

Buffett stated that he would talk to CEOs in an industry and ask them, if you wanted to invest in one company in your industry who would it be and why? This methodology allowed him to learn about the leaders in each industry.

There was no magical test to determine the value of a company, but Buffett appeared to have a good handle on the various tactics he used to help him value companies.

BUFFETT'S KEYS TO SUCCESS

Buffett has been described by many as a genius, brilliant with numbers, photographic memory, honest, loyal, frugal, smart, rich, etc. Peter Buffett, Buffett's youngest of three, stated that his dad had the most integrity and was the most honest man that he had ever met.

Buffett was not an ostentatious man. He lived in the same house in Omaha that he purchased in 1957 for $31,500 and drove a Lincoln Town Car with license plates that said THRIFTY. A few years ago he auctioned off the car on e-Bay. Buffett stated, "My suits are old, my wallet's old, my car's old and I've lived in the same house since 1957, so I hang on to things" (Kilpatrick, 2000, p. 16).

In a recent talk to University of Florida students Buffett stated, "There is no difference between you and me: We all go to McDonald's…better yet Dairy Queen, we all live in cool houses in the summer and warm houses in the winter. Our lives are not that different. You will get decent medical care if something happens to you and so will I. The only difference is that I travel around on this little plane and that is the only difference. If you leave this aside, what can I do that you cannot do? I get to work in a job that I love and I think you are out of your mind for taking jobs you do not love. Take a job that if you were independently wealthy you would do. If you think you are going to be a lot happier with 2x instead of x, you are probably making a big mistake. Find something you like, you will get in trouble if you think that making 10x or 20x will make you happy because then you will do things you should not do like cut corners. Do something you enjoy and be associated with people you like. If I could make $100 million dollars with some guy that made my stomach churn I would say no. It is like marrying for money, which if you are already rich, is crazy" (Buffet, 2006).

Buffett did not believe in high CEO pay. He consistently spoke out about the abuses of management in relation to pay and stock options. Since 1980, Buffett made $100,000 a year, which he stated was more than enough to live on. He never cashed in a share of Berkshire stock for personal use. Exhibit 16 showed some of Buffett's more famous quotes.

Exhibit 16: Warren Buffet Quotes

"Shares are not mere pieces of paper. They represent part ownership of a business. So, when contemplating an investment, think like a prospective owner."

"All there is to investing is picking good stocks at good times and staying with them as long as they remain good companies."

"Look at market fluctuations as your friend rather than your enemy. Profit from folly rather than participate in it."

"If, when making a stock investment, you're not considering holding it at least ten years, don't waste more than ten minutes considering it."

"A public-opinion poll is no substitute for thought."

"Of the billionaires I have known, money just brings out the basic traits in them. If they were jerks before they had money, they are simply jerks with a billion dollars."

"It takes 20 years to build a reputation and five minutes to ruin it. If you think about that, you'll do things differently."

"I always knew I was going to be rich. I don't think I ever doubted it for a minute."

"What good is money? It buys time and flexibility to do what you want (work how you want). But, it doesn't really make a huge difference in other things."

"It's better to hang out with people better than you. Pick out associates whose behavior is better than yours and you'll drift in that direction."

"The business schools reward difficult complex behavior more than simple behavior, but simple behavior is more effective."

"Our favorite holding period is forever."

"Price is what you pay. Value is what you get."

"Risk comes from not knowing what you're doing."

"There seems to be some perverse human characteristic that likes to make easy things difficult."

"Time is the friend of the wonderful company, the enemy of the mediocre."

"We enjoy the process far more than the proceeds."

"We simply attempt to be fearful when others are greedy and to be greedy only when others are fearful."

"When a management with a reputation for brilliance tackles a business with a reputation for bad economics, it is the reputation of the business that remains intact."

"Why not invest your assets in the companies you really like? As Mae West said, "Too much of a good thing can be wonderful."

"You only have to do a very few things right in your life so long as you don't do too many things wrong."

"Your premium brand had better be delivering something special, or it's not going to get the business."

"Wide diversification is only required when investors do not understand what they are doing."

"I don't look to jump over 7-foot bars: I look around for 1-foot bars that I can step over."

"If past history was all there was to the game, the richest people would be librarians."

Source: Warren Buffett Quotes. http://www.brainyquote.com/quotes/authors/w/warren_buffett. html. Accessed December 3, 2008.

Forever a student, Warren Buffett stated that if you want to become a successful investor you need to read all of the time. In 1965 he wrote, "We derive no comfort because important people, vocal people, or great numbers of people agree with us. Nor do we derive comfort if they do not. A public opinion poll is no substitute for thought. When you find a situation you understand, where the facts are ascertainable and clear, then act, whether the action is conventional or unconventional and regardless of whether others agree or disagree. When you are dead sure of something and are armed with all the facts, then everyone else's advice is only confusing and time-consuming" (Cunningham, 2001).

Buffett stated that we like to buy businesses at reasonable prices. He also stated that the secret to making money was to avoid making mistakes and bet big, but seldom. Buffett kept his investments secret until the publication of the Berkshire Hathaway's Annual Report or until he was required by the Securities and Exchange Commission to disclose his transactions.

A Wall Street money manager with First Manhattan Co. in New York reported to his wife after a lunch with Buffett "I think I just met the smartest investor in the country". Phil Carret, an investor, called Buffett "the smartest man in the U.S." Sequoia Fund's Bill Ruane dubbed Buffett "the smartest guy in the country". Former GE CEO Jack Welch called Buffett "the smartest guy in any room". Executive Jet CEO Rich Santulli said, *"There is not a person in the world that is smarter than Warren Buffett"* (Kilpatrick, 2000, p. 23).

Buffett disliked schedules, meetings, company rituals, and managing people. His office was in a simple building called Kiewit Plaza for over 30 years.

Buffett had an incredible high level of integrity (e.g., he mouthed no threats and never participated in hostile takeovers). Buffett considered character the most important ingredient of a hire, but he also wanted someone who was intelligent with a high level of energy. Other characteristics he admired were generosity; people that gave credit to other people even if they did the work, people that had strong leadership capabilities, and people that were not greedy. Buffett also believed in the philosophy that if you admire someone, you should behave like them.

Buffett was also a debt adverse person and had a strong dislike for being in debt. Buffett had two rules that he considered rich seekers must learn: Rule no 1: never lose money. Rule no 2: never forget rule no 1 (Buffet, zimbio.com).

One of the keys to Buffett and Berkshire's success was the interest free leverage from the insurance premiums the company received. For example, Geico customers would pay their premiums and then Berkshire was free to use the money for other investments, such as the acquisition of successful companies like See's Candies or Nebraska Furniture Mart. Of course, Geico would have to pay claims, but until then, they were free to use the cash on other investments.

BUFFETT AND CHARITY

What made Buffett especially happy was giving most of his fortune to the Bill & Melinda Gates Foundation and four other philanthropies (*New York Times*, 2008). More than 99% of the monetary proceeds and 100% of the human proceeds of his life were to be returned to society. Buffett stated, "I want my trustees to swing for the fence on a few projects that do not have natural funding constituencies, but that are important to society. I tell them that if they start giving half a million to this hospital and a million to that college, I will come back and haunt them" (Kilpatrick, 2000, p. 26).

Buffett also stated that his children would not inherit a significant proportion of his wealth and that his great fortune would not be transferred from one generation to the next. Buffett stated, "I want to give my kids just enough so that they would feel that they could do anything, but not so much that they would feel like doing nothing. I do not have a problem with guilt about money. The way I see it is that my money represents an enormous number of claim checks on society. It is like I have these little pieces of paper that I can turn into consumption. If I wanted to, I could hire 10,000 people to do nothing but paint my picture every day for the rest of my life. And the GNP would go up. But the utility of the product would be zilch, and I would be keeping those 10,000 people from doing AIDS research, or teaching, or nursing. I do not do that though. I do not use very many of those claim checks. There is nothing material I want very much. And I am going to give virtually all of those claim checks to charity when my wife and I die" (Kilpatrick, 2000, p. 1775-1783).

Buffett always felt best when he was giving and helping others. Buffett's value system was a major reason why he was so successful. Every year for the past several years Buffett invited approximately 15 universities and colleges from all over the world to his corporate headquarters. He shared his thoughts on business and more importantly his lessons on how to live your life. Buffett donated one class A share to each school to cover their expenses.

Buffett also auctioned off a lunch with himself every year on eBay. He gave the proceeds to Glide Foundation, a non-profit organization in San Francisco that helped the homeless and poor. This past year a Chinese investment fund manager won the bidding at $2.1 million.

Buffett stated that he was the luckiest person in the world because he loved what he did for a living and was surrounded by people that loved him. When he was recently asked in an interview about the key to happiness, Buffett made no mention of money or any materialistic things, but mentioned the importance of surrounding yourself with people that love you.

Buffett's value system stressed the importance of being honest and forthright; something his father had taught him. His honesty was legendary. Buffett always stated that it was better to make less profit if it meant doing it honestly rather than questionably. As a result, it was not uncommon for leading investors and media to contact Buffett first to get his opinion on critical issues. People knew that when Buffett spoke, they got an honest, intelligent, and forthright answer.

ECONOMIC ENVIRONMENT

In late 2008, the U.S. economy was muddled with a drop off in consumer spending, the housing bust, and the subprime financial disaster. At the heart of the economic mess was one of the biggest financial disasters in the history of the U.S., the housing bust and the subprime mortgage collapse. The U.S. was in the worst housing correction since the Great Depression. By 2009, the average net worth of households headed by homeowners age 45 to 54 will be almost 25% less than it was in 2004 (*Money Magazine*, 2008).

The factor that led up to the housing bust that began in 2006 was the U.S. recession from 2001-2003. To stimulate the economy, the former Chairman of the Federal Reserve, Alan Greenspan, dropped the Federal funds rate to 1%, making it easier for people to borrow money at a very cheap rate. The lowering of interest rates, compounded with little regulations, and greed within the financial industry, created a housing boom.

New innovations along with low interest rates allowed consumers easy access to funding to purchase real estate. Buyers were allowed to purchase real estate with no money down without lenders checking employment records or their ability to pay their debt obligations. The easy access to capital created a housing boom. Some areas of the country (e.g., California, Florida, Arizona, Nevada, etc.) saw their housing values increase in double digits for several years.

This level of growth was not sustainable and eventually led to the collapse of the housing industry. People borrowed money to purchase houses with adjustable rate mortgages (ARMs) with the hope that the values of real estate would continue to go up. Unfortunately, that gamble came to an end in 2006 when prices started to fall and people could not refinance their ARMs due to falling home values.

According to the latest S&P/Case-Schiller Index, the most respected U.S. housing index indicator, the average U.S. home price dropped 21% from its peak in the second quarter 2006 to September 2008. On a year-to-year basis, the average home in the U.S. dropped 16.6% from September 2007 to September 2008. Some areas of the country have been hit especially hard. Phoenix, Las Vegas, Miami, Los Angeles and San Francisco saw their average home prices decline 39%, 38%, 36%, 33%, and 33% from their highs in mid 2006 and were still dropping.

The collapse in housing values cost U.S. homeowners $4 trillion in lost equity. Many analysts have estimated that home values could drop another 10-20% before the crisis is over. Some analysts also state that just because the housing crisis bottoms, does not necessarily mean that price appreciation will come back any time soon.

According to Bill Gross, CEO of Pimco Investments, "The housing market is going down because quite simply, they went up too much and were financed with excessive debt. The housing bubble was well inflated by low interest rates, easy, and in some cases fraudulent credit, a lack of federal and state regulation, and a gullible public who read the history books for the past half century and knew full well that home prices never, ever go down. Not much of an enigma there. No riddle to be solved it would seem. It was simply a fairy tale too good to be true. Yet housing, unlike other asset classes, carries with it an aura more like a bad dream than a fairy tale. That is because it is the most levered asset class and the one held by more "investor" citizens than any other. U.S. homes are market valued at over 20 trillion dollars with nearly half of the value supported by mortgage finance of one sort or another. At first blush that appears to be reasonably levered, but at the margin, homes purchased in 2004 and beyond are now at risk of turning upside down – negative equity – and there are some 25 million or so of those. The "upsidedownness" in many cases results in foreclosures, or outright abandonment and most certainly serves as an example of what not to do for millions of twenty-somethings or new citizens choosing between homeownership and renting. PIMCO estimates a total of 5 trillion dollars of mortgage loans are in risky asset categories and that nearly 1 trillion dollars of cumulative losses will finally mark the gravestone of this housing bubble. The problem with writing off 1 trillion dollars from the finance industry's cumulative balance sheet is that if not matched by capital raising, it necessitates a sale of assets, a reduction in lending or both that in turn begins to affect economic growth, creating what Mohamed El-Erian fears as a "negative feedback loop" (Gross, 2008).

"I worry a lot about what's happening in housing," Martin Feldstein, Professor of Economics at Harvard University and President Emeritus of the National Bureau of Economic Research. Feldstein stated, "The number of negative-equity homes is exploding. Housing prices will continue to go down, driven by the large oversupply of houses and the increasing number of foreclosures" (Chandra, 2008).

In an interview on August 22, 2008 on CNBC Buffett was quoted, "The economy continues to be in a recession, by my definition, and will continue to be for at least several more months. The ripples of the credit crunch are continuing to cause problems in financial businesses and the economy. We found out that Wall Street has been kind of a nudist beach. You always find out who has been swimming naked when the tide goes out. We found out that Wall Street has been kind of a nudist beach. I am confident the country will be doing better five years from now, but the economy could be worse five months from now. The economy is in a recession because most Americans are not doing as well today as before. The technical definition of a recession most economists use is two consecutive quarters of negative growth in the country's gross domestic product. The current economic struggles in the U.S. create investment opportunities, and my phone is ringing more lately than it was three months ago. However, many of those calls have come from desperate people and did not represent good investment opportunities" (Funk, 2008).

BUFFETT'S NEXT MOVE

As Buffett finished his Buster Bar at Dairy Queen his second wife, Astrid Menks, (Buffett's first wife, Susie, passed away in 2004) asked him a few questions, "Warren, Berkshire Hathaway's stock price is down 48% this year and you keep telling me that we are in a recession. I am very concerned about the economy. I have never seen it this bad before. What are you going to do next, Warren? Buffett thought to himself, this was the worst economic period of his investment career. He pondered about what his next moves should be.

DISCUSSION QUESTIONS

1) What is the background and personality of Warren Buffett?

2) Is Warren Buffett an entrepreneur?

3) What did Warren Buffett do to make Berkshire Hathaway, Inc. so successful? What was Buffett's investment philosophy?

4) Perform a SWOT analysis on Berkshire Hathaway.

5) Analyze the financial ratios for the company. Is the firm financially healthy? Why or why not?

6) What were the major problems and/or opportunities facing Berkshire Hathaway, Inc. in 2008?

7) What recommendations would you make to Warren Buffett? Why? What do you recommend that Berkshire Hathaway, Inc. do over the next 5-10 years to increase shareholder wealth?

REFERENCES

1. "The World's Billionaires." *Forbes*. March 5, 2008. Available at http://www.forbes.com/2008/03/05/richest-billionaires-people-billionaires08-cx_lk_0305intro.html.

2. Hamilton, J. (2008). Buffett's Berkshire Discloses Stake in NRG Energy. *Bloomberg.com*, Available at http://www.bloomberg.com/apps/news?pid=newsarchive&sid=ambd9i WGLjGA

3. Kilpatrick, A. (2008). *Of Permanent Value: The Story of Warren Buffett/2008*. Andy Kilpatrick Publishing Empire. Birmingham, Alabama. Page 13.

4. Buffett: Economy in a recession will be worse than feared. *USA Today.com*, April 4, 2008. Available at http://www.usatoday.com/money/economy/2008-04-28-buffett-recession_N.htm

5. Crippen, A. (2008). *Three Hours with Warren Buffett*. Transcript/Video Parts One-Six Live From Omaha. Available at http://www.cnbc.com/id/19206666/?sky=GGL|CAMP0 29CNBC_CoreTerms+Blogs_Dec+2007|ADGP028CNBC_CoreTerms_warrenbuffett|K WRD014warren+buffett&__source=SI_28965575_999685666_1

6. Schroeder, A. (2008). *How Warren Buffett Made His First Dime*. Available at: http://www.parade.com/hot-topics/0809/how-warren-buffett-made-his-first-dime.

7. Miles, R. (2004). *Warren Buffett Wealth: Principle and Practical Methods used by the World's Greatest Investor*. Page 25.

8. Schroeder, A (2008). *The Snowball: Warren Buffett and the Business of Life.*

9. Steele, J. (1999). *Warren Buffett: Master of the Market.* Page 28.

10. Vick, T. (2000). *How to Pick Stocks like Warren Buffett.* Page 10.

11. Mazzocco, D. (1999). *Networks of Power: Corporate TV's Threat to Democracy.* Page 94.

12. Fridson, M. (1999). *How to Be a Billionaire.* Page 179.

13. Gurufocus.com. *"GuruFocus Tracks the Stock Picks of Gurus,"* accessed August 4, 2008 http://www.gurufocus.com/ListGuru.php?GuruName=Warren+Buffett

14. Buffett, W. (2008). *Chairman's 1997 Annual Letter to Shareholders*. Available at http://www.berkshirehathaway.com/letters/letters.html. Accessed August 25, 2008.

15. Warren Buffett MBA Talk. *Presentation at the University of Florida*. September 4, 2006. http://video.google.com/videoplay?docid=-6231308980849895261 Accessed August 29, 2008.

16. *Margin of Safety*. Available at http://www.investopedia.com/terms/m/marginofsafety.asp. Accessed September 1, 2008.

17. *Warren Buffett's Investment Philosophy.* Available at http://www.investmentu.com/IUEL/2008/February/warren-buffett.html. Accessed August 28, 2008.

18. Buffett, M. and Clark, D. (2001). *The Buffettology Workbook: Value Investing the Warren Buffet Way.* Simon and Schuster, NY, NY.

19. Cunningham, Lawrence (2001). *The Essays of Warren Buffett: Lessons for Corporate America.* (Essays by Warren Buffet; Selected, Arranged, and Introduced by Lawrence Cunningham).

20. *Warren Buffett: Rule No. 1 – Never Lose Money.* Available at http://www.zimbio.com/Self+Improvement/articles/125/Warren+Buffett+Rule+No+1+Never+Lose+Money. Accessed August 24, 2008.

21. Buffett to Give Bulk of His Fortune to Gates Charity. *New York Times.com.* June 26, 2006. Available at http://www.nytimes.com/2006/06/26/business/26buffett.html. Accessed August 8, 2008.

22. How the Housing Crisis Hurts Your Retirement. *Money Magazine.* September 2, 2008. http://money.cnn.com/2008/08/29/real_estate/housing_retirement.moneymag/index.htm?postversion=2008090207 Accessed September 1, 2008.

23. Gross, B. (August, 2008). Investment Outlook by Bill Gross. *Pimco Investment.* Available at: http://www.pimco.com/LeftNav/Featured+Market+Commentary/IO/2008/Investment+Outlook+Bill+Gross+Mooooooo+August+2008.htm. Accessed August 7, 2008

24. Chandra, S. (2008). *U.S. Existing Home Sales Rose 3.1% in July to 5 Million Rate.* Available at http://www.bloomberg.com/apps/news?pid=20601068&sid=ad9i9FnnYhDw&refer=home. Accessed August 25, 2008.

25. Funk, J. (2008). *Buffett: Recession Will Continue for at Least Several More Months.* Available at http://www.huffingtonpost.com/2008/08/22/buffett-recession-will-co_n_120754.html. Accessed August 22, 2008.

26. Graham, Benjamin (1934). *Security Analysis.* Harper & Brothers, New York, NY.

27. Graham, Benjamin (1949). *The Intelligent Investor.* Harper & Brothers, New York, NY.

CORPORATE ENTREPRENEURSHIP & INNOVATION IN SILICON VALLEY: THE CASE OF GOOGLE, INC.

Todd A. Finkle, Gonzaga University

ABSTRACT

In May 2009, Sergey Brin and Larry Page, co-founders of Google, Inc., were trying to determine how they were going to navigate Google through the worst recession since the Great Depression. Their primary problem was how to maintain the company's culture of corporate entrepreneurship and innovation in the face of stagnant profits and a host of other issues. Google sought answers on how to increase corporate entrepreneurship and innovation during the worst economic environment that the company had ever experienced.

INTRODUCTION

In May 2009, Sergey Brin and Larry Page, co-founders of Google, Inc., watched Green Day in concert at the famous Shoreline Amphitheatre in Mountain View, California. The brilliant young entrepreneurs had many things on their minds. They tried to determine how they were going to navigate Google during the worst recession the United States had seen since the Great Depression (Willis, 2009). The Standard and Poor's 500 (S&P 500), one of the most popular indicators of the U.S. economy, had dropped to an intra-day low of 666.79 on March 6, 2009 from an intra-day high of 1576.09 on October 11, 2007 for a collapse of 57.7% (S&P 500 Index, 2009). World-wide stocks had decreased on average by approximately 60%.

Warren Buffett, Chairman of Berkshire Hathaway and one of the most prolific investors of all time, foresaw the current economic turmoil in early 2008. Buffett stated, "Even though the numbers do not state it, the United States was in for a deep long-lasting recession (*USA Today*, 2008)."

By early 2009, U.S. retirement accounts also dropped by an average of 40% or $3.4 trillion (Brandon, 2009). Many U.S. retirees saw their pensions cut in half and many were forced to go back to work or rely on their families to support them.

Brin and Page had never witnessed anything like this in their young lives. Even the ever successful company they created in 1998, Google, Inc., was feeling the effects of the crisis. At its low point, Google's stock price dropped 51.35% from an intra-day high of $713.587 on November 2, 2007 to an intra-day low of $259.56 on November 20, 2008. The stock price picked up momentum recently and traded at $410 as of May 28, 2009.

As the young entrepreneurs listened to the Bay Area band Green Day, they pondered their next moves. Google had problems. The company's primary problem was how to maintain the culture of corporate entrepreneurship and innovation in the face of flat net profits from 2007 to 2008. As a result of this, the firm had to fire several employees for the first time in the company's history and eliminate products that made no money (Blodget, 2009). Furthermore, employees left for a variety of reasons (e.g., lack of mentoring and formal career planning, too much bureaucracy, low pay and benefits, high cost of living in the area, desire to start their own business, etc.).

In a little over 10 years, Google had grown to a company with over 20,000 employees. If Google wanted to continue its main strategy of growth through innovation, it would have to find a way to recruit the best employees and retain them.

Exhibit 1: Google - Income Statements 2004-2008 (in millions)

	2008	2007	2006	2005	2004
Period End Date	*12/31/08*	*12/31/07*	*12/31/06*	*12/31/05*	*12/31/04*
Revenue	21,795.55	16,593.99	10,604.92	6,138.56	3,189.22
Total Revenue	**21,795.55**	**16,593.99**	**10,604.92**	**6,138.56**	**3,189.22**
Cost of Revenue, Total	8,621.51	6,649.09	4,225.03	2,577.09	1,468.97
Gross Profit	**13,174.04**	**9,944.90**	**6,379.89**	**3,561.47**	**1,720.26**
Selling, General, & Administrative	3,748.88	2,740.52	1,601.31	854.68	483.9
Research & Development	2,793.19	2,119.99	1,228.59	599.51	395.16
Unusual Expense (Income)	1,094.76	0	0	90	201
Operating Income	**5,537.21**	**5,084.40**	**3,550.00**	**2,017.28**	**640.19**
Other, Net	4.52	-4.65	3.46	4.14	-5.09
Income Before Tax	**5,853.60**	**5,673.98**	**4,011.04**	**2,141.68**	**650.23**
Income Tax – Total	1,626.74	1,470.26	933.59	676.28	251.12
Net Income	**4,226.86**	**4,203.72**	**3,077.45**	**1,465.40**	**399.12**

Source: http://www.google.com/finance?fstype=bi&cid=694653

Exhibit 2: Google Cash Flow 2004-2008 (in millions)

	2008	2007	2006	2005	2004
Period End Date	*12/31/08*	*12/31/07*	*12/31/06*	*12/31/05*	*12/31/04*
Net Income/Starting Line	4,226.86	4,203.72	3,077.45	1,465.40	399.12
Depreciation/Depletion	1,212.24	807.74	494.43	256.81	128.52
Amortization	287.65	159.92	77.51	37	19.95
Deferred Taxes	-224.65	-164.21	0	0	0
Non-Cash Items	2,055.44	489.44	-112.83	656.47	682.66
Other Non-Cash Items	960.68	489.44	-123.63	634.43	470.32
Changes in Working Capital	295.32	278.8	43.96	43.74	-253.21
Accounts Receivable	334.46	-837.25	-624.01	-372.29	-156.93
Accounts Payable	-211.54	70.14	95.4	80.63	-13.52
Taxes Payable	626.03	744.8	398.41	87.4	-125.23
Other Liabilities	41.43	70.33	30.8	39.55	22
Other Operating Cash Flow	-31.91	-39.74	1.67	0	0
Cash from Operating Activities	**7,852.86**	**5,775.41**	**3,580.51**	**2,459.42**	**977.04**
Capital Expenditures	-2,358.46	-2,402.84	-1,902.80	-853.04	-355.9
Purchase of Fixed Assets	-2,358.46	-2,402.84	-1,902.80	-838.22	-319
Purchase/Acquisition of Intangibles	0	0	0	-14.82	-36.91
Other Investing Cash Flow Items, Total	-2,960.96	-1,278.75	-4,996.35	-2,505.16	-1,545.46
Acquisition of Business	-3,320.30	-906.65	-402.45	-86.49	-21.96
Purchase of Investments	-15,403.46	-16,031.57	-27,701.04	-12,675.88	-4,134.58
Cash from Investing Activities	**-5,319.42**	**-3,681.59**	**-6,899.15**	**-3,358.19**	**-1,901.36**
Financing Cash Flow Items	159.09	379.21	581.73	0	4.3
Other Financing Cash Flow	159.09	379.21	581.73	0	4.3
Total Cash Dividends Paid	0	0	0	0	0
Issuance (Retirement) of Stock, Net	-71.52	23.86	2,384.67	4,372.26	1,195.03
Issuance (Retirement) of Debt, Net	0	0	0	-1.43	-4.71
Cash from Financing Activities	**87.57**	**403.07**	**2,966.40**	**4,370.83**	**1,194.62**
Foreign Exchange Effects	-45.92	40.03	19.74	-21.76	7.57
Net Change in Cash	**2,575.08**	**2,536.92**	**-332.5**	**3,450.30**	**277.88**
Net Cash - Beginning Balance	6,081.59	3,544.67	3,877.17	426.87	149
Net Cash - Ending Balance	8,656.67	6,081.59	3,544.67	3,877.17	426.87

Source: http://www.google.com/finance?fstype=bi&cid=694653

Exhibit 3: Google Balance Sheet 2004-2008 (in millions)

	2008	2007	2006	2005	2004
Period End Date	*12/31/08*	*12/31/07*	*12/31/06*	*12/31/05*	*12/31/04*
Assets					
Cash and Short Term Investments	15,845.77	14,218.61	11,243.91	8,034.25	2,132.30
Total Receivables, Net	2,642.19	2,307.77	1,322.34	687.98	382.35
Total Inventory	0	0	0	0	0
Prepaid Expenses	1,404.11	694.21	443.88	229.51	159.36
Other Current Assets, Total	286.11	68.54	29.71	49.34	19.46
Total Current Assets	**20,178.18**	**17,289.14**	**13,039.85**	**9,001.07**	**2,693.47**
Property/Plant/Equipment, Total - Net	5,233.84	4,039.26	2,395.24	961.75	378.92
Goodwill, Net	4,839.85	2,299.37	1,545.12	194.9	122.82
Intangibles, Net	996.69	446.6	346.84	82.78	71.07
Long Term Investments	85.16	1,059.69	1,031.85	0	0
Note Receivable - Long Term	0	0	0	0	0
Other Long Term Assets, Total	433.85	201.75	114.46	31.31	47.08
Total Assets	**31,767.58**	**25,335.81**	**18,473.35**	**10,271.81**	**3,313.35**
Liabilities and Shareholders' Equity					
Accounts Payable	178	282.11	211.17	115.58	32.67
Payable/Accrued	0	0	0	0	0
Accrued Expenses	1,824.45	1,575.42	987.91	528.94	269.29
Notes Payable/Short Term Debt	0	0	0	0	0
Current Port. of LT Debt/Capital Leases	0	0	0	0	1.9
Other Current Liabilities, Total	299.63	178.07	105.51	100.87	36.51
Total Current Liabilities	**2,302.09**	**2,035.60**	**1,304.59**	**745.38**	**340.37**
Total Long Term Debt	0	0	0	0	0
Deferred Income Tax	12.52	0	40.42	35.42	0
Other Liabilities, Total	1,214.11	610.53	88.5	72.05	43.93
Total Liabilities	**3,528.71**	**2,646.13**	**1,433.51**	**852.86**	**384.3**
Common Stock	0.32	0.31	0.31	0.29	0.27
Additional Paid-In Capital	14,450.34	13,241.22	11,882.91	7,477.79	2,582.35
Retained Earnings (Accumulated Deficit)	13,561.63	9,334.77	5,133.31	2,055.87	590.47
Other Equity, Total	226.58	113.37	23.31	-115	-244.03
Total Equity	**28,238.86**	**22,689.68**	**17,039.84**	**9,418.96**	**2,929.06**
Total Liabilities & Shareholders' Equity	**31,767.58**	**25,335.81**	**18,473.35**	**10,271.81**	**3,313.35**
Total Common Shares Outstanding	315.11	313.28	309	293.03	266.92

Source: http://www.google.com/finance?fstype=bi&cid=694653

Exhibit 4: Google's Stock Price from IPO through May 28, 2009

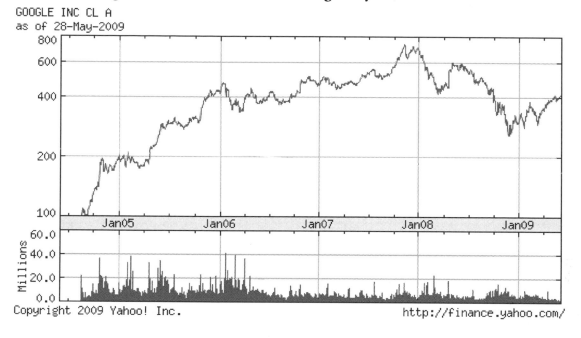

BACKGROUND OF FOUNDERS

Google was founded by Larry Page and Sergei Brin who met in 1995 while they were Ph.D. students in computer engineering at Stanford University. Page was born in Lansing, Michigan on March 26, 1973 and was the son of a computer science professor at Michigan State University who specialized in artificial intelligence. Page's mother also taught computer programming at the Michigan State University (Thompson, 2001, page 50).

Page spent his youth learning about computers and immersed himself into multiple technology journals that his parents read. Page had a very impressive educational background. He attended a Montessori school initially, and then went to a public high school. He later went on to earn a Bachelor of Science Degree (with honors) in computer engineering from the University of Michigan. Page was then accepted to graduate school at Stanford where he met Brin and began his study of website linkages. Nicola Tesla, a Serbian inventor who was a contemporary of Thomas Edison, was Page's inspiration. Tesla was superior to Edison in some respects; however, he failed at commercializing his inventions. Page wanted to do both.

In 1973, Sergey Brin was born in Moscow Russia. At age six, Brin and his family who were Jewish, fled Russia to the United States to escape anti-Semitism. Brin's father was a mathematics professor at the University of Maryland and his mother was a research scientist at NASA's Goddard Space Flight Center. Brin attended a Montessori high school and graduated with a degree in computer science and mathematics with honors from the University of Maryland. He then began to study computer science at Stanford University until he dropped out to form Google with Page. Brin was the more gregarious, however both were strong willed and opinionated.

At Stanford they began their quest to "organize the world's information and make it universally accessible (Miller, 2006, page 10). Google began as a research project at Stanford University in January, 1995.

Page started his research under the tutelage of Dr. Terry Winograd, a computer science professor at Stanford. His research focused on which web pages linked to a given page. His initial problem was trying to determine the number of citations in academic publishing. He called his research project "BackRub." Brin soon joined Page on the project. Page began exploring the web in March 1996 by using Page's Stanford home page. It was at this point that Page and Brin developed PageRank, an algorithm that ranked the importance of the sites that were relevant to the entry.

Page and Brin did not create the algorithm with the intention of making money, but they wanted to have a significant impact on the world. As time went on they decided that they did not want to create their own company, but they wanted to sell their invention to one of the existing search companies (e.g., WebCrawler, AltaVista, Yahoo!, etc.). However, all of these companies stated that there was no money in search and rejected them.

By 1996, Brin and Page had servers and computers stacked in their dorm room. Initially targeted at Stanford students, the two consulted with two former Stanford students that started Yahoo!, Jerry Yang and David Filo. They encouraged Brin and Page to create their own company. So the two decided to drop out of school and start their own business. In 1998, Sun Microsystems co-founder Andy Bechtolsheim, who also dropped out of Stanford to become a successful entrepreneur, wrote a check for $100,000 to Brin and Page and they formed a new company called Google, Inc.

GROWTH OF GOOGLE

Since its founding in 1998, Google was one of the most innovative companies in the world. The company ranked at the top with other leading companies like Apple in the development of innovative products and technologies. Corporate entrepreneurship and innovation was the heart and soul of the company's success.

Google initially set up its business in a garage at 232 Santa Margarita, Menlo Park, California in 1998. Later that year, Google was named Search Engine of Choice by PC Magazine in the Top 100 Sites of 1998 (Lowe, 2009, page 282). In 1999, Google moved to a new office space in Palo Alto to make room for several new employees. Palo Alto was the location of Stanford University. The city was in the heart of Silicon Valley and was the location where the first semiconductor chip was created in 1956 by Fairchild Semiconductor.

In 1999, Google received its first significant influx of capital, $25 million in venture capital financing from Sequoia Capital and Kleiner, Perkins, Caufield, and Byers, both located in Silicon Valley. Members of both firms sat on the board of directors of Google.

In 1999, the term "googler" was termed for "people who used Google". In August, 1999 Google moved to Mountain View, just south of Palo Alto. Google moved into an empty building next door to Silicon Graphics, a firm that was founded by a former Stanford electrical engineering professor, Dr. James Clark and seven graduate students and staff from Stanford. Clark would go on to found Netscape Communications, my-CFO, and Healtheon. A review of the history of Google can be seen below.

Exhibit 5: Google's Corporate History

Aug-98   Sun co-founder Andy Bechtolsheim writes a check for $100,000 to an entity that doesn't exist yet: a company called Google Inc.

Sep-98   Google files for incorporation in California on September 4. Larry and Sergey open a bank account in Google's name and deposit check.

Dec-98   "PC Magazine" reports that Google "has an uncanny knack for returning extremely relevant results" and names it the search engine of choice.

Jun-99   Google's first press release announces a $25 million round from Sequoia Capital and Kleiner Perkins

May-00   The first 10 language versions of Google.com are released targeting the Western European market from Spain up to Denmark. (New Market)

Jun-00   We forge a partnership with Yahoo! to become their default search provider. (Partnership)

Sep-00   We start offering search in Chinese, Japanese and Korean, bringing our total number of supported languages to 15. (New Market)

Oct-00   Google AdWords, the self-service ad program with keyword targeting, launches with 350 customers - revenue stream. (New Product)

Dec-00   Google Toolbar is released. It's a browser plug-in that makes it possible to search without visiting the Google homepage. (Innovation)

Feb-01   Acquires Deja.com's Usenet Discussion Service, adds search and browse features, and launches it as Google Groups. (Acquisition)

Mar-01   Google.com is available in 26 languages. (Foreign)

Jul-01   Image Search launches, offering access to 250 million images. (New Product)

Aug-01   Google opens its first international office, in Tokyo. (International)

Aug-01   Eric Schmidt becomes CEO, and Larry and Sergey are named presidents of products and technology, respectively

Oct-09   A new partnership with Universo Online (UOL) makes Google the major search service for millions of Latin Americans. (Partnership)

Feb-02   The first Google hardware is released, the Google Search Appliance. (Related Diversification - Hardware)

Feb-02   Google releases a major overhaul for AdWords, including new cost-per-click pricing. (Innovation)

May-02   Partnership with AOL to offer Google search and sponsored links to customers using CompuServe, Netscape, and AOL.com. (Partnership)

Sep-02   Google News launches with 4000 news sources. (New Product)

Oct-02   Google opens its first Australian office in Sydney. (International)

Dec-02   Google launches Froogle to buy stuff (later called Google Product Search). (New Product)

Feb-03   Acquires Pyra Labs, the creators of Blogger. (Acquisition)

Mar-03   We announce a new content-targeted advertising service called AdSense. (New Product)

Apr-03   Acquires Applied Semantics, whose technology bolsters AdSense. (Acquisition)

Apr-03   Google launches Google Grants, an advertising program for nonprofit organizations to run ad campaigns for their cause. (New Product)

Dec-03   Google launches Google Print (later renamed Google Book Search), indexing small excerpts from searched for books. (New Product)

Jan-04   Google launches Orkut as a way to tap into the sphere of social networking. (New Product)

Mar-04   Google formalizes its enterprise unit with the hire of Dave Girouard to run the enterprise search business. (Related Diversification)

Mar-04   Google introduces Google Local (later part of Google Maps), offering business listings, maps, and directions. (New Product - Maps)

Jul-04   Acquires Picasa, a digital photography company. (Acquisition)

Aug-04   Google's Initial Public Offering of 19,605,052 shares of Class A common stock with opening price of $85 per share. (IPO)

Oct-04   Google opens an office in Dublin, Ireland. (International)

Oct-04   Google launches SMS (short message service) to send search queries to GOOGL or on a mobile device. (Related Diversification - Phone)

Oct-04   Google opens new engineering offices in Bangalore and Hyderabad, India. (International - Outsourcing)

Oct-04   Google Desktop Search is introduced so users can search for files and documents stored on their own hard drive. (New Product)

Oct-04   Acquires Keyhole, a digital mapping company whose technology will later become Google Earth. (Acquisition - Maps)

Dec-04   Google opens an R&D center in Tokyo, Japan to attract bright Asian engineers. (International - Outsourcing)

Feb-05   Google Maps goes live. (New Product - Innovation - Maps)

Mar-05   Google launches code.google.com, a new place for developer-oriented resources, including all of our APIs. (New Product)

Mar-05   Acquires Urchin, a web analytics company whose technology is used to create Google Analytics. (Acquisition)

Apr-05   Google Maps features satellite views and directions. (Innovation - Maps)

Apr-05   Google Local goes mobile, and includes SMS driving directions. (Related Diversification - Phone)

May-05   Google releases Blogger Mobile, enabling mobile phone users to post and send photos to their blogs. (Related Diversification - Phone)

May-05   Google launches Personalized Homepage (now iGoogle) enabling users to customize their own Google homepage. (New Product)

Jun-05   Google Mobile Web Search is released, specially formulated for viewing search results on mobile phones. (Related Diversification - Phone)

Jun-05   Google launches Google Earth: a satellite imagery-based mapping service. (New Product - Innovation - Maps)

Aug-05   Google launches Google Talk, which enables Gmail users to talk or

IM over the Internet for free. (New Product)

Sep-05   Google opens new R&D center in China. (International - Outsourcing)

Sep-05   Google Blog Search goes live to facilitate finding current and relevant blog postings. (New Product)

Oct-05   Google launches Google.org, a philanthropic arm of the firm, to address energy and environmental issues. (Diversification - Charity)

Oct-05   Google introduces Google Reader, a feed reader. (New Product)

Nov-05   Google release Google Analytics, formerly Urchin, for measuring the impact of websites and marketing campaigns. (Innovation)

Nov-05   Google opens of our first offices in São Paulo, Brazil and Mexico City, Mexico. (International)

Dec-05   Gmail for mobile launches in the United States. (Innovation - Phone)

Jan-06   Acquires dMarc, a digital radio advertising company. (Acquisition - Unrelated Diversification)

Jan-06   Google launches Google.cn, a local domain version of Google in China. (International – Multi-domestic Competition)

Jan-06   Google introduces Picasa in 25 more languages. (New Market)

Feb-06   Google releases Chat in Gmail, using the instant messaging tools from Google Talk. (New Product)

Feb-06   Google launches Google News for mobile launchers. (New Product - Phone)

Mar-06   Acquires Writely, a web-based word processing application that subsequently becomes the basis for Google Docs. (Acquisition)

Mar-06   Google launches Google Finance, our approach to an improved search experience for financial information. (New Product)

Apr-06   Google launches Google Calendar, complete with sharing and group features. (New Product)

Apr-06   Google releases Maps for France, Germany, Italy and Spain. (New Market)

May-06   Google releases Google Trends, a way to visualize the popularity of searches over time. (New Product)

Jun-06   Google announces Picasa Web Albums, allowing Picasa users to upload and share their photos online. (Innovation)

Jun-06   Google announces Google Checkout, a fast and easy way to pay for online purchases. (New Product)

Jun-06   Gmail, Google News and iGoogle become available on mobile phones in eight more languages. (New Markets - Phone)

Aug-06   Google releases Apps for Your Domain, a suite of applications including Gmail and Calendar for any size organization. (New Product)

Aug-06   Google Book Search begins offering free PDF downloads of books in the public domain. (Innovation)

Oct-06   Acquires YouTube. (Acquisition)

Oct-06   Acquires JotSpot, a collaborative wiki platform, which later becomes Google Sites. (Acquisition)

Dec-06   Google releases Patent Search in the U.S., indexing more than 7 million patents dating back to 1790. (New Product)

Jan-07   Google partners with China Mobile, world's largest mobile telecom carrier, to provide mobile searches in China. (International - Partnership)

Feb-07   Gmail is opened up to everyone, no longer by invitation only. (New Market)

Feb-07   Google launches Google Apps Premier Edition, bringing cloud computing to businesses. (Innovation)

Feb-07   We introduce traffic information to Google Maps for more than 30 cities around the US. (Innovation- Maps)

Jun-07   Google partners with Salesforce.com, combining that company's on-demand CRM applications with AdWords. (Partnership)

Jul-07   Acquires of Postini. (Acquisition)

Aug-07   Google launches Sky inside Google Earth, including layers for constellation information and virtual tours of galaxies. (New Product - Maps)

Sep-07   Google introduces AdSense for Mobile, giving sites for mobile browsers the ability to host same ads as on computers. (Innovation - Phone)

Sep-07   Google adds Presently, a new application for making slide presentations, to Google Docs. (New Product)

Nov-07   Google (with Open Handset Alliance) announces Android, first open platform for mobile devices. (Related Diversification - Phone)

Nov-07   Google.org announces RE<C, an initiative designed to create electricity from renewable sources. (Unrelated Diversification - Energy)

Mar-08   Acquires DoubleClick, which provides internet ad services. (Acquisition)

May-08   Google releases Google Health to the public, allowing people to manage their medical records and health information online. (New Product)

Jul-08   Google releases first downloadable iPhone app. (Related Diversification - Phone)

Sep-08   Unveils G1, the Google Phone on the Android operating system, available through T-Mobile. (Forward Vertical integration - Hardware)

Oct-08   Google introduces Google Earth for the iPhone and iPod touch. (New Market)

Jan-09   Google launches of Picasa for Mac. (New Market)

Feb-09   Google introduces Google Latitude, that lets users share their location with friends. (New Product - Maps)

Feb-09   Adding new languages enables Google Translate to accommodate 41 languages, covering 98% of Internet users. (Innovation - New Markets)

Stages of Growth

Hamel and Breen (2007) described the growth of Google into five stages:

Google 1.0:–Brin and Page invented a search engine that searched the Web, won millions of eyeballs, but generated no real revenue.

Google 2.0:–Google sold its search capacity to AOL, Yahoo!, and other major portals. These partnerships generated revenue and sparked a surge in search requests. Suddenly, Google started to look like a business.

Google 3.0:–Google crafted a clever model for selling ads alongside search results called AdWords. Unlike Yahoo! and others, it eschewed banner ads, and took a newspaper's "church-and-state" view of advertising and content by clearly differentiating between ads and search results. Moreover, advertisers paid only when users actually clicked on a link. Google was well on its way to becoming the Internet's leading retailer of ad space.

Google 4.0:–Google's initially controversial Gmail service, which served up ads based on a computer analysis of each incoming message, provoked a serendipitous bit of learning that led to the creation of AdSense. This breakthrough gave Google the ability to link its ads to virtually any sort of Web content, not just its own search results. AdSense gave webmasters a new way of monetizing content and vastly expand the scope of

Google's business model.

Google 5.0:–Google used its windfall from advertising to fund a flock of new services, including Google Desktop (a cluster of information utilities accessible directly from a user's PC screen), Google Book Search (an ambitious plan to digitize the books from the world's greatest libraries), Google Scholar (a tool for searching academic papers), and Google Chrome, a new Internet search browser.

The company also purchased a number of other firms over the years including, Keyhole (which became Google Earth), Writely (which became Google Docs), YouTube, and Android (which went on to become the Android Operating System for Google's new phone launch called the Android in 2008).

In 2008, Google had more than $4 billion in revenues with the majority of it coming from the company's AdWords business model or click through advertising. AdWords was one of the most revolutionary developments in the media world since television itself, said author John Battelle (2009): "AdWords was what made Google… Google." AdWords was what generated the ads – or "Sponsored Links," you see on a Google results page. You only have to pay for the link when someone actually clicks on the link and goes to the advertiser's web site. It was called "pay-per-click."

STRATEGIES AT GOOGLE

Google's primary corporate strategy was related diversification. Google achieved its diversification strategy through corporate entrepreneurship and innovation and acquisitions. This enabled Google to increase its offerings and decrease its competition. As the industry leader, Google used offensive strategies by constant innovation of its product lines and expansion into other industries like mobile phones, maps, blogging, news, health, etc.

Google provided internet users with the most relevant search results on as many topics as possible. This included going international to outsource and expand markets by providing its products in foreign languages. Google's business level strategy was a broad differentiation strategy, because it offered features that other search engines did not, such as translating from one language into another, while still providing the most relevant search results.

PHILANTHROPY AT GOOGLE

Philanthropy was widespread at Google. The company gave 1% of its equity and yearly profits to philanthropy. Google's five primary areas that it focused on were: (1) Google.org which used Google's information and technology to build products and advocate for policies that address global challenges; (2) Engineering Awards and Programs that supported the next generation of engineers and maintained strong ties with academic institutions worldwide pursuing innovative research in core areas relevant to its mission; (3) Information and Tools to Help You Change the World that were used to promote causes, raise money, and operate more efficiently; (4) Charitable Giving that supported efforts in the local communities and around the globe; and (5) Google Green Initiatives where Google gave back to the community through financing humanitarian efforts in Africa and research on alternative fuels and global warming (Google.org, 2010).

Exhibit 6: Google Philanthropic Initiatives

Google.org - Google.org used Google's strengths in information and technology to build products and advocate for policies that address global challenges.

Google Flu Trends - A tool that uses aggregated Google search data to estimate flu activity in near real-time for 20 countries.

Google PowerMeter - A home energy monitoring tool that gives you the information you need to use less electricity and save money.

Earth Engine - A computational platform for global-scale analysis of satellite imagery to monitor changes in key environmental indicators like forest coverage.

RE<C - An effort to develop utility-scale renewable energy at a price cheaper than that of coal.

Google Crisis Response - A team that provides updated imagery, outreach through our web properties, and engineering tools such as the Person Finder application, in the wake of natural and humanitarian crises.

All For Good - A service, developed by Google and other technology companies, that helps people find volunteer opportunities in their community and share them with their friends. All for Good provides a single search interface for volunteer activities across many major volunteering sites and organizations.

Engineering Awards and Programs

Google supported the next generation of engineers and maintained strong ties with academic institutions worldwide pursuing innovative research in core areas relevant to its mission.

Google Research - Awards for world-class, full-time faculty pursuing research in areas of mutual interest.

BOLD Scholarships - Diversity internships to encourage those who are historically under-represented in the technology industry to explore a new career opportunity.

Google Code University - Tutorials and sample course content so computer science students and educators can learn more about current computing technologies and paradigms.

Google PhD Fellowship Program - Recognition for outstanding graduate students doing exceptional work in computer science, related disciplines, or promising research areas.

Google RISE Awards (Roots in Science and Engineering) - Awards to promote and support science, technology, engineering, mathematics (STEM) and computer science (CS) education initiatives.

Google Scholarships - Scholarships to encourage students to excel in their studies and become active role models and leaders.

Summer of Code - Stipends to student developers to write code for various open source software projects.

Information and Tools to Help You Change the World

Google tools were used to promote causes, raise money, and operate more efficiently.

Google for Non-Profits - Information on free Google tools for creating awareness, fundraising, and operating more efficiently.

Google Grants - In-kind online advertising for non-profit organizations.

Apps for EDU/Non-Profits - Free communication, collaboration and publishing tools, including email accounts, for qualifying non-profits.

Checkout for Non-Profits - A tool to increase online donations for non-profit organizations.

Custom Search for Non-Profits - A customized search experience for non-profit organizations.

Sketchup for EDU - A product allowing educators to create, modify, and share 3D models.

YouTube for EDU - An educational channel for two- and four-year degree granting public and private colleges and universities.

YouTube for Non-Profits - A designated channel, premium branding, and additional free features to drive non-profit fundraising and awareness.

YouTube Video Volunteers - A platform to connect non-profit organizations with volunteers who can help them to create videos.

Google Earth Outreach - Resources to help non-profits visualize their cause and tell their story in Google Earth and Maps.

Google MapMaker - A tool that allows users to contribute, share and edit map information for 174 countries and territories around the world.

Charitable Giving

Googler-led giving to support efforts in our local communities and around the globe.

Corporate Giving Council - A cross-Google team that coordinates support for Googler-led partnerships on causes such as K-12 science/math/technology education and expanding access to information.

Holiday gift - A $22 million donation in 2009 to a couple dozen deserving charities from around the globe in order to help organizations who have been stretched thin by increasing requests for help at a time of lower donations. Gift was in lieu of giving holiday gifts to clients and partners.

Community Affairs - Investments in local communities where Google has a presence, creating opportunities for Googlers to invest their time and expertise in their communities, engage in community grant making, and build partnerships with stakeholders in the community.

Google employee matching - Up to $6,000 company match for each employee's annual charitable contributions and $50 donation for every 5 hours an employee volunteers through the "Dollars for Doers" program.

Google Green Initiatives

Google implemented innovative and responsible environmental practices across the company to reduce its carbon footprint, to ensure efficient computing, and to help its employees be green.

Source: Philanthropy at Google. Accessed May 18, 2010, http://www.google.org/googlers.html

COMPETITION

Google operated in markets that changed rapidly. Google faced the possibility of new and disruptive technologies and faced formidable competition in every aspect of its business, particularly from companies that sought to connect people with information on the web. The company considered Microsoft Corporation and Yahoo! Inc. to be their primary competitors.

Exhibit 7: Yahoo! Financial Ratios 2004-2008

Liquidity Ratios	2008	2007	2006	2005	2004
Quick Ratio	1.97	1.12	1.70	1.79	1.10
Current Ratio	2.78	1.41	2.54	2.86	3.46
Operating Cash Flow Ratio	0.01	0.30	0.64	0.92	0.58
Debt to Equity	0.22	283.00	0.26	0.27	0.30

Profitability Ratios	2008	2007	2006	2005	2004
ROA	3.27	5.56	6.73	18.95	11.08
ROE	4.07	7.06	8.48	24.21	14.61
ROI	0.12	7.15	9.79	12.90	10.59
EBITDA Margin	12.29	21.64	25.49	50.46	37.24
Revenue per employee	528,589	487,362	563,656	536,497	469,046
Net Profit Margin After Tax	-2.31	7.35	9.96	36.10	20.90

Asset Management Ratios	2008	2007	2006	2005	2004
Total Asset Turnover	0.55	0.59	0.58	0.53	0.47
Receivables Turnover	6.79	7.02	7.78	8.75	9.35
Accounts Payable Turnover	43.83	48.86	71.63	88.74	89.01

Google faced competition from other web search providers, including start-ups as well as developed companies that were enhancing or developing search technologies. Google competed with internet advertising companies, particularly in the areas of pay-for-performance and keyword-targeted internet advertising. The company also competed with companies that sold products and services online because these companies were trying to attract users to their web sites to search for information about products and services. Google also provided a number of online products and services, including Gmail, YouTube, and Google Docs, which competed directly with new and established companies offering communication, information, and entertainment services integrated into products or media properties.

Google competed to attract and retain relationships with users, advertisers and

Google Network members and other content providers in different ways (see below, Google's 2008 Annual Report):

• Users. Competed to attract and retain users of their search and communication products and services. Most of the products and services Google offered to users were free, so the company did not compete on price. Instead, the company competed in this area on the basis of the relevance and usefulness of search results, features, availability, and ease of use of products and services.

• Advertisers. Google competed to attract and retain advertisers. Google competed in this area principally on the basis of the return on investment realized by advertisers using the company's AdWords and AdSense programs. Google also competed based on the quality of customer service, features and ease of use of its products and services.

• Google Network members and other content providers. Google competed to attract and retain content providers (Google Network members, as well as other content providers for whom the company distributed or licensed content) primarily based on the size and quality of its advertiser base, and its ability to help these partners generate revenues from advertising and the terms of the agreements.

SILICON VALLEY

Culture & Location

Google was located in the heart of Silicon Valley, Mountain View, California. According to Randy Komisar, an entrepreneur-turned-venture capitalist at Kleiner, Perkins, Caufield, and Byers, "In Silicon Valley we have created a culture that attracts the sort of people who prosper in ambiguity, innovation, and risk taking" (Harris, 2009). Other parts of the U.S. have also been successful at building innovative technology corridors like Boston, Massachusetts and Austin, Texas.

Silicon Valley was often called South San Francisco, but was really comprised of about 60 miles of suburbs immediately to the south of the city of San Francisco. Some of the more prominent cities and companies included (North to South) South San Francisco (Amgen and Genentech), San Mateo (YouTube), Redwood Shores (Oracle Corporation, Electronic Arts, and Sun Microsystems), Menlo Park (most venture capital firms), Palo Alto (Hewlett-Packard and Facebook), Mountain View (AOL, Intuit, RedHat, Symantec, and VeriSign), Sunnyvale (Yahoo!, Ariba, NetApp, and Advanced Micro Devices), Santa Clara (Applied Materials and Nvidia Corporation), Cupertino (Apple, Inc.), San Jose (McAfee, eBay, Adobe Systems, and Cisco Systems), and Los Gatos. Hundreds of prestigious high technology companies were located here.

Exhibit 8: Map of Silicon Valley

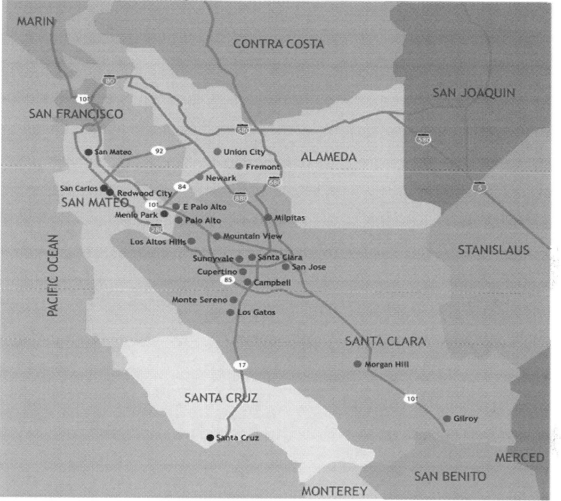

Source: Silicon Valley Cities and Counties, Retrieved May 19, 2009,
http://www.siliconvalleyonline.org/cities.html

Exhibit 9: Leading Public Companies in Silicon Valley

Company	Symbol
AGILENT TECHNOLOGIES, Inc.	A
APPLE	AAPL
ACTEL	ACTL
ADOBE SYSTEMS	ADBE
ADAPTEC	ADPT
AFFYMETRIX	AFFX
ALIGN TECHNOLOGY	ALGN
ALTERA CORP	ALTR
APPLIED MATERIALS	AMAT
APPLIED MICRO	AMCC
ADVANCED MICRO DEVICES	AMD
APPLIED SIGNAL TECH	APSG
ARIBA	ARBA
ARUBA NETWORKS	ARUN
ATHEROS COMMS	ATHR
BIGBAND NETWORKS	BBND
BROCADE COMM	BRCD
CADENCE DESIGN	CDNS
CHORDIANT SOFTWARE	CHRD
Credence Systems Corp	CMOS
COHERENT	COHR
CISCO SYSTEMS	CSCO
CYPRESS SEMICONDUCTOR	CY
CYBERSOURCE	CYBS
DATA DOMAIN	DDUP
DSP GROUP	DSPG
EBAY	EBAY
ELECTRS FOR IMAGING	EFII
ECHELON	ELON
EQUINIX	EQIX
ELECTRONIC ARTS	ERTS
EXTREME NETWORKS	EXTR
Foundry Networks, Inc.	FDRY
FINISAR	FNSR
GILEAD SCIENCES	GILD
GOOGLE-A	GOOG
GRANITE CONSTRUCTION, Inc.	GVA
HARMONIC	HLIT

Company	Symbol
Hewlett-Packard Company	HPQ
INTEGR DEVICE TECH	IDTI
INFORMATICA	INFA
Intel	INTC
INTUIT	INTU
IPASS	IPAS
INTERSIL-A	ISIL
INTUITIVE SURGICAL	ISRG
INTEGR SILICON SOL	ISSI
INTEVAC	IVAC
Interwoven, Inc.	IWOV
SUN MICROSYSTEMS	JAVA
JDS UNIPHASE	JDSU
JUNIPER NETWORKS	JNPR
KLA-TENCOR	KLAC
LINEAR TECHNOLOGY	LLTC
LAM RESEARCH CORP	LRCX
LSI CORPORATION	LSI
MICREL	MCRL
MCAFEE, Inc.	MFE
MONOLITHIC POWER	MPWR
MACROVISION SOLNS	MVSN
NANOMETRICS INC	NANO
NETFLIX	NFLX
NEKTAR THERAPEUTICS	NKTR
NATIONAL SEMICONDUCTOR	NSM
NETAPP	NTAP
NETGEAR	NTGR
NVIDIA	NVDA
NOVELLUS SYSTEMS	NVLS
OMNICELL	OMCL
OPLINK COMMS	OPLK
OPENWAVE SYSTEMS	OPWV
ORACLE	ORCL
OMNIVISION TECH	OVTI
PALM	PALM
VERIFONE HOLDINGS, Inc.	PAY
PDL BIOPHARMA	PDLI
PMC-SIERRA	PMCS

Company	Symbol
POWER INTEGRATIONS	POWI
PERICOM SEMICONDCTR	PSEM
QUANTUM CORPORATION	QTM
RACKABLE SYSTEMS	RACK
ROBERT HALF INTERNATIONAL, Inc.	RHI
RAMBUS	RMBS
Silicon Graphics, Inc.	SGIC
SILICON IMAGE	SIMG
SYMYX TECHNOLOGIES	SMMX
SANDISK	SNDK
SYNOPSYS	SNPS
SYNNEX CORPORATION	SNX
SUNPOWER-A	SPWR
SILICON STORGE TECH	SSTI
SYMANTEC	SYMC
SYMMETRICOM	SYMM
SYNAPTICS	SYNA
TIVO	TIVO
TRIDENT MICROSYSTEM	TRID
TRIMBLE NAVIGATION	TRMB
TESSERA TECH	TSRA
VARIAN MEDICAL SYSTEMS, Inc.	VAR
VARIAN	VARI
VMWARE, Inc.	VMW
VERISIGN	VRSN
XILINX	XLNX
YAHOO	YHOO

Cost of Living

Silicon Valley was one of the most expensive places to live in the U.S. During the recent housing boom, the average house in the region sold for $800,000. Prices differed depending on the city. For example, during the height of the housing boom an average house in San Jose sold for $710,000. However, by 2009, the price had fallen to $475,000 or a 33% plunge. Real estate in Palo Alto held up better than other parts of Silicon Valley. The average price of a home at the housing peak was $1.2 million versus $1.1 million in early 2009. Several factors contributed to Palo Alto's resilience: (1) The city was sunny and beautiful; (2) its proximity to Stanford; (3) the limited amount of housing available (no space for new homes); (4) its proximity to all of the top high-tech companies in the region (Google and Apple were 15 minutes away), and (5) the prestigious K-12 school system. Steve Jobs, CEO of Apple Inc., Steve Young, former star quarterback of the San Francisco 49rs, and Page all lived in Palo Alto.

The average per capita personal income in the U.S. was $39,751, however in Silicon Valley salaries were 30% above the average. While this may sound encouraging, the cost of living in Silicon Valley was significantly higher than most places in the U.S. For example, if you made $100,000 a year in Dallas, Texas and took a job at Google and moved to Palo Alto you would have to make a salary of $252,226 to afford the same lifestyle. The high cost of living was a barrier that the company had to overcome when recruiting employees.

Education and Employees

There were a number of universities and colleges in the San Francisco area, however there were only two world class research universities; Stanford University and the University of California at Berkeley. Some of the brightest minds from all over the world came to Silicon Valley to work and/or attend these schools. San Jose State University, which was also located in Silicon Valley, was also a major feeder of engineers to high tech companies in the region. Furthermore, several of these engineers went on to become leaders in their respective companies (e.g., Gordon Moore, founder of Intel Corporation in 1968).

The region was a breeding ground for some of the brightest minds in the world. The area had a forward looking energy. People were more entrepreneurial because they had witnessed great wealth creation. According to Bill Powar, one of the founders of VeriSign, "I worked at Visa for 30 years, but when the internet was created we saw an opportunity to create the first internet security system that is still used today." Powar made millions on the initial public offering and retired.

Access to Capital & Legal Infrastructure

Money was another key variable for the success of Silicon Valley. Sand Hill Road in Menlo Park was famous for the large number of venture capital firms in a very small area. During the dot.com boom, real estate there was the most expensive in the world. A small number of employees worked in very small office buildings that were often hidden by trees and brushes. At Kleiner, Perkins, Caufield, and Byers, one of the premier venture capital firms in the world, bottlebrush trees hid the name of the firm. Other prestigious venture capital firms there were Sequoia Capital, Interwest Partners, Kohlberg Kravis Roberts, Draper Fisher Jurveston, etc. This proximity to venture capital gave Google a competitive advantage since venture capital firms liked to be close to their investments and sit on their boards.

As Silicon Valley grew, the number of law firms specializing in funding, litigation, resolving disputes, high tech companies, and intellectually property grew enormously. Many of these firms were located in San Francisco and Palo Alto.

CORPORATE ENTREPRENEURSHIP & INNOVATION

Corporate entrepreneurship (Guth & Ginsberg, 1990) is a term used to describe entrepreneurial behavior inside established mid-sized and large organizations. Corporate entrepreneurship can be formal or informal activities aimed at creating new businesses in established companies through product and process innovations and market developments (Zahra, 1991). Innovation is a key ingredient of corporate entrepreneurship where one can take an idea or invention and create something new of value. For example, an innovation of the toothbrush is the electric toothbrush.

Rule and Irwin (1988) stated that companies established a culture of innovation through: the formation of teams and task forces; recruitment of new staff with new ideas; application of strategic plans that focused on achieving innovation; and the establishment of internal research and development programs that were likely to see tangible results.

The roots of corporate entrepreneurship proliferated at 3M Corporation. 3M was the first company that introduced "organizational slack" as a key factor enabling their engineers and scientists to spend 15% of their time on projects of their own design. As a result of this many inventions came out of 3M (e.g., Post it Notes and Scotch Tape).

CORPORATE ENTREPRENEURSHIP & INNOVATION AT GOOGLE

Google's mission was not based on money alone; rather it was to improve the world. The heart and soul of Google was based on entrepreneurship and innovation. The philosophy of the company started at Stanford University. Stanford had a program dedicated to the formation of technology oriented ventures called the STVP or the Stanford Technology Ventures Program in the School of Engineering. The school had a rich 100 year history of students and faculty that created fledging organizations like Federal Telegraph and Telephone, Hewlett-Packard, Varian Associates, SRI International, Yahoo!, Cisco, Sun Microsystems, Silicon Graphics, Varian Medical Systems, and VMware.

Stanford encouraged their professors to create companies based on their research. According to Dr. Thomas Lee, the founder of Stanford's Integrated Circuits Laboratory, "Entrepreneurship is built into the DNA of Stanford." When Lee arrived, he said that colleagues told him that he would have to do a startup. He said there was a kind of peer pressure on campus to start a business. The President, John L. Hennessey, had prospered as an entrepreneur in MIPS Computer Systems (now MIPS Technologies) and Silicon Graphics (Harris 2009). Stanford also encouraged their professors to take equity stakes in companies. This culture fostered entrepreneurial ventures throughout the region. In the

2009 student business plan competition there were 235 entries, double the amount during the dot.com boom.

Google's management model was similar to other high-tech companies like Microsoft, Apple, and Cisco. Google bought many of the buildings around its original office. The make-up, location, and culture of the company were similar to that of a college or university. It was not uncommon to see many bicycles around the campus traveling from building to building along with people playing volleyball outdoors.

According to current CEO Eric Schmidt (2009), "I looked at Google as an extension of graduate school; similar kinds of people, similar kinds of crazy behavior, but people who were incredibly smart and who were highly motivated and had a sense of change, a sense of optimism. It was a culture of people who felt that they could build things; they could actually accomplish what they wanted and ultimately people stay in companies because they can achieve something."

Brin and Page created a company that had some of the brightest minds in the world. Similar to a top flight university, they hired the brightest minds, worked in small teams, received feedback, and their mission was to improve the world. The culture of Google had similar values as academia in the sense that everything was questioned. Ideas were critiqued by your peers not just your managers. At Google, position and hierarchy seldom won an argument, and the founders wanted to keep it that way (Hamel and Breen, 2007).

Another factor that contributed to the success of Google was their flat, open organizational structure. Typical corporate models had many layers of management and strategy was driven top down. However at Google, the company was highly democratic and employees were encouraged to question anyone. Strategy tended to come from bottom up. Company President, Eric Schmidt, stated that he talked with many employees every day about their various projects. The culture and structure of Google initiated from Brin and Page's attitude, "We do not like authority and we do not like being told what to do." Brin and Page understood that breakthroughs come from questioning assumptions and smashing paradigms (Hamel and Breen, 2007).

In order to increase the effectiveness of communication, the company developed an intranet, called "MOMA," or Message Oriented Middleware Application." MOMA was a Web page and threaded conversation for each of the company's several hundred internal projects, making it easy for teams to communicate their progress, garner feedback, and solicit help. The company also created a program called Snippets; a site where all Google engineers could post a summary of their activities. Any Googler could search the Snippets list to locate individuals working on similar projects, or to simply stay abreast of what was happening (Hamel and Breen, 2007).

Google also had a policy of giving outsized rewards to people who came up with outsized ideas, a team-focused approach to product development, and a corporate credo that challenged every employee to put the user first (Hamel and Breen, 2007).

Support from Top Management

Google sought out the best and brightest from all over the world. Google was committed to having one of the most open and entrepreneurial environments in the world. Evidence of this could be seen in a recent study of MBA graduates who were interviewed about which company they wanted to work for and Google was number one, where 20% of all MBA graduates said they wanted to work for Google after graduation (CNNMoney.com, 2009).

Corporate Culture and Employees

The most critical factor in stimulating entrepreneurship within Google was the culture. Keys to success included forming an innovative and loose structure with quality employees. It was also essential to reward entrepreneurship and innovation.

Exhibit 10: Example of an Employee's Desk at Google

COURTESY: GOOGLE

Google's hiring process was based upon the belief of Brin and Page that A-level talent wanted to work with A-level talent and B-level talent tended to hire B-level talent or lower. This can ruin an organization. As a result, Google's hiring process could be painful to applicants. Interviews often extended several weeks and potential employees were often given scientists Mensa-level problems to solve on the spot. Decisions on candidates were made by veteran associates and executives. It was an admittedly brutal process, but it weeded out anyone who was merely average (Hamel and Breen, 2007).

Brin and Page tried to keep the layers of management to a minimum. They also tried to keep the communication channels narrow so people could act quickly. They disliked taking orders from people and hated being managed. According to Brin and Page, "Our management philosophy amplified that quality employees who are motivated do not need to be managed." Similar to academia, Google gave their employees a lot of freedom.

Google's web site stated that its philosophy was, "Never Settle for the Best." Google's persistence, along with enormous amounts of energy and ambition brought about its success. The company's website listed "Ten Things Google Has Found to be True:"

1. Focus on the user and all else will follow.

2. It is best to do one thing really, really well.

3. Fast is better than slow.

4. Democracy on the web works.

5. You do not need to be at your desk to need an answer.

6. You can make money without doing evil.

7. There is always more information out there.

8. The need for information crosses all borders.

9. You can be serious without a suit.

10. Great is not good enough.

(Source: http://www.google.com/corporate/tenthings.html, Accessed May 17, 2009).

Page and Brin placed heavy emphasis on providing a relaxed and fun work environment. They believed that employees should create their own hours and work them as they felt they were most productive. Google's staff worked 80% of their hours on regular work and the other 20% on noncore projects (organizational slack). The company estimated that it developed 10-12 new service offerings every quarter. According to Marisa Mayer (2009), Vice President of Search Product and User Experience and the first female engineer hired at Google, "The 20% was one of the keys to our success. It gave the engineers the ability to work on whatever they were passionate about. You never know when you are going to create great products. That was why we gave them the opportunity to be creative. That was how Google News and Gmail were born. You have to try a number of different things. Certainly we are in the business of searching and advertising, but basically we are in the business of innovation. Our innovation strategy has been three fold:

(1) allow small teams to work together, (2) allow ideas to come from everywhere, and (3) give employees 20% free time to work on any projects they have a passion for. These have all contributed to our success."

Google prided itself on its open, social environment but many people felt that Google had turned increasingly "corporate". The environment in which engineers were able to create their own products and services was decreasing since it had to go through a full review process that could take months before the product was released to market. Although engineers enjoyed being creative, they might as well create a product/service that they can monetize on their own.

Despite these factors, Google had problems related to the rapid growth of the company. As of May, 2009 Google had over 20,000 employees. This had a negative effect on the company's ability to maintain an entrepreneurial culture. The most often heard complaint was that the employees' skills were not being utilized. As one Ivy League graduate stated, "I have an Ivy League education and I was hired to shuffle papers in Human Resources. I quit after six months."

Small, Self-Managed Teams

The majority of Google's employees worked in teams of three engineers when working on product development. Big products like Gmail could have 30 or more people with three to four people on a team. Each team had a specific assignment (e.g., building spam filters or improving the forwarding feature). Each team had a leader, however leaders rotated on teams. Engineers often worked on more than one project and were free to switch teams. According to Shona Brown, Google's VP for operations, "If at all possible, we want people to commit to things, rather than be assigned to things," (Hamel and Breen, 2007).

Reward Structure

Google was called a playground on steroids where there were 18 cafes staffed with 7 executive chefs. Google was known for offering its staff incredible free perks: volleyball court, gyms, gourmet lunches and dinners (although leaving after eating dinner was frowned upon); Ben & Jerry's Ice Cream, yoga classes, employees could bring their dogs to work, onsite masseuse, office physician, laundry service, travel back and forth to work, etc. This made Google one of the most sought after companies to work for. Google offered great perks to their employees because they wanted the brightest and most qualified employees focusing their attention on their jobs all of the time.

Google employees earned a base salary that was on par with, or slightly lower than the industry average, however the standard deviation around that average was higher at Google than it was at most other companies. At Google, annual bonuses amounted to 30% to 60% of base salary, but the financial upside could be much, much bigger for those that came up with a profit-pumping idea (Hamel and Breen, 2007).

Google understood that entrepreneurs were motivated by money. Therefore in 2004, they created the "Founders Awards." These were restricted stock options (sometimes worth millions) that were given quarterly to teams that came up with the best ideas to increase the profitability of the company. The largest such award to date went to a team led by Eric Veach. His team created a new advertising algorithm, dubbed "Smart-Ads" and won $10 million (Hamel and Breen, 2007).

DECISION POINT

As Brin and Page sat through the concert they thought, "Look at Green Day. These guys have been successful for years and they still ROCK!! If Green Day can do it, so can Google." But Brin and Page realized that in order to accomplish their goals they would need to figure out how to solve their corporate problems. Their primary problem was how to maintain their culture of corporate entrepreneurship and innovation in the face of flat net profits from 2007 to 2008. Additionally, a multitude of other issues faced the company: (1) a decrease in advertising revenue, (2) the firing of several employees for the first time in the company's history and the elimination of products that made no money, and (3) the loss of employees for a variety of reasons (e.g., lack of mentoring and formal career planning, too much bureaucracy, low pay and benefits, high cost of living in the area, desire to start their own business, etc.). If Google wanted to continue its main strategy of growth through innovation, it would have to find a way to recruit and retain the best employees.

Google had to figure out how to maintain its culture of corporate entrepreneurship and innovation in an era of stagnant profitability. Furthermore, the company had grown to over 20,000 employees. How could it maintain its culture with so large an organization?

DISCUSSION QUESTIONS

1. What are the major problems facing Google in 2009?

2. Given the economic environment in 2009 as described in the case, what implications, opportunities and threats does this context pose for Google currently? What about in 2012?

3. Based on the content of the case, what was the primary Strategic Inflection Point for Google? Why did you select this point?

4. What were Google's keys to success?

5. What recommendations would you make to Google? Why?

REFERENCES

1. 100 Top MBA Employers. *CNNMoney.com,* Accessed May 28, 2009, http://money.cnn.com/magazines/fortune/mba100/2009/full_list/

2. Battelle, J. (2009). *Inside the Mind of Google.* CNBC Interview. December 3, 2009.

3. Blodget, H. (2009). Google Announces Layoffs (GOOG). *Silicon Valley Insider.* Accessed May 15, 2009, http://www.businessinsider.com/2009/1/google-announces-layoffs-goog.

4. Brandon, E. (2009). Retirement Accounts Have Lost $3.4 Trillion. *USNews.com.* Accessed May 28, 2009. Accessed May 28, 2009, http://www.usnews.com/blogs/planning-to-retire/2009/03/13/retirement-accounts-have-now-lost-34-trillion.html

5. Buffett: Economy in a Recession Will Be Worse Than Feared. *USA Today.com,* April 4, 2008. Accessed May 15, http://www.usatoday.com/money/economy/2008-04-28-buffett-recession_N.htm

6. Christie, L. (2009). Homes Almost 20% Cheaper. *CNNMoney.com.* Accessed May 24, 2009, http://money.cnn.com/2009/05/26/real_estate/CaseShiller_home_prices_Q1/index.htm?cnn=yes

7. Google Milestones (2009). Accessed on March 31, 2009, http://www.google.com/corporate/history.html

8. Google.org (2010). *Philanthropy at Google.* Accessed May 18, 2010, http://www.google.org/googlers.html.

9. Guth, W. & Ginsberg, A. (1990). "Guest Editors' Introduction: Corporate Entrepreneurship", *Strategic Management Journal,* 11, 297-308.

10. Hamel, G. & Breen, B. (2007). Aiming for an Evolutionary Advantage. *Harvard Business Review*. Harvard Business School Press, Boston, MA.

11. Harris, S. (2009) Stanford's Rich Entrepreneurial Culture Still Bursting with Ideas, Nurturing Minds. *San Jose Mercury News*, May 10, pages 1, 19.

12. Lowe, (2009). *Google Speaks: Secrets of the World's Greatest Billionaire Entrepreneurs.* John Wiley & Sons. Page 282.

13. Miller, M. (2006). *Googlepedia: The Ultimate Google Resource.* Que. Page 10

14. Pinchot, G. & Pellman, R. (1999) *Intrapreneuring in Action: A Handbook for Business Innovation.* Berrett-Koehler.

15. Pohle, G. & Chapman, M. (2006). IBM Global CEO Study 2006: Business Model Innovation Matters. *Strategy and Leadership*, 34, 5, 34-40.

16. Rule, E & Irwin, D. (1988). Fostering Intrapreneurship: The New Competitive Edge. *Journal of Business Strategy.* 9, 3, 44–47.

17. S&P 500 Index (2009). Accessed October 24, 2009, http://finance.yahoo.com/q/hp?s=^GSPC&a=0&b=3&c=1950&d=9&e=25&f=2009&g=d&z=66&y=132.

18. Schmidt, E. (2009). *Inside the Mind of Google.* CNBC Interview. December 3, 2009.

19. Thompson, C. (2001). *Current Biography Yearbook.* Hw Wilson Co. Page 50

20. Willis, B. (2009). *U.S. Recession Worst Since Great Depression*, Revised Data Show. Accessed November 27, 2009, http://www.bloomberg.com/apps/news?pid=20601087&sid=aNivTjr852TI.

21. Wolcott, R. & Lippitz, M. (2007). The Four Models of Corporate Entrepreneurship. *MIT Sloan Management Review.* Fall, 49, 1, 74-82.

22. Zahra, S. (1991). Predictors and Financial Outcomes of Corporate Entrepreneurship: An Exploratory Study. *Journal of Business Venturing*, 6, 4, 259-285.

WAYNE HUIZENGA: THE TALE OF A CLASSIC ENTREPRENEUR

Todd A. Finkle, Gonzaga University

INTRODUCTION

It was a stormy day on April 9, 2010 in South Florida where famous businessman H. Wayne Huizenga lived. Huizenga was listed as the 463th richest man in the world with a net worth of $2.3 billion according to *Forbes Magazine* (2010). Huizenga was a self-made entrepreneur who made his fortune in garbage hauling, video rentals, automobile sales and rentals, security alarms, professional sports franchises, hotels, portable toilets, lawn care, bottled water, pest control, billboards, and machine parts washing service (Fridson, 2010).

His career started with a single garbage truck in 1962, from which he was the only person in history to build three Fortune 1000 companies and the only person to build six NYSE-listed companies. He is also the only person to ever own three professional sports teams in a single market (*Young Entrepreneur,* 2009).

Despite all of these accomplishments, Huizenga was getting the entrepreneurial itch once again. He was contemplating what opportunities were available in today's economic environment. After all, he had a net worth of $2.3 billion dollars.

H. WAYNE HUIZENGA

H. Wayne Huizenga was born on December 29, 1937 in Evergreen Park, Illinois, a suburb of Chicago. Huizenga referred to his childhood as miserable, chaotic, and dangerous. His father Harry was the son of a Dutch immigrant named Harm Huizenga. His grandfather, Harm, founded the first garbage-hauling business in Chicago in 1894. Huizenga's father Harry declined to enter the family's garbage business and became a carpenter and homebuilder.

In his youth, Huizenga went to Dutch private schools. He described his family life growing up as difficult, as his father's quick temper and mother's emotions led to a volatile combination (DeGeorge, 1996, p. 4). His family had financial troubles which contributed to a volatile family life. As a result, Huizenga became independent and intense at a very young age. Huizenga's friend Dick Molenhouse stated, "From the time his folks' problems started, he was basically on his own. He did his own thinking then as he does today" (DeGeorge, 1996). Huizenga was a curious person that had the ability to talk to everyone and anyone.

Huizenga was extremely hard working. At age 14, he helped out in the family business while his father was in the hospital. Huizenga also helped out the family by working at gas stations and driving a truck in high school.

Huizenga's parents fought constantly when he was a teenager. As a result of the physical and mental abuse from his father, Huizenga's mother had a nervous breakdown in 1953. In an attempt to save his marriage, Huizenga's father moved the family to Fort Lauderdale, Florida. South Florida was booming; Huizenga loved the area and his father entered the construction industry. Harry was moderately successful, but faced financial problems when he focused on larger custom homes. This increased the financial stress on the household.

The financial stress peaked when his father attacked his wife, daughter, and Huizenga himself. Following this incident, his wife filed for divorce in July, 1954.

In a divorce petition filed in 1954, Jean Huizenga accused her husband of ongoing mental and physical abuse that eventually landed her in a mental hospital (Almond 2004). The troubles got even worse after the divorce as Huizenga's father, at times, was unable to pay alimony.

Based on his family's constant financial troubles, Huizenga learned a valuable lesson at a young age; the value of cash and paying your bills. He also learned that you have to learn how to take care of yourself at a very young age. This was the foundation of Huizenga's drive for success.

In Florida, Huizenga attended high school at the Private Pine Crest School. He was the poorest student at the affluent school, which was the only preparatory school in the area. Huizenga was not a great student. He needed much assistance with his classes to pass.

During high school he became the class treasurer and business manager for the yearbook and newspaper. He was also the third baseman on the baseball team and linebacker and center for the football team. Huizenga was a perfectionist and had the ability to understand people quickly, which benefited him enormously in business. During summer vacations, Huizenga moved to Chicago to work for family friends, driving a dump truck.

After high school, Huizenga obtained a loan from his Uncle to purchase a dump truck. He used the truck for various projects until it broke down. He then moved back to Chicago to work in construction. After a brief stint at this, he was approached by his Uncle Pete who offered to pay for him to go to college. Huizenga took him up on the offer and attended Calvin College in Grand Rapids, Michigan for three semesters. But he dropped out and moved back to Florida where he worked construction for his father. After this, he served in the Army Reserve to avoid the Vietnam War draft. When he returned from the Army, he got a job working as a manager for a family friend's garbage business.

HUIZENGA AND WASTE MANAGEMENT INC.

At the age of 23 years old, Huizenga married his high school sweetheart, Joyce Vander-Wagon. While he was managing his father's friend's garbage business, Huizenga saw an ad in the paper for a refuse business for sale with $500 a month in revenues. Huizenga met the owner, Wilbur Porter, and said, "Wilbur I want to buy your business but I do not have any money. I bugged Porter for months and he finally said that he would finance me. That was my first leverage buyout" (Huizenga, 2009). In 1962, Porter sold the young entrepreneur a snub-nosed truck and $500 worth of customers. On February 14, 1962, Huizenga incorporated Southern Sanitation Service with $5,000 he borrowed from his father-in-law to purchase a single used garbage truck and 20 commercial accounts from Wilbur Porter of Porter's Rubbish Service in Broward County, Florida (Huizenga, 10 March 2010).

Huizenga's work habits were epic, as his secretary, Judy Balfoort recalls, "He was always there before anyone else and he was always the last one to leave and in between he just did everything" (DeGeorge, 1996, p. 15). In the beginning, a typical day for Huizenga consisted of him collecting trash from 2:30 a.m. until 12 p.m. He then went home and showered, put on a suit, and went out to build new accounts. His business model was based on two streams of revenue. First he would make money by hauling trash and second he would make money through renting receptacles (bins).

Huizenga's brother-in-law, Harris Whit Hudson once said with respect to Huizenga, "The most important thing to him was the customer . . . you had better do right by the customer. No matter what it took and no matter what it cost you. If you lose that one customer, you are going to lose more customers." Huizenga prided his operation on its sharp appearance, ensuring that the garbage trucks were clean and painted. He also made it a point to have clear communication with everyone, making sure that there were no surprises (DeGeorge, 1996, p. 16).

Huizenga's operation was a success, however his first marriage failed. Huizenga built up his company to 40 trucks by 1968. That same year, Huizenga merged his garbage business with the garbage company of his three widowed aunts and Dean Buntrock, from Chicago. According to Huizenga, "Buntrock became a family member by marrying one of Huizenga's cousins, B.J." (Huizenga, 8 May 2010). Together they created a new company called Waste Management, Inc. Within six months the firm went public at $16 a share and raised $3 million. Over the next nine months, Huizenga was the driving force behind acquiring 100 competitors through stock swaps. Stock swaps entailed buying the competitors with stock from Waste Management, Inc.

In 1972, Huizenga married his former secretary, Marti Goldsby, a widow with two children. Huizenga already had two children from his previous marriage. By 1983,

Waste Management, Inc. was the largest garbage hauling business in the United States. In 1984, the company had $10 billion in revenues while Huizenga was the COO and president of the company.

In 1984, Huizenga resigned at the age of 46, taking with him 3.7 million shares of stock worth approximately $23 million. He retired for only a few weeks before starting his next venture; he began buying hotels, office buildings, pest control businesses, warehouses, and lawn care services. By the end of 1986, Huizenga and his new company, Huizenga Holdings, had bought more than 100 businesses that generated $100 million in annual income (Huizenga, 10 March 2010).

HUIZENGA AND BLOCKBUSTER INC.

In 1985, David Cook and his wife, Sandy created Blockbuster Video in Dallas, Texas. Blockbuster competed in the fragmented video rental industry at that time. The Cooks had created a successful concept where their niche was longer hours and a larger inventory of videos combined with a brighter atmosphere than other traditional stores. The store was 6,000 square-feet, had 6,500+ titles in an x-rated free environment, and was a refreshing change from the traditional video business (Huizenga, 10 March 2010). Cook expanded to three stores by the summer of 1986.

The company was set to have an initial public offering in 1986. However, before it was able to raise additional capital, Barron's Magazine came out with an article questioning the Cook's business skills and the viability of the business (*Barron's*, 1986). According to Cook, "The article's impact was the single changing point in my life" (DeGeorge, 1996, p. 100). Blockbuster lost $3.2 million in 1986.

In November, 1986, John Melk, a previous employee at Waste Management Inc., contacted Huizenga about Blockbuster. He stated that this was a great investment opportunity that Huizenga needed to investigate. Huizenga finally took him up on the offer and visited a Blockbuster store in Chicago in February of 1987. Huizenga, Melk, and Donald F. Flynn (a Waste Management executive), purchased a 35% stake in Blockbuster for $18.5 million. Cook and Huizenga differed in their philosophies of how Blockbuster would be run, with Cook more interested in franchising and Huizenga seeing growth through corporate store ownership (*Hoovers, Inc.*, 2009). By April of 1987, Cook was bought out for $20 million and the Blockbuster headquarters moved to Fort Lauderdale, Florida (DeGeorge, 1996, p. 108). Huizenga was now in charge. He recognized the potential and followed the growth-by-acquisition playbook honed in his Waste Management days. Huizenga purchased dozens of video chains all over the United States. The stock soared and Huizenga took a $1 salary a year for the first three years. The majority of his income was based on stock options.

Huizenga and his partners bought into Blockbuster when it owned 19 stores. Huizenga grew Blockbuster through aggressive acquisitions and franchising. Blockbuster's philosophy was to purchase local and regional video store chains, and then maintain a familiar atmosphere in the stores (Greenberg, 2008, p. 128). The stores were bright, selling only rentals, candy, soda, and popcorn. The breakneck pace of expansion was in full-gear. Blockbuster had everything needed to build and stock a new store packed in a tractor-trailer. Empty stores to ready ones could occur in just a day. As Richard Nathenson, a former worker once said referencing Blockbuster's efficiency, "It was an amazing company… I'm not saying good or bad, but I'm just saying amazing" (Greenberg, 2008, p. 129). According to Allen Klose, former Vice President of Marketing Research for Blockbuster, "Huizenga was amazing. We would have board meetings in the morning and in the afternoon we would be implementing our strategies."

According to Huizenga, "We broke down the country into eight regions and hired a manager in: marketing, operations, real estate, construction, and regional vice president to oversee each region" (Huizenga, 2009). Huizenga's goal was to open 250 stores a year. Over the next six years one store opened every 17 hours.

Huizenga wanted to raise additional funding in a secondary offering, but the combination of another negative Barron's article in September of 1987 and the stock market collapse on Black Monday, forced Huizenga to ask his friends and family for additional capital (Alpert, 1987). Huizenga's wife, Marti, noted that this was a turning point for Huizenga. "He felt such a [great] sense of responsibility to the people who invested their money… I think it still would be what it is today, but maybe not in the same time frame" (DeGeorge, 1996, p. 125).

What made the expansion possible was Huizenga's willingness to hire people that were better than him. Huizenga stated, "You always hear about delegation," he says, "but people make the mistake of delegating and not following up. I give authority, but I stay in touch. Otherwise it does not work" (DeGeorge, 1996, p. 125).

Huizenga's legendary 12- to 14-hour workdays were a model for what he expected of others. "This place," said Thomas A. Gruber, a former Blockbuster chief marketing officer, "is run like a presidential campaign, 24 hours a day. We get in early, go home late, travel after hours, have meetings on the plane. Huizenga sets the pace and everybody needs to move at that pace" (DeGeorge, 1996, p. 125).

The Blockbuster culture was very conservative under Huizenga. The company forbade employees to speak to reporters without corporate permission and also forbade male employees from wearing their hair long. Employees at Blockbuster were instructed on how to greet customers and referred customers to printed recommendations instead of their personal video recommendations (Greenberg, 2003).

Blockbuster dominated the suburbs, but found the urban environment challenging and the rural environment unprofitable. The Blockbuster model changed the video store culture, from one that was a community, to one that was business-like in approach, but making the experience more family friendly (Greenberg, 2003).

By 1990, Blockbuster's revenues surpassed $1 billion. Blockbuster generated $89 million in profit on $1.5 billion in sales in 1991 and by the end of that year, there were Blockbuster owned stores in Japan, Chile, Venezuela, Puerto Rico, Spain, Australia, New Zealand, and Guam. By 1993, there were more than 3,400 video stores worldwide, about one-third of them overseas (*Hoovers, Inc.*, 2009). During this year, Blockbuster acquired a one-third, controlling share in Republic Pictures, a movie and television production and Distribution Company (SunSentinel.com). In March 1993, Blockbuster acquired a 53.8 percent stake in Spelling Entertainment for $141.5 million dollars (*Associated Press*, 1993). Huizenga bought up competitors Errol's Video Inc., then the third largest video store chain, and Major Video (*Hoovers, Inc.*, 2009).

Though Blockbuster was international and had diverse holdings, Huizenga was worried that evolving technology could make video tape rental obsolete. An exit strategy appeared in January of 1994. Blockbuster was able to sell itself to Viacom Inc. in a deal valued at $8.4 billion (*Columbia Business Review*, 2010). Huizenga's $18.5 million investment in Blockbuster, along with options, was worth $600 million when he stepped down as CEO in 1994. An investment of $25,000 in Blockbuster in 1987 would have been worth $1 million seven years later (Sexton, 2001, p. 41).

HUIZENGA AND PROFESSIONAL SPORTS

During the Blockbuster years, Huizenga purchased 15% of the professional football's Miami Dolphins in 1989. In 1990, he purchased 50% of Miami's Joe Robbie Stadium in Dade County, Florida. By 1994, Huizenga purchased all of the stadium and the football team for $138 million. In 1991, Huizenga beat out 10 other cities to gain Major League Baseball's (MLB) newest franchise and the first professional baseball team in Florida history, the Florida Marlins (Huizenga, 10 March 2010). The Marlins cost $95 million in 1993 and within four years they became World Series Champions in 1997. Several months before the championship games, however, on June 27, 1997, Huizenga had announced that he would sell the Marlins and take a $39 million loss, but would not sell them to anyone who would take them away from Miami.

Realizing also that, southern Florida was home to millions of transplanted northeasterners and Canadians, Huizenga spent $50 million to win Miami a National Hockey League (NHL) expansion team, the Florida Panthers, in 1992 (Huizenga, 10 March 2010).

Huizenga made no secret of his view of sports franchises as businesses and his disappointment over the financial performance of both teams. The man who was a hometown hero for bringing the franchises to South Florida became the object of fan disappointment and anger when the championship teams were dismantled to cut costs.

In 1999, Huizenga sold the Marlins to commodities trader John Henry (the team was later sold in 2002 to Jeff Loria, an art dealer). After expressing interest in selling the Panthers, Huizenga instead took the team public in 1997, folding into the public company four resorts to create a company called Boca Resorts Inc., which owned the Boca Raton Hotel & Club, Hyatt Pier 66, and Radisson Bahia Mar among other properties. In 2001, Huizenga sold the Florida Panthers to ex Cleveland Browns quarterback Bernie Kosar and Alan Cohen at a reduced price. However, Huizenga still owned the building where they played, the BankAtlantic Center. In 2004, he sold Boca Resorts Inc. to the Blackstone Group.

In 2009, Huizenga sold 95% of his stake in the Miami Dolphins to Stephen Ross, a real estate magnate, for $1.1 billion, seven times what he paid for the team in 1994. He still owns 5% of the team.

HUIZENGA AND REPUBLIC INDUSTRIES

The next venture that Huizenga entered was a revisit to the sanitation industry. In 1995, he invested $64 million of his own money and raised an additional $168 million and bought the Atlanta-based sanitation company Republic Waste Industries (*Entrepreneur. com,* 2010). Huizenga renamed the company Republic Industries, a small business that was struggling in the garbage and electronic-security industries. In 1995, Huizenga became the chairman of the Board of Directors.

As he did with Waste Management, he expanded the business and used the cash flow to enter the retail automotive industry. Huizenga's next venture was to create a network of new and used car outlets throughout the United States. Republic began opening AutoNation used car megastores and over a period of six months, he bought 65 auto dealerships with 109 outlets selling 31 brands, opened 11 used-car superstores called AutoNation USA, and purchased three rental-car agencies, including Alamo, National, and CarTemps USA (*Entrepreneur.com*, 2010).

Huizenga propelled the company from $48 million in sales in the early 1990s to over $10.3 billion in 1997. Republic became the nation's largest auto retailer in a $1 trillion industry, owning just shy of 320 new car dealerships, a fleet of over 310,000 rental cars in the United States, Canada, the Caribbean, Latin America, Australia, Europe, Africa, and the Middle East, 26 AutoNation USA superstores, and had plans to add the 12-outlet Driver's Mart chain to the fold in 1998 (*Entrepreneur.com,* 2010).

In 1999, Huizenga renamed Republic to AutoNation Inc. He had deals to acquire about 400 new-car dealerships and more than 40 used-car stores, and operated approximately 4,000 rental car locations worldwide, making it the world's number-one auto retailer and the United States' second-largest provider of vehicle-rental services (Republic Industries, 2010). In January 2003, Mike Jackson replaced Huizenga as Chairman of the company.

HUIZENGA'S KEYS TO SUCCESS

Huizenga stated, "My father always said working for somebody else never amounted to anything. You have to be an entrepreneur... I do not want to be just a voice on the phone. I have to get to know these guys face-to-face and develop a sincere relationship. That way, if we run into problems in a deal, it does not get adversarial. We trust each other and have the confidence we can work things out...I do not think we are unique; we are certainly not smarter than the next guy. So the only thing I can think of that we might do a little differently than some people is we work harder and when we focus in on something we are consumed by it. People are what determine your success in the future. Surround yourself with good people and you will not fail... Have a passion for what you do, work hard, have great people with good personalities, enjoy the ride" (Carmichael, 2009) Huizenga grew up in a business where there were no excuses. He was not inclined to give or take excuses. He believed in hard work.

Huizenga added, "Overcoming hardships and working around and through their obstacles to achieve an education is what I call a true success" (Horation Alger Foundation, 2010). Huizenga had a few rules that he used: keep meetings short and master the executives' areas of expertise and constantly challenge them.

Success in Huizenga's mind was enabled by "creativity, endurance, and a willingness to stick to one's convictions" (Kadlec, 2009). Huizenga would place himself in the other person's shoes when making a deal. He treated them fairly, so it was a win-win situation. Huizenga did not develop companies for money, but for the challenge and excitement. All the jobs that we have created, all the companies that we have created – a lot of people have made a lot of money.

Huizenga stated, "The most important factor is people... Everybody I hire is smarter than I am...I have never been frightened by hiring people who are more intelligent than I am, that are smarter than I am. There is a difference between being intelligent and being smart. People have to have both" (Jacobs, 2005).

Another key to his success was his ability to delegate responsibilities to others that have greater expertise than he does in certain areas than he does. When he bought into Blockbuster, he saw it as a sort of video McDonald's—a one-product venture that could easily be duplicated and franchised. However, Huizenga had little knowledge of the retail business, so he sought help from the ranks of fast-food giants, where he found and recruited former McDonald's and Kentucky Fried Chicken (KFC) real estate manager Luigi Salvaneschi (*Entrepreneur.com*, 2010). According to Huizenga, "Salvaneschi was the architect behind the real estate masterpiece of McDonald's and KFC. He was the President of Blockbuster from 1988-1990" (Huizenga, 8 May 2010). Huizenga recruited top management from some of the best companies offering them more money and perks. He persisted until they would come aboard.

The key to Huizenga's success was a formula that worked time and time again. He focused on service industries that had recurring income: dumpster rental, trash collection, video rental, etc. Even with AutoNation, there was no big manufacturing plant, and an emphasis was on customer service. Most of all, Huizenga focused on finding industries that were not meeting customer needs. Each of his companies set a new standard of highly professional service in its industry.

In an interview about his keys to success with the different businesses he stated, "In each business, there was a customer-service aspect that could be improved. My approach has always been to do those things that keep the customer happy. The opportunity for customer service in waste collection was to pick up the trash at the same time each week and to use clean trucks and equipment. At AutoNation, it was the one-price, no-hassle selling process" (Sexton, 2001, p. 41).

In a more recent interview, Huizenga talked about his management style related to performance, "If there is someone in the bottom 10 percent of the company, they out to know. I am not looking at the company's side of it, but the employee's side. I think the employee needs to know that management thinks they are in the bottom 10 percent. Early on in my career I had a guy named Bill working for me that worked really hard but just did not fit; did not make the right decisions. We kept him around for a while because he was a good guy and we wanted to be loyal to him. We actually did him a disservice by keeping him around. We should have let him go and get a job with another organization where he could rise to the top. I learned from that experience that you have to be fair with the employees and tell them up front" (Huizenga, 20 March 2010).

Some final remarks from Huizenga were, "I am from the old school. The first thing that an entrepreneur needs to do is to believe in what he or she is doing and work hard to sell the business concept. It is hard work, and you must believe in an idea to be able to sell it to others. You must be committed to what you are doing. You should wake up in the morning excited to go to work. If you find yourself in a position where you are not sure or you do not like it, do something else. I could not go to work unless I felt very passionate about what I was doing. I also think you have to be lucky, because timing is everything in life. The key is to be in the right place at the right time. Many people have had a great idea, but at the wrong time. Interest rates may have been too high, or the economy was down. The key is to have the right idea and roll it out as the economy is going up. We cannot dictate when the economy is going to be strong and when it is not. I have been fortunate and lucky. I have been in the right place at the right time, and have been prepared to pursue the opportunity. It is more than just being good it is being good at the right time" (Sexton, 2001, p. 48).

HUIZENGA AND CHARITY

Huizenga has given over $100 million dollars to charity over his life. Huizenga has donated $9 million to Nova Southeastern University's business school, which was named the H. Wayne Huizenga School of Business and Entrepreneurship. Huizenga also donated money to fund a new Huizinga Science Building to his high school, Pine Crest School. In 2009, he gave $1 million to the Martin Memorial Foundation in Florida. Huizenga gave $2 million to the Hurricane Charley relief fund in 2004 and gave $2 million to the Junior Financial Achievement Center in Coconut Creek, Florida to fund educational institutions.

Mr. Huizenga was inducted into the Junior Achievement U.S. Business Hall of Fame in 2006. Huizenga received the prestigious Horatio Alger Association of Distinguished Americans Award in 1992 based on his millions of dollars of college scholarship donations to the National Scholar Scholarships which are presented by the Horatio Alger Association every year. More recently, Huizenga gave $8 million to two churches in South Florida.

HUIZENGA TODAY

Huizenga remains one of the world's richest men. Ironically, money is not his primary motivator. What drives Huizenga is the thrill he gets from one-on-one competition between himself and a rival. That's why at a time when most people his age are considering retirement, Huizenga presses on and promises to remain one of the business' most influential and successful entrepreneurs well into the next century (Sexton 2001, p. 48).

Huizenga still has business interests but also collects antique cars and spends time with his family in Fort Lauderdale and at a Golf Club in Martin County. He is now diversified: bonds, real estate, AutoNation, Republic Services, private jets, plush Gary Player-designed golf course.

When asked if he was going to retire, Huizenga retorted, "Are you kidding me! I will never retire. I am in the process of searching for new opportunities. Do you know of any?"

Exhibit 1: Chronology of H. Wayne Huizenga

1939: Born.

1953: Moved to Fort Lauderdale, Florida.

1962: Created Southern Sanitation Service.

1968: Renamed company Waste Management, Inc.

1972: Waste Management, Inc. became largest trash collecting business.

1984: Resigned from Waste Management, Inc.

1987: Purchased Blockbuster Video.

1991: Granted baseball expansion team Florida Marlins.

1992: Granted hockey expansion team Florida Panthers.

1993: Purchased Spelling Entertainment Group and Republic Pictures Corporation.

1994: Sold shares of Blockbuster Entertainment Corporation.

1994: Became sole owner of NFL's Miami Dolphins and Joe Robbie Stadium.

1997: Announced proposed sale of Florida Marlins.

Source: Huizenga, H. Wayne - Overview, Personal Life, Career Details, Chronology: H. Wayne Huizenga, Social and Economic Impact, 9 March 2010, <http://encyclopedia.jrank. org/articles/pages/6278/Huizenga-H-Wayne.html#ixzz0he3GTxvD>

Exhibit 2: Question and Answer with Wayne Huizenga

1. What do you eat for breakfast?

Cereal and/or fruit.

2. What was your nickname in high school?

Wayne.

3. What was your first job?

A gas station attendant while in high school in Fort Lauderdale, Fla.

4. How often do you exercise?

Three times a week.

5. Who was your mentor?

My father, Harry.

6. How many hours a day do you read?

Approximately two hours.

7. What motivates you?

Working with great people who make it happen, and seeing the results.

8. What is more important: the idea or the execution?

The execution, because there are many great ideas, but you must be able to execute to succeed.

9. Worst day of your life?

The loss of my parents.

10. Do you pray?

Yes, often.

11. What was your biggest mistake?

Going into baseball and hockey--although I love the game.

12. Worst business idea you ever heard? (Did it succeed?)

Heard some doozies, hard to pick just one.

13. What can't you live without?

Love, faith and family.

14. What is your favorite way to relax?

Being on a boat--anywhere.

15. What is the best part about being the boss?

It's like being the quarterback on the team or the head coach. You pick your players, develop the game plan and together, you must execute.

16. What is "success" to you?

Success is obtaining your goals and objectives. Doing what others do not.

17. What is the best investment advice you ever heard?

Cash flow.

18. Is there any reason to get an MBA?

Yes, education is the most important thing to obtain the edge.

19. If you could be anything else, what would it be?

I really would not change anything.

20. What is your advice to young entrepreneurs?

Have a passion for what you do, work hard, have great people with good personalities, enjoy the ride, but balance work and family.

Source: Wayne Huizenga, 21 September 2006, 9 March 2010, <http://www.forbes. com/2006/09/20/ent-manage_biz_06rich400_self_made_entrepreneurs_wayne_huizenga. html>

Exhibit 3: Huizenga Quotes

Harry Huizenga, Huizenga's father once said, "Working for somebody else never amounted to anything. You have to be an entrepreneur."

"I don't think we are unique, we're certainly not smarter than the next guy. So the only thing I can think of that we might do a little differently than some people is we work harder and when we focus in on something we are consumed by it. It becomes a passion".

"The enormous potential of the AutoNation concept will complement Republic's strategy of building a diversified group of growth businesses in highly fragmented industries."

A friend said, "He (Wayne) was always a perfectionist, whatever he got into he would carry through on it."

We're looking for something where we can make something happen: an industry where the competition is asleep, hasn't taken advantage. It's going to be hard to find another Blockbuster, but that doesn't mean you can't have three good companies growing. The point is, we're going to be busy.

I don't want to be just a voice on the phone. I have to get to know these guys face-to-face and develop a sincere relationship. That way, if we run into problems in a deal, it doesn't get adversarial. We trust each other and have the confidence we can work things out.

I busted my butt all my life building companies. I have a friend who's my age, and the last thing we say when we hang up is QTR – quality time remaining. I don't know how many years I'll be able to play golf, so I'm going to enjoy every minutes of this.

Overcoming hardships and working around and through their obstacles to achieve an education is what I call a true success. People are what determine your success in the future. Surround yourself with good people and you won't fail.

I really would not change anything. Have a passion for what you do, work hard, have great people with good personalities, enjoy the ride."

Sources:

1. Entrepreneur's Hall of Fame: Wayne Huizenga 1March 2010 <http://www.ltbn.com/hall_ of_fame/Huizenga.html>

2. Evan Carmichael, Working for Someone Else Never Amounted to Anything, youngentrepre-neur.com, 24 February 2009, 1 March 2010 <http://www.youngentrepreneur.com/blog/model-ing-masters/working-for-somebody-else-never-amounted-to-anything-wayne-huizenga/>

Exhibit 4: Key Thoughts for Entrepreneurs Based on Wayne Huizenga

Find a niche that interests you. Then do your homework. While Huizenga looks to play the big niches, we can each look in our local areas for opportunity. And who knows where it can go with passion and hard work?

Wayne is an instinctual driver that doesn't stop until he's done. Sure he's brash, aggressive and thick skinned but that's what it takes. As one of his original employees once said, "He was always there before anyone else and he was always the last one to leave and in between he just did everything".

He is prepared to put in the time and the dollars to make things happen. His partners and financiers trust him implicitly for his character, ability, and performance.

As you might guess, Huizenga was not without hard times. As a child of divorced parents, he had great difficulty often denying himself a paycheck in the early years. He was accused of having connections to the mafia and even accusations of illegal disposition of harmful toxins (later disproved) while at Waste Management.

It is a long and hard road that your spouse, family and employees need to under-stand. Huizenga is known to use the word "we" often as it is only with the assistance of others that great things can be accomplished. People such as Huizenga are driven to succeed at everything they attempt. And if they don't, NEXT!!!

Source: Entrepreneur's Hall of Fame: Wayne Huizenga, LTBM.com, 15 February 2010
<http://www.ltbn.com/hall_of_fame/Huizenga.html>

DISCUSSION QUESTIONS

1) Describe the background and personality of Wayne Huizenga. What events happened during his youth that contributed to his success as an entrepreneur as an adult.

2) How did Huizenga start and grow Waste Management Inc.? What was his business model? How did he grow the business?

3) What was the history of Blockbuster Video pre Huizenga? How did Huizenga come across the opportunity? What strategies did he use to grow Blockbuster?

4) What were H. Wayne Huizenga's Keys to Success?

5) What recommendations would you make to Huizenga today? What industry not mentioned in the case would you recommend that Huizenga invest in and why?

Sources

1. #463 H. Wayne Huizenga - The Forbes 400 Richest Billionaires in the World 2010, *Forbes.com*, 10 March 2010, 15 March 2010 <http://www.forbes.com/lists/2010/10/billionaires-2010_H-Wayne-Huizenga_E353.html>

2. Martin Fridson. *How to be a Billionaire: Proven Strategies from the Titans of Wealth.* 1 May 2001, 10 March 2010 <http://books.google.com/books?id=iPWjNoSS9vUC&pg=PA146&dq=wayne+huizenga&cd=3#v=onepage&q=wayne%20huizenga&f=false>

3. Working for Somebody Else Never Amounted To Anything – Wayne Huizenga, *YoungEntrepreneur.com,* 24 February 2009, 5 March 2010 <http://www.youngentrepreneur.com/blog/modeling-masters/working-for-somebody-else-never-amounted-to-anything-wayne-huizenga/>

4. Gail DeGeorge. *The Making of a Blockbuster.* (Hoboken, NJ: John Wiley & Sons, Inc., 1996).

5. Steven Almond. Citizen Wayne: The Unauthorized Biography, *Miami New Times*, 9:33 (2004). <http://blogs.browardpalmbeach.com/pulp/2009/03/h_wayne_huizenga.php>

6. H. Wayne Huizenga on Getting Started, Presentation at the H. Wayne Huizenga School of Business at Nova Southeastern University, 3 September 2009, 10 March 2010

7. <http://www.youtube.com/watch?v=REgV2RP_LeU>

8. Huizenga, H. Wayne - Overview, Personal Life, Career Details, Chronology: H. Wayne Huizenga, *Social and Economic Impact*, 10 March 2010

9. <http://encyclopedia.jrank.org/articles/pages/6278/Huizenga-H-Wayne.html>

10. H. Wayne Huizenga (8 May, 2010). Interview on Huizenga's background and companies.

11. Up & Down Wall Street, *Barron's,* 1 September 1986.

12. Hoover's Report on Blockbuster, *Hoover's Inc.*, www.hoovers.com, accessed December 2009.

13. Joshua Greenberg. *From Betamax to Blockbuster: Video Stores and the Invention of Movies on Video.* (Cambridge, MA: MIT Press, 2008). 15 April 2010

14. H. Wayne Huizenga on Acquiring Blockbuster, 9 September 2009, 30 April 2010 <http://www.youtube.com/watch?v=13XIdWavY7U>.

15. William M. Alpert, "What's Wrong with This Picture? Too Many Companies Are Making the View Scene," *Barron's*, September 21, 1987.

16. Joshua M. Greenberg, p. 128 (Richard Nathanson interview with Joshua M. Greenberg, March 13, 2003).

17. H. Wayne Huizenga, SunSentinel.com. February 17, 2011. < http://www.sun-sentinel.com/topic/economy-business-finance/h.-wayne-huizenga-PEBSL000167.topic>

18. Associated Press, "Spelling Gets New Officers," *New York Times,* April 10, 1993, p. 136.

19. Columbia Business Review, "Resources: Who Owns What, Viacom Inc., Timeline," http://www.cjr.org/resources/index.php? c=viacom , 19 February 2010.

20. Donald Sexton, "Wayne Huizenga: Entrepreneur and wealth creator," *Academy of Management Executive*, 15:1 (2001).

21. H. Wayne Huizenga, Entrepreneur.com, 11 March 2010 <http://www.entrepreneur.com/growyourbusiness/radicalsandvisionaries/article197648.html>

22. Republic Industries, Inc., *Answers.com,* 10 March 2010 <http://www.answers.com/topic/republic-industries-inc>

23. Evan Carmichael. Working for somebody else never amounted to anything-Wayne Huizenga, *Young Entrepreneur.* 24 February 2009, 15 March 2010 <http://www.evan-carmichael.com/Famous-Entrepreneurs/3640/Lesson-1-Service-is-the-Secret-to-Success.html>

24. H. Wayne Huizenga, Horatio Alger Foundation, 15 March 2010 <http://www.horatioalger.com/member_info.cfm?memberid=hui92>

25. Daniel Kadlec. *Introduction by Wayne Huizenga, Masters of the Universe: Winning Strategies of America's Greatest Deal Makers,*(United Kingdom: HarperCollins, 2009), p. x.

26. Daniel Jacobs. Smart Business Miami/Broward/Palm Beach, www.sbnonline.com. (September, 2005).

27. H. Wayne Huizenga on Management Style. 20 March 2010 <http://www.youtube.com/watch?v=rX_txW9DIys>

Timko Export Management Company: The Dynamics of International Entrepreneurship

Andrew Thomas, The University of Akron
Todd A. Finkle, Gonzaga University
Tim Wilkinson, Montana State University

INTRODUCTION

In June of 1997, Tom Wilson and Dave Richards congratulated themselves on the success of their company, Timko Export Management. Thanks to their hard work, ability to read international markets, and willingness to risk millions of dollars in deals, their business was very successful. They were a formidable pair: Richards, 20 years older than Wilson, had already made a small fortune before they formed their dynamic partnership. Wilson brought three key assets to the table: several years of experience in international trade, fluency in Spanish, and an MBA that gave him an understanding of business management.

Timko Export Management had posted $30.7 million in pre-tax earnings in 1996 with sales of $127.5 million. At this rate of growth, they projected that their company would soon reach $200 million in sales.

Exhibit 1: Pro Forma Income Statement: 1992-1998 (in millions)

	1992	1993	1994	1995	1996	1997	1998
SALES (millions US$)	20.90	32.67	37.80	65.80	127.50	52.90	47.00
COST OF GOODS SOLD (millions US$)	11.70	17.68	19.70	38.90	78.80	49.80	55.60
GROSS PROFIT (millions US$)	9.20	14.99	18.10	26.90	48.70	3.10	-8.60
OPERATING EXPENSES (millions US$)							
Employee Wages	0.51	0.51	0.53	0.63	1.70	1.90	1.90
Management Wages	0.40	0.40	0.40	0.40	0.40	0.40	0.40
Health Insurance	0.25	0.25	0.26	0.36	0.59	0.59	0.62
Real estate taxes	0.03	0.03	0.03	0.03	0.03	0.03	0.03
Utilities	0.04	0.04	0.04	0.04	0.05	0.05	0.05
Errors & Omissions Insurance	0.01	0.01	0.01	0.01	0.07	0.07	0.09
Bank fees	0.05	0.05	0.05	0.08	0.24	0.11	0.20
Postage / UPS	0.12	0.15	0.08	0.11	0.14	0.10	0.14
Telephone / Fax	0.29	0.27	0.15	0.45	0.65	0.74	0.69
Telex	0.04	0.04	0.04	0.03	0.03	0.03	0.03
Depreciation	0.10	0.10	0.10	0.10	0.10	0.10	0.01
Travel	2.80	2.80	1.10	1.90	4.60	5.90	4.70
Regional Distributor Conferences	0.00	0.00	0.25	0.70	1.70	1.90	1.70
Legal Expenses	2.60	2.60	1.60	3.40	3.20	2.10	1.95
Miscellaneous	1.70	1.70	2.50	3.90	4.50	3.20	2.70
TOTAL EXPENSES	8.94	8.95	7.12	12.12	17.99	17.21	15.21
PRE-TAX PROFITS (millions US$)	0.26	6.04	10.98	14.78	30.71	-14.11	-23.81

They could not believe their good fortune. What they did was fairly simple. They saw an opportunity to export low-cost motorcycles to Latin America and Africa. In order to achieve this opportunity, they created a partnership with a Chinese manufacturer and developed an international distribution network.

In June of 1997, when they decided to send $5 million to the manufacturer in China for their next order, they appeared to be lucky, brilliant, and successful entrepreneurs. Unfortunately, they had no idea that several large financial institutions in Thailand were about to default on loans that they had taken from international banks. Nor did they know that foreign investors would soon begin a selling spree on the Thai stock market, which would lead to a perception of risk everywhere in Asia. Soon, everything would change.

In July, most of the economies of Southeast Asia suffered a major meltdown, later called the Asian Flu where currencies plummeted in Asia, Africa, and Latin America. Wilson and Richards soon realized that their situation had become desperate. The devaluation in the currencies meant that the market for imported motorcycles had vanished virtually overnight. Unfortunately, they had the $5 million in inventory that they had already paid for, with no prospects for recuperating their investment. When the partners met in December, it soon became clear that they only had three options:

1. They could sell their stake in their joint venture to their Chinese manufacturing partner for pennies on the dollar.

2. They could ship the motorcycles to their distributors, who would be compelled to take the merchandise -- effectively dumping it on their customers -- even though they would not be able to sell anything in the foreseeable future. While this move could result in a rebound, it also had the potential of failure and the appearance of being unethical.

3. They could do nothing and simply absorb the costs associated with the disaster, which would mean losing millions of dollars.

As 1997 came to a close, the partners asked themselves how they could have gone from being brilliant successful businessmen to being distraught and desperate. What could they have done? More importantly, what should they do next?

HISTORY OF TIMKO EXPORT MANAGEMENT COMPANY

Timko Export Management Company was founded in January 1992. It was the second company that evolved out of a partnership between Wilson and Richards.

Wilson and Richards were very different people. Richards, 46 years old, was 20 years older than Wilson. A high-school dropout, Richards was the quintessential "up by your own bootstraps" story. Leaving an abusive family in the Midwest when he was only 16, Richards headed to California in search of a better life. He pumped gas, washed dishes, parked cars, and even walked dogs. At 18, he took a job as a salesman at a truck parts outlet in Los Angeles. He excelled. Richards possessed an uncanny ability to read customers and their needs within a few seconds. Within a year, he was made sales manager. Working sometimes 20 hours a day, Richards doubled the sales of the company within 18 months. Eventually, Richards became frustrated with the office politics and left to start his own company. He quickly built one of the largest firms specializing in wholesale truck parts on the West Coast. By age 30, Richards was a multi-millionaire.

When interviewed, Richards had this to say, "Frankly, I never thought about becoming wealthy. I loved to work – and still do. I started my own company because I really thought I could do things better and wanted to control my own destiny."

As his sons became older, they began racing motorcycles. Frustrated by the poor level of service from the local motorcycle dealerships in Los Angeles, Richards bought one. The first shop, in Torrance, was a representative of Honda, Yamaha, Suzuki, and Kawasaki. Richards jumped in with both feet and turned the store into one of the most profitable in Southern California. He later bought two more dealerships, and by the early 1990's, was one of the biggest motorcycle dealers in the entire country.

Richards added, " I got into the motorcycle business on a whim. I spent a lot of time and money at these dealerships; a small fortune on parts, accessories, and repairs, and got lousy service in return. I knew that I could run a business better than they did."

Wilson, on the other hand, was an army brat. His father was a logistics officer who moved the family 10 times in his 22 year career. Richards and Wilson were introduced to each other through Richards' sister, an army wife whose best friend was Wilson's mother. Wilson was an ROTC cadet in college for two years before deciding that a military career was not for him. He decided, instead, to study economics, and by the time he was 22, had a Master's Degree. Wilson also learned several languages as a child. He was a product of the elitist culture found in the officer corps of the military. Wilson noted, "I was a cocky young kid who had grand visions. I really thought I could do anything. My family taught me that with hard work, anything was possible."

In early 1991, the two began to export Japanese brand motorcycles out of Richards' three motorcycle dealerships in Los Angeles, California. The motorcycles they exported were initially targeted for sale within the U.S. dealer network. However, Wilson and Richards saw opportunities elsewhere. The first country that they targeted was Argentina. Argentina had closed its borders to motorcycle imports as well as almost every other consumer product, for many years. These restrictions began to ease up in early 1990 as the military junta, which was in charge of the country, changed to a more democratic and open trade policy.

Figure 1: Example of Motorcycle Sold

Pent-up demand in Argentina for the high-end, Japanese-made bikes was exacerbated by the fact that even after the import restrictions had been eased, availability of the product within the country's distribution network was extremely limited. For Timko Export Management Company, the timing could not have been better. The U.S. dealer network had an abundance of available Japanese motorcycles. Evidence of the demand in Argentina was the number of Argentines who would travel to Los Angeles with suitcases full of cash to purchase motorcycles from local dealers at prices often 30-40 percent above manufacturer's suggested retail price (MSRP)!

Seeing this tremendous opportunity, the partners quickly decided to "go direct". Wilson got ready to leave for Buenos Aires where he set out to establish a small import office. Still, the partners were clueless when it came to knowing how to accomplish this. Neither one had set up a foreign company before. Although Wilson was bilingual and had lived many years across South America, the company needed to build the infrastructure necessary to begin receiving the U.S.-spec Japanese-manufactured motorcycles from Richard's dealerships.

Ultimately, they reached out to their bankers in the U.S., ABN AMRO, and explained what they wanted to do. ABN AMRO was and remains one of the most global of all banks. This turned out to be a brilliant move. In international business, it is extremely difficult to build mutually beneficial relationships. For many companies, this becomes a major cause of failure in their global ventures. By aligning with their bank – an already-existing strategic alliance partner- they were able to tap the tremendous resources of ABN AMRO and get a business created in Argentina in a very short period of time.

The U.S. branch introduced the partners to the Buenos Aires office, which facilitated the proper introductions with the right law firms, accountants, and governmental officials. Both parties benefitted. The partners were able to seamlessly lay the foundation they needed, and the bank took care of an important client who would make them a lot of money in the coming years.

Even with this forward-thinking strategy and the fact that every motorcycle they imported sold within hours at two or three times the price in the U.S., they still had seriously underestimated the market. Timko imported and sold nearly 3,000 motorcycles in six months – and could have easily sold more than 4,000.

According to Richards, "There was no way in our wildest dreams that we could have anticipated the demand for these bikes. My gut instinct said that there had to be a market, but I had no idea of the magnitude of the built up demand. Sometimes being an entrepreneur has to do with a little luck; being in the right place at the right time."

By the end of 1991, the supply /demand curve began to stabilize. However, Richards and Wilson would continue to sell Japanese-made motorcycles in Argentina for the next several years at a nice level of profit.

The initial revenue generated from Argentina prompted the partners to consider expanding their operations. Based on their initial success in Argentina, they formed a company called the Timko Export Management Company.

THE GLOBAL MOTORCYCLE INDUSTRY

The motorcycle was invented through a succession of experiments carried out in Europe and the U.S. in the late 19th century. A series of inventors strapped an array of motors onto bicycles until Swedish immigrant Carl Hedstrom, fitted a 1.75-horsepower single-cylinder engine to a bike thereby creating the first modern motorcycle. Hedstrom and his business partner George Hendee, began building and selling what was called the Indian Motorcycle in Springfield, Massachusetts, in 1901. In the same year, bicycle racer Glenn Curtiss also began making motorcycles and in 1907 he became the fastest man alive by strapping himself to a 40-hp V8 engine and then shooting down the road at 135 mph.

Soon motorcycles were the trend with over 50 new companies successfully building and selling this new form of transportation. Among this group was a firm founded by William Harley, an engineering student at the University of Wisconsin-Madison, and Arthur Davidson, a pattern maker in a railroad shop. The Harley-Davidson Motor Company, was incorporated in 1907 and was financed by the life savings of Davidson's 80 year old bookkeeper uncle.

The Harley Davidson Company marketed its motorcycle as a less expensive alternative to the popular motor car. The first model sold for $200, and got approximately 180 miles per gallon. By 1914, the firm was producing 1,600 units each year of its new 45-degree V-twin engine model.

Because the motorcycle had become popular in law enforcement circles, it was only natural that the military would see its wartime potential. General Pershing ordered 20 machine gun laden Harleys to the Southern border to drive Pancho Villa's raiding parties out of Texas. This was followed by a yearly deployment of a 20,000 bikes to the European theatre during WW I.

JAPANESE ENTRY INTO THE MARKET

The Japanese entry into the motorcycle industry began in 1938 when Soichiro Honda and Takeo Fujisawa began their business through the perfection of a piston ring in Honda's Japanese machine shop. In order to facilitate Honda's interest in motorcycle racing, the two formed a motorcycle production company called Honda Motor Company in 1948. A year later Honda's engineering genius paid off. Honda created a technological innovation that doubled the horsepower of the four-stroke engine used with Japanese motorcycles of the day.

In 1956, Honda decided to build a commercial motorcycle focused on a specific market segment, Japanese housewives. The Honda 50cc Super Cub featured a three-speed transmission, an automatic clutch, and most importantly, an automatic starter. By the end of the decade the bike was the bestselling motorcycle in Japan, with sales of $55 million.

The Japanese firm's introduction of the Super Cub was a new conceptualization of the motorcycle. Instead of being solely the purview of racers, warriors, police, stuntmen, and gangsters, the motorcycle was transformed into an inexpensive form of transportation for consumers around the world. By 1997, the company reached the production milestone of 100 million motorcycles produced during its 60 year history. By the late 1990s the firm was producing motorcycles in India, Vietnam, Turkey, Brazil, and Indonesia. Today, Honda is by far the largest manufacturer of motorcycles in the world (Honda Motor Co. Annual Report, 2007).

MOTORCYCLES AND EMERGING MARKETS

In most of the emerging markets in the world, motorcycles have historically been viewed differently. Motorcycles were treated as a means of basic transportation. Whether in India, China, South America, Sub-Sahara Africa, or Southeast Asia, small-engine motorcycles were widely held to be an attainable alternative to other forms of transport such as walking, burros, or buses. This was due to the fact that most people in these places did not have the financial wherewithal to purchase their own automobile. As a result, an affordable, low-end motorcycle became the primary option for people who sought to have their own motorized transportation. In 1992, it was estimated that 15-20 million motorcycles were sold all over the world. China sold eight million bikes domestically.

Viewing China as a viable export option in 1992 was not a popular choice. At that time, Japan, not China, was perceived as one of the biggest global opportunities for U.S. companies. China still had the political after effects of Tiananmen Square in the summer of 1989.

Still, the partners were convinced that China held the future, especially in the area of small, basic transportation motorcycles. Corporate decisions by Honda, Yamaha and Suzuki, were pushing those companies away from the manufacture of small motorcycles. Honda and Suzuki had decided to focus on building automobiles, while Yamaha shifted its emphasis to electric-domestic products.

The scaling back of these major players created a hole in the marketplace. At the same time there was rising growth in many emerging markets around the world. In Latin America, sub-Saharan Africa, India, and China, demand for inexpensive modes of transportation was rising.

Wilson pointed out the following, "At that time, there was little confidence that China could build anything of quality, -except t-shirts. Everyone kept saying Japan, Mexico or South Korea. As a kid, I remember the famous shortstop Pee Wee Reese saying, 'Hit em where they ain't.' The first time I went to China in 1991, I landed at Beijing International Airport. Our plane was the only flight. I remember the lights were turned on when we entered the immigration and customs area. Nothing was working. I saw this as an opportunity. Little or no competition."

Wilson began a research project with the goal of identifying one or more markets where demand for motorcycles would be high. He was astonished to learn, in an examination of U.N. documents, that only about one out of five people on the planet had ever been inside an automobile. His reading further convinced him that the vast majority of people could not conceptualize a car as easily as they could a basic transportation motorcycle.

As incomes increased in those countries, consumers desired automobiles. However, because they could not afford cars, the pent up demand for individual means of transportation was focused upon motorcycles. Ironically, just as the Japanese started to phase out of the small motorcycle business, the demand for motorcycles began to take off. While demand was great, the supply was limited. Timko Export Management Company was at the right place at the right time.

In other words, the low-end motorcycle market that had served tens of millions of customers around the world for decades was undergoing a significant change. In light of this, the partners came up with a simple strategy; provide basic, low-end motorcycles for the people of the developing world using China as the manufacturing source. In late 1992, Timko Export Management Company reached an agreement with a joint venture partner after extensive market research and interviews with prospective motorcycle manufacturers in China.

Timko soon realized that the Chinese companies they spoke with were generally unsophisticated with regard to Western business concepts of service, consistency, and quality. They did, however, know how to build things at a very low price.

JOINT VENTURE WITH A CHINESE MANUFACTURER

In 1992, Timko established a joint venture with Shanghai Jaiek Motorcycle Limited in Shanghai. This company was part of the giant Shanghai Automotive Industrial Corporation (SAIC). Shanghai Jaiek Motorcycle Company was the first company in the history of China to go public on the New York Stock Exchange. Half of its holdings were owned by the Chinese government, or the SAIC division, and the other half of the company was held as a joint venture of CP Group in Bangkok.

Timko formed a joint venture with Shanghai Jaiek Motorcycle Limited for the production, exportation and ultimate distribution of a line of motorcycles. The motorcycles were very similar to domestic models, except they were modified to ensure higher performance and quality for the international market.

Timko knew the quality issue would be critical. If they could develop a quality product at an affordable price then they knew that success would be within reach.

The motorcycles were sold under the Jaiek brand, as they were in China. Timko initially exported motorcycles to existing customers in Argentina. Within a short time, the firm exported the motorcycles to other parts of South America, Central America, and Mexico. Leveraging previously established relationships, the firm rapidly built an exclusive distribution network. Business was very good throughout 1993 and the first half of 1994. Several exclusive distributors were established in Argentina, with others established in Brazil, Peru, Chile, Bolivia, Paraguay, Uruguay, Columbia, and Ecuador.

The firm then turned its attention to the Caribbean, and found distributors for its motorcycles in Haiti and the Dominican Republic. The biggest markets during the initial phase of operations (from 1993 to mid-1994) were Argentina, Brazil, Peru and increasingly Mexico.

The partners felt good about the timing of their venture. Not only had they jumped into the motorcycle business as the major players were pulling out, but their target markets were exhibiting new signs of economic growth and stability. Latin America was recovering from the debt crisis of the 1980s. For example, Argentina had beaten back inflation and was growing at an annual rate of 5.7 percent, Brazil replaced a military dictatorship with a democratic government, and Mexico initiated a privatization program and an attack on its age-old policy of import substitution (Hill 2006, p. 358). It appeared that the partners had made the right move when they decided to meet the growing demands of emerging market consumers with a new line of motorcycles.

PAYMENT STRUCTURE

Figure 2 shows the Timko Export Purchase Order Processing Process. Timko set up a payment structure that was fairly conventional. A purchase order would be sent from a distributor, processed, and then submitted to the Chinese partner for production. After a formal purchase order was established and sent to China, production would begin. At the same time, the financing mechanism of the entire transaction, in U.S. dollars, was executed. Either a wire transfer cash payment or a letter of credit originating from one of the Latin American distributors would be sent to the United States. In order to enhance sales, Timko required distributors to provide on the front end only one-half of the cost of the motorcycles. They fronted the rest, waiting to cash the Letters of Credit after the shipment to receive the balance. This financing mechanism, it was believed, would give distributors the ability to sell more units and fill the pipeline much sooner. Having plenty of available cash on hand, the partners were willing to assume the risks in order to grow the business.

Figure 2: Timko Export Purchase Order Processing

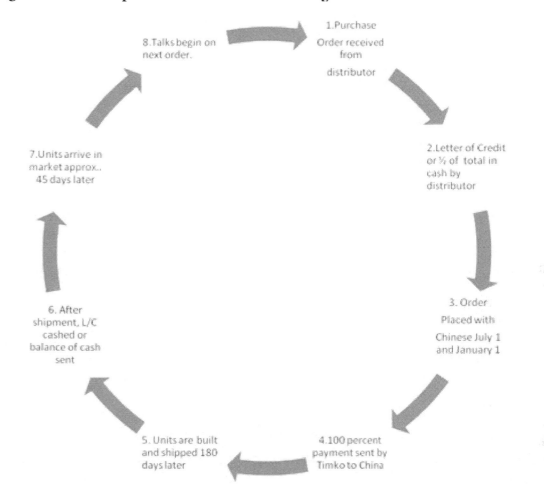

Calculating the gross profit was not complicated. The gross profit was simply the difference between what the distributor would send and the amount required by the Chinese joint venture partner to produce the motorcycles. Operating in this manner made it easy to handle the accounting and taxes. The Chinese were not sophisticated about global trade so they liked the simplicity of the arrangement.

The motorcycles were shipped on the first of July and the first of January. Purchase orders were obtained, money was collected, motorcycles were produced and manufactured, and then money was sent and the product was shipped. The letters of credit could be cashed after the shipment was confirmed by presenting the export documents to the negotiating bank.

The simple way of operating that Timko and its Chinese manufacturers adopted had left the partners vulnerable. With a letter of credit, a firm does not get paid until after a shipment is delivered. As a result, in many cases the partners would send on a bi-quarterly basis $5-10 million dollars in cash to China. This would pay for a shipment of motorcycles and cover the Chinese partner's expenses. Several months would pass before they were able to recuperate their money, including their profits. The partners were seemingly aware of the risks.

ECONOMIC CLIMATE IN SOUTH AMERICA

In the beginning, the loose operational mode of Timko worked well. The countries of Latin America experienced economic stability throughout 1992 and early 1993. However, trouble was around the corner.

In the early 1980s the International Monetary Fund bailed Mexico out of a financial crisis. As a condition of the bailout the IMF forced the Mexican government to "peg" the peso to the dollar within a band of plus or minus three percent. The band was also allowed to "crawl" downward daily. This created an annual depreciation of the peso against the dollar of about four percent.

On January 1, 1993 the Mexican government instituted the Nuevo peso – the new peso – in response to the extreme devaluation that had occurred during the 1980s. One new peso was worth 1,000 of the obsolete Mexican pesos. In the international community, there was grave concern that the new peso was being artificially maintained by the Mexican government. Currency speculators began to put pressure on the Mexican government to float the peso on the open market in order to determine the true value of the currency, especially relative to the U.S. dollar. The partners did not pay attention to any of this.

The first half of 1994 was a great time for Timko Export Management Company. They were able to coordinate the shipment of three quarterly orders of motorcycles, $45 million to their distributors in Latin America. The partners had began to think of expanding into new markets with a broader product line. They had even drawn up plans for opening assembly plants in local markets around the region. Unfortunately for them, the global economy was about to teach them a painful lesson.

Timko was approaching the quarterly manufacturing cycle. A shipment of motorcycles worth $3.3 million dollars was to be sent on January 1, 1995. Over the previous six-month period purchase orders had been received from distributors along with wire transfers and letters of credit. More than $10 million dollars had been sent to China to fund the manufacturing of the motorcycles.

During the second half of 1994, pressure began to be exerted against the Mexican peso vis a vis the U.S. dollar. The exchange rate, which was 3.111 Nuevo pesos to $1 U.S. dollar, was widely considered artificial and unsustainable. As Christmas approached, the Mexican government indicated that it might do something short of floating the peso. This timing was likely due to a slowdown in the financial markets during the holidays. On December 20, 1994, the Mexican government decided to devalue the peso by 13 percent. By the end of the month it fell another 15 percent. On December 20th the peso was worth 3.940, on March 19, 1995 it stood at 7.220 per dollar. Over the course of the previous several months, 50 percent of the value of the peso evaporated.

The sudden devaluation of the peso, and the subsequent realization that Mexico was in the midst of a currency crisis, sent shock waves throughout the Latin American distribution network of Timko Export Management Company. The problem was the motorcycles were bought and sold in dollars on the international market (by Timko, the Chinese, and the distributors) and were sold in local currencies in the home market (to retail customers). Projections in terms of pricing and financing were based on the valuations of those currencies prior to what had happened in Mexico. In what came to be called the "Tequila Effect", the Mexican financial crisis soon spread throughout Latin America. As a result, Timko's motorcycles became cost prohibitive for its distributors.

For example, in Mexico, the cost to the local distributor of the motorcycles before the peso devaluation was approximately 3,100 pesos (the sale price from Timko was US$1,000 per unit x 3.11 pesos). A few months after the devaluation, the cost to the local distributor had jumped to over 7,200 pesos. Although the sale price from Timko remained US$1,000 per unit to the Mexican distributor, the cost in the local market had increased by over 40%! This scenario repeated itself across Latin America, where currencies across the region fell spectacularly against the U.S. dollar.

After wallowing in self-pity over the holidays, the partners decided that the only solution to a warehouse full of motorcycles was to come up with new customers. Wilson thought back to a conversation he had with an individual he met on one of his trips to Brazil. James Boachie-Adjei was a Ghanaian who had expressed an interest in selling Timko motorcycles in Africa. Because no other options came readily to mind, Wilson flew to Ghana and visited Mr. Boachie-Adjei.

After a long lunch, it became evident that Boachie-Adjei did not have the resources or capacity to do business. However, he did tell Wilson about an area in northern Ghana, on the border with Burkina Faso, where there was a huge market for small-end motorcycles, especially Japanese motorcycles. Wilson made the 18-hour trip in the back of a small pick-up. Wilson was encouraged by the consumer demand that he witnessed and began a year and a half of travels that took him to 50 countries throughout Africa.

According to Wilson, "It was paradise! I knew we were going to make it. Of course the amount of work required was monstrous. But I was convinced we could survive."

His mission was simple, set up new distributors and liquidate the inventory remaining in Shanghai from the Tequila effect debacle. By mid-1995, Timko sold its way out of the Mexican currency crisis by meeting the demand for low-end motorcycles in Africa. By this time, things were looking up in Latin America. Currencies in the region had stabilized and economic growth was beginning to take off. The Mexican economy had revived; Both Brazil and Argentina began to experience near double digit growth, and the Tequila Effect had rapidly dissipated.

The economic crisis hangover was gone, and with new African distributors on line, Timko Trading, in conjunction with its Chinese partner, had visions of expanding markets, increased revenue and fat profit margins. Things had never been in better shape- or so it seemed.

The partners remained convinced that they could overcome whatever obstacles the global economy threw in front of them. Richards called himself "The Terminator" when he closed a deal and Wilson began to think himself a kind of management guru in the making. They often joked about how "all the so-called experts never had the guts to do what they had done."

Despite the difficulties of the previous months, none of the parties voiced concern over the payment structure. To better manage economic risk, the partners decided to change the product/payment sequence from six months to a three month cycle. In other words, motorcycles would be ordered, shipped, and paid for in three months instead of six. The Chinese were amicable, their customers were cooperating, and business was booming.

From 1995 to 1996 100,000 motorcycles were manufactured and sold. Spare part sales were in the millions of dollars. The company was approaching $200 million a year in sales.

ASIAN MONETARY CRISIS

In 1997, the partners were once again so fixated on business, that they did not notice new rumblings in the international financial markets – rumblings about the valuations of the currencies in Southeast Asia, particularly in Thailand, Malaysia, Indonesia, and South Korea. Both partners were logging about 500,000 miles a year, flying all over the world.

Wilson would be gone two-to-three weeks at a time in Africa or Latin America, only to return home for a few days, and get back out on the road. They were managing their Chinese partner, helping successful distributors grow their business, axing non-productive ones, and looking for new ones.

At this time, Wilson and Richards were thinking about how smart they had been. Having overcome the "Tequila Effect" they were sure that a billion dollar business was not that far off. They were already talking about an IPO and spin-offs around the world.

The Asian export boom of the 1980s had led to a boom in commercial and residential property investment. As the valuation of real estate in major Asia cities soared, a "bubble" was created. Heavy borrowing from banks financed huge infrastructure projects throughout the region. However, because the underlying economic fundamentals were unsound, pressure from international financial markets began to build.

In mid-1997 it became evident that several large financial institutions in Thailand were about to default on loans they had taken out from international banks for the purpose of financing local development. Sensing a financial meltdown, investors began a selling spree on the Thai stock market, with some individuals even shorting the Thai baht. Suddenly, investors began to perceive risk everywhere in Asia. What came to be known as "contagion" spread throughout the region, as investors sold their positions in Asian markets, demanded dollars, and exited the area. Because there were not enough dollars to cover the dollar-denominated debt, Asian governments began to rapidly devalue their currencies. The "Asian Flu" of 1997 had arrived.

It was déjà vu for Timko. Now shipping on a quarterly basis to their customers in Africa and Latin America, the partners had experienced a good first two quarters of 1997. In October, at the beginning of the third quarter as the partners waited for their motorcycles to arrive, the economies of Asia suffered their meltdown.

During the previous month, $5 million had been sent to China. As the Asian Flu hit, currencies plummeted relative to the U.S. dollar, not only in Asia, but also in Sub-Saharan Africa and Latin America. Because of the millions of dollars that had been sent overseas during the previous month, Timko Trading faced an even graver, more dangerous situation than it had in 1993.

Timko now had to decide what to do. They had $5 million in inventory, which they had already paid for and had no prospects for recuperating their investment. The partners narrowed their options down to three options:

1. They could sell their stake in their joint venture to their Chinese manufacturing partner for pennies on the dollar.

2. They could ship the motorcycles to their distributors, who would be compelled to take the merchandise -- effectively dumping inventory on their distributors -- even though they would not be able to resell any of it in the foreseeable future. While this move could result in a rebound for Timko, it also had the potential of failure and the appearance of being unethical.

3. They could simply absorb the costs associated with the disaster, which would mean losing millions of dollars.

DISCUSSION QUESTIONS

1. The owners took a calculated risk when they set up the payment structure for their business. Why did it succeed initially? Why did it ultimately fail?

2. Together, the owners of Timko Export Management Company had the following assets: cash, experience, and education. What didn't they have, which may have prevented their mistakes?

3. What strategies could Timko have put in place to hedge the potentially damaging effects of rapid or drastic currency value fluctuations within international financial markets?

4. Conduct a SWOT analyses of the Timko's position in the motorcycle market in 1992 and 1997. Do any of the 1992 points remain relevant in 1997?

5. In Behaving Badly: Ethical Lessons from ENRON, Denis Collins provides an ethics decision making framework. The full framework consists of six questions, but ultimately an ethical decision comes down to the answers to two questions:

1. Is the action for the greatest good of the greatest number of people affected by it?

2. Are the motives behind the action based on truthfulness and respect/integrity toward each stakeholder? (You will need to consider all the people affected by the decision.)

According to Collins, if the answers to both questions are "yes" then taking this action is the most ethical decision. If the answers to both questions are "no" then taking this action is the least ethical decision. If the answers to both questions are mixed, then taking this action is moderately ethical and you may have to consider legal, social, and personal affects.

Discuss each of the following decisions made by the Timko partners in terms of Collins' ethical decision making framework:

(a) Selling motorcycles in Argentina which the Japanese OEM designed, built, and intended for sale in the U.S. market.

(b) Selling motorcycles in Argentina for 200 percent to 300 percent over MSRP.

(c) Salvaging the value of motorcycles intended for customers in Mexico by selling them instead to customers in Africa.

(d) Continuing to incur expenses appropriate for a $127 million business in the face of an economic crisis created by unstable currency valuations.

(e) Establishing a payment structure that required distributors (buyers) to put down only 50 percent of the value of what they purchased.

6. What should Timko do now? Why?

REFERENCES

1. Hill, Charles (2006). *Global Business Today* (McGraw-Hill, Irwin. p. 358.

2. Honda Motor Co. Ltd. Annual Report 2007, (accessed on February 10, 2008, http://www.honda.com)

The Crowne Inn: A Classic Case of a Family Business in Turmoil

Todd A. Finkle, Gonzaga University

INTRODUCTION

It was clear cool fall day in late 2000 when Barbara Johnston, a retired nurse, was confronted with one of the biggest challenges of her life. Her son Bruce, had entered her dilapidated house, threw down his keys and blurted out the following,

> *You are all plotting behind my back. You are trying to bankrupt and steal the bar away from me. Well, you can have the keys to my house, car, and the lousy bar. But you will lose your son and two grandchildren forever.*

> *No one wanted the bar. I made the bar what it is today. If I leave, the business will collapse and then you will have nothing. I have already talked to the employees and they will all walk out. After this is over, I am going to disown this whole family. I have had it with all of you!!*

Barbara's family was on the verge of being torn apart over the family's largest asset, a bar called The Crowne Inn located in Kansas City, Missouri. Since the death of her husband Harvey in 1997, Barbara had problems with Bruce's inability to meet his previously agreed upon oral agreement to take care of her. On the day of his father's retirement in 1995, Bruce made an oral agreement to pay off the second mortgage of his parent's house ($23,500), give them $500 in cash per month and pay their health insurance and medical bills for the rest of their lives. He made this oral agreement in front of his parents and their attorney, Bobby Free. However, despite repeated warnings from Free, Harvey refused a formal written contract. As a result of the agreement, Bruce received all of the proceeds from the bar.

After five years, Bruce had not lived up to his agreement with his parents. The family was trying to work out a deal with Bruce's lawyer and accountant to sell him the business. The family's attorney, Bobby Free, devised three possible solutions to the problem: (1) have Bruce pay a lump sum, (2) have Bruce pay a smaller lump sum and $500 per month, or (3) sell the bar outright to an outside party.

Bruce stated that he would pay a lump sum of not more than $60,000 to his mother. The family was unsure whether this was a fair offer. And if not, what was a fair offer? Also, was the lump sum method the best way to handle the problem? Furthermore, would Bruce be willing and/or able to pay a higher lump sum? Previously, he told his older brother Karl that he refused to pay $75,000. He stated that he would be better off going into business with someone else rather than pay $75,000.

The real challenge was solving the family crisis without alienating Bruce and his family. Furthermore, Bruce only had one good relationship with his four brothers, Karl. Barbara was looking to her sons and her attorney for an answer to this complicated, nerve-racking, family crisis.

THE JOHNSTON FAMILY

Born in Kansas City in 1934, Barbara Johnston grew up in a lower middle class Lutheran family and was a by-product of the depression. Despite her challenging upbringing, Barbara was a gregarious, warm, friendly, family-oriented woman.

During her junior year in high school, she fell in love with a senior named Harvey Johnston. Harvey married Barbara four years after she graduated from high school. The marriage proved to be very tumultuous, but produced five healthy boys and six grandchildren. Most of the boys had similar personality characteristics as their father, which included a very high need for independence, an extremely strong work ethic, and an entrepreneurial flair. The oldest son, Karl, a twice divorced, 47-year old, was currently married (Caren). Karl was a street-smart, successful entrepreneur who owned a 3M dealership in Seattle, Washington. He had grown the business to over $1.5 million in sales in four years. His salary, not including the profits from the business, was around $85,000 a year.

Her second son, Cal (Jessica), had been married for 22 years. His marriage produced three children; Jason, Jennifer, and Jim. Cal was a religious, optimistic, and successful 45-year old cardiologist who lived in Kansas City. Of the five brothers, Cal was the most financially successful. His independent medical practice has sales of $1,000,000 with an annual net income of $250,000.

The middle child, Bruce (Sharon) had been married since 1985 and had two children, Albert and Bob. Bruce and Sharon were currently running the family-business, The Crowne Inn. Bruce enjoyed partying with his friends from the bar. Bruce and Sharon worked at the bar and made a combined salary of $84,000 (1999), not including the profits from the bar.

Exhibit 1: Annual Salaries for Bruce and Sharon Johnston and The Crowne Inn's Net Income (Pre Tax) from 1997-2000

YEAR	BRUCE	SHARON	BAR'S NET INCOME PRE TAX	TOTALS
1997	53,500	20,000	-500	73,000
1998	60,000	20,000	3,440	83,440
1999	62,000	22,000	6,450	90,450
2000	64,000	24,000	6,500	94,950

The fourth son, Tyler, was a single (never married), 40-year old dentist living in Las Vegas, Nevada. He was a hard working free spirit who enjoyed his freedom and convertibles. His dental practice was very successful and he made approximately $100,000 a year.

Danny, the last son, was also single (37 years old). He was extremely creative and enjoyed working with his hands. He had just started his own entertainment company that specialized in decorations for holidays and special events.

THE CROWNE INN

Harvey and Barbara Johnston were married in 1952. Before their marriage, Johnston's father, Norm, realized that his son needed a profession to support his new wife. Norm approached his 22-year old son and asked him what profession he wanted to enter. After some thought, Johnston stated that he wanted to start his own bar. The loose, free lifestyle appealed to him.

Before opening the bar, Johnston asked his best friend, Leo Smith, if he wanted to be his partner. Smith had been bartending with Johnston for the past two years and enjoyed it so he agreed. Smith also had more experience in the bar business so it was a good match. He was a warm, friendly man who was married with one daughter.

In 1952, Johnston and Smith took out a $10,000 loan and started a bar called Leo and Harvey's in downtown Kansas City. The bar was structured as an S-Corporation where both Johnston and Smith owned 50 percent of the stock in the company.

After seven years of moderately successful business, they made a decision to move the business to the northeast part of Kansas City. The downtown area had become increasingly dangerous with an increase in crime and an increase in the number of homeless people. The new location had fewer competitors, less crime, and a better clientele. The partners purchased the land and building and moved into the new location in 1959, renaming the bar, The Crowne Inn.

The Crowne Inn was unique from other bars because it was patterned after the old West. Old wooden barrels lined the front of the building. The building itself was made of wood boards and signs were placed all over the front of the building that ranged from "Dance Girls Wanted" to "Whisky Served Here" to "Coldest Beer in Town." On the top of the building was a 7 Up sign.

At the entrance of the smoke filled bar there was a shiny, dark stained, wooden bar with 10 swinging stools for customers. A pair of small swinging doors led to the back of the bar where a small cooler held mugs, cans, and bottles of beer and wine. There were five taps: one for Champagne, Cold Duck, Miller High Life, and two for Budweiser (their best selling beer). On the other side of the bar were a small grill, refrigerator, office, and cooler for kegs and cases of beer. A limited supply of hard alcohol and food items were also for sale behind the bar.

The Crowne Inn differentiated itself from other bars in a number of ways. First, the bar had a very homey atmosphere with approximately 15 tables and a total capacity of 70 people. This gave customers the ability to converse without all the hassles (e.g., fights, loud music) of a typical bar. The bar also served lunch (hamburgers, hot dogs, chili dogs, and chips) and snacks (slim jims, beef jerky, bags of peanuts). The bar initially had a pool table and color TV, however they dropped the pool table due to fights.

The historic ambiance of the bar was enhanced through the shellacking historic newspaper clippings on the walls. Actual articles on the Japanese surprise attack at Pearl Harbor, the sinking of the Lusitania, and the D-Day invasion were all exhibited on the wall. The bar was also full of historic relics, which included old menus, beer trays, political buttons, and beer cans. Jim Bean bottles (novelty bottles filled with whiskey) were also located all over the bar.

The Crowne Inn's busiest times were weekdays for lunch (11-1 PM), happy hour (5-7 PM), and weekend evenings (8-1 AM). Business professionals made up the largest segment of customers at lunch. During the late afternoon and evenings the customers were primarily local blue-collar workers.

Johnston and Smith worked alternating, two-week shifts: day (10 AM-6 PM) and evening (6 PM-2 AM). As their business slowly grew, so did their families. Smith eventually had four girls and moved into a beautiful four-bedroom house, while Johnston had five boys, moved into a small three-bedroom house, and struggled to pay his bills.

TRANSITIONAL YEARS

In 1981, Harvey bought out Smith's stock in the company for $50,000 cash. At the age of 28, Karl joined the business full-time. Karl brought a new ambiance to the bar. He had a high level of energy, creativity, and numerous innovative ideas to enhance the sales of the bar. One of the first things that he did was add a large cooler that contained over 80 imported beers from all over the world. He also created an advertising campaign in the local entertainment papers, bought a popcorn machine, a stereo system, and a VCR to play movies. These ideas along with Karl's jovial personality bolstered sales and changed the culture of the bar from a primarily neighborhood blue-collar establishment to a younger, trendier 25-40 year old crowd.

By late 1982, Karl had grown weary of the long hours, drunks, and low pay.

Furthermore, he had recently been married and his wife, Jessica, wanted him to leave the bar business. Despite the rise in sales of the bar to $125,000, he was not making as much money as he had hoped. He quit the bar and moved to San Diego, California.

TURNAROUND

By late 1982, Johnston's middle son, Bruce, started working part-time for the bar;

however, Harvey still worked the majority of the hours. In 1984, Karl returned from San Diego as a divorcee and started working at the bar again. Karl and Bruce came up with some innovative ideas to increase sales. They started selling warm roasted peanuts at $.75 a bowl and ice-cold pints of imported beer on tap (e.g., Guinness, Heineken, Bass Ale). They also started selling pickles, inserted video games, a pinball machine, a jukebox CD player and a big screen television.

After two years of working together, sales had increased to $185,000. Despite the increased success of the bar, Karl decided to quit. He had been robbed twice at gunpoint, including one time where the robbers took all of the money and jewelry from the customers. He also got remarried and his second wife, Judy, was pushing him to get out of the bar business. Karl and Judy moved to San Diego at the end of 1986.

By the end of 1986, Bruce was working full-time with his father. Bruce continued his entrepreneurial flair over the next 10 years. One of his most innovative moves was a strategic alliance with an Italian restaurant across the street, called Pappa's Pizza. The take out or dine in restaurant consisted of tasty Italian food. Since the bar did not serve food (besides snacks) in the evenings, it was an ideal strategy to allow people to order food from Pappa's Pizza and bring it into the bar. This strategy beefed up sales for both businesses.

Bruce also had promotional events where guest DJs would come in and play music. One of his most innovative special events was Crownewood. Crownewood was held every year on the night of the Oscars. Customers would vote on which stars would win. If they guessed correctly, they would win prizes. Other events focused on sporting events. For example, free chili was served during Monday Night Football.

These activities combined with advertising in the local entertainment paper, Rebel, attracted two new market segments, the college crowd and young urban professionals. The Crowne Inn had transformed itself from a primarily blue-collar neighborhood bar into one of the most progressive bars in Kansas City. As a result, the Johnston's increased their prices and sales. Under Harvey and Bruce's tenure, the sales of the bar increased from $145,000 in 1984 to $200,000 in 1994 (4 percent increase in sales a year).

Exhibit 2: The Crown Inn Sales from 1982-2000

YEAR	SALES ($)
1982	$125,000
1983	135,000
1984	145,000
1985	165,000
1986	185,000
1987	170,000
1988	175,000
1989	180,000
1990	185,000
1991	190,000
1992	192,500
1993	197,500
1994	200,000
1995	225,000
1996	250,000
1997	295,000
1998	326,000
1999	346,000
2000	366,000

One of the keys to Bruce's success in turning around the bar around was his girlfriend, Sharon, who he eventually married in 1985. Sharon was a very savvy businessperson with a very strict authoritarian management style with tight controls. This was in contrast to Harvey and Bruce's laid-back personalities, which led Sharon to take control the bar.

FAILURE OF THE ORAL AGREEMENT

In 1994, after 42 years of running the bar, Harvey was ready to retire. Harvey had emphysema, diabetes, and was obese. He approached his sons to see who wanted the bar. Bruce was the logical person to purchase the bar since he had been running it successfully for the past 11 years.

On the day of his father's retirement, Bruce made an oral agreement with his parents. In exchange for the future proceeds from the bar, Bruce made an oral agreement to pay off the $23,500 left on the second mortgage of his parent's house, give them $500 in cash per month, and pay for their health insurance and medical costs for the rest of their lives. Harvey refused to have a written contract.

Harvey remained the President of the company and owned all of the stock. If he passed away, the stock would move into his wife's name. After they both passed away, the stock would then pass on to Bruce. The remainder of the estate's assets would then be divided among the other four siblings. The estimated amount of the remainder of the estate in 2001 was $50,000 (house), $80,000 (cash and securities), automobile ($10,000), and miscellaneous ($5,000).

Bruce had paid his parent's health care premiums with the most inexpensive policy up until his father's death in 1997. By 1998, when Barbara was eligible for Medicare, Bruce did not pay for any of her health care costs, which included Medicare ($46 per month) and medications ($300 per month). Cal ended up paying for the medications, which caused resentment from Cal and his wife. Barbara paid for her Medicare.

From 1994-1998, Bruce paid his mother $500 per month, however he treated her as an employee. Therefore, taxes were deducted from her paycheck of $500, which resulted in a final sum of approximately $400. Bruce did pay $500 cash for one year, but in 2000 he treated his mother as an employee again. Furthermore, Barbara often complained that Bruce missed paying her on time (5th of the month). However, Barbara stated that after a phone call to Bruce, he always paid her by the end of the month. She insisted that he never missed a payment. To make matters worse, the bar's accountant was also Bruce and Barbara's personal accountant.

In April 2000, Bruce told his mother that she owed $10,000 in taxes for the tax year 1999. He stated that she owed this because she cashed in $15,000 in stock (initial cost basis of $1,352 in 1965) to refurbish parts of her house. Barbara's total income and taxes paid for 1999 can be seen in Exhibit 3.

EXHIBIT 3: BARBARA JOHNSTON'S SOURCES OF INCOME AND TAX SUMMARY FOR THE TAX YEAR 1999

SOURCE OF INCOME	AMOUNT ($)
TAXABLE INTEREST	2,294
DIVIDENDS	2,752
CASHED IN STOCK (CAPITAL GAIN)	13,648
TAXABLE PENSION	5,778
TAXABLE S-CORP INCOME (BAR)	2,299
TOTAL INCOME	26,771
ADJUSTED GROSS INCOME	26,771
STANDARD DEDUCTION	5,350
PERSONAL EXEMPTIONS	2,750
TOTAL STATE TAX	942
TOTAL TAX	$3,518

Bruce and Sharon recommended that Barbara take out a $10,000 loan for the taxes that she owed. This was done within a 24-hour period of time. When Barbara informed her sons about this, they were suspicious. They decided to obtain a copy of the financial statements of the bar from 1997-1999. In October 2000, Danny requested a copy of the financial statements from Bruce. Bruce vehemently refused, stating that Danny was not a shareholder in the bar so he could not receive a copy of the financials. The next day Danny and Barbara visited Bruce's accountant and demanded a copy of the financial statements for the past three years. The accountant reluctantly gave copies to Barbara.

Exhibit 4

Income Statement
The Crowne Inn

	1997		1998		1999	
	$	%Sales	$	%Sales	$	%Sales
Sales	$295,621	100.00%	$326,352	100.00%	$345,669	100.00%
Cost of Goods Sold	$156,100	52.80%	$157,231	48.18%	$174,139	50.38%
Gross Profit	$139,521	47.20%	$169,121	51.82%	$171,530	49.62%
Operational Expenses						
Advertising	$8,318	2.81%	$8,277	2.54%	$5,777	1.67%
Bank Charges	$892	0.30%	$1,094	0.34%	$1,592	0.46%
Insurance—General	$9,762	3.30%	$7,024	2.15%	$11,555	3.34%
Payroll—General	$94,951	32.12%	$96,027	29.42%	$98,383	28.46%
Professional Expense	$1,083	0.37%	$1,424	0.44%	$2,341	0.68%
Repairs and Maintenance	$2,096	0.71%	$9,211	2.82%	$1,687	0.49%
Taxes—Other	$7,813	2.64%	$23,312	7.14%	$27,308	7.90%
Utilities	$7,011	2.37%	$7,689	2.36%	$6,883	1.99%
Other	$5,678	1.92%	$7,882	2.42%	$6,369	1.84%
Total SG&A Expense	$137,604	46.55%	$161,940	49.62%	$161,895	46.84%
Operating Profit	1917	0.65%	$7,181	2.43%	$9,632	2.79%
Depreciation Expense	$1,753	0.59%	$2,353	0.72%	$2,086	0.60%
Interest Expense	$664	0.22%	$1,387	0.43%	$1,096	0.32%
Pretax Profit (Loss)	($500)	-0.17%	$3,441	1.05%	$6,451	1.87%

Exhibit 5	Balance Sheet The Crowne Inn		
	1997	**1998**	**1999**
Current Assets			
Cash & Marketable Securities	$6,280	$5,359	$8,118
Inventory	$6,250	$7,325	$6,785
Total Current Assets	$12,530	$12,684	$14,903
Property, Plant, & Equipment	$80,790	$82,315	$86,467
Less: Accumulated Depreciation	$60,791	$63,144	$69,384
Total Net Fixed Assets	$19,999	$19,171	$17,083
Total Assets	$35,529	$31,855	$31,986
Current Liabilities			
Accounts Payable	$5,146	$3,183	$3,456
Sales & Income Tax Payable	$1,460	$1,481	$1,827
Total Current Liabilities	$6,606	$4,664	$5,283
Long Term Liabilities	$14,045	$11,872	$9,085
Total Liabilities	$20,651	$16,536	$14,368
Common Stock or Owner's Equity	$6,000	$6,000	$6,000
Retained Earnings	$5,878	$9,319	$11,618
Total Equity	$11,878	$15,319	$17,618
Total Liabilities and Owner's Equity	$32,529	$31,855	$31,986

Exhibit 6	Cash Flow Statement The Crowne Inn		
	1997	**1998**	**1999**
Total Sales	$295,621	$326,352	$345,669
Total Cash Available	$295,621	$326,352	$345,669
Total Purchases	$156,100	$157,231	$174,139
Increase (Decrease) in Inventory	$820	$1,075	($540)
Cash Available After Purchase	$156,920	$158,306	$173,599
Uses of Cash:			
Operating Expenses:			
Total Per Income Statement	$137,604	$161,940	$161,896
Financing Activities:			
Interest Expense	$664	$1,387	$1,096
Principal Payments (Loan Additions)	($14,045)	$2,173	$2,787
Assets Additions	$16,917	$1,525	$0
Other Decreases (Increases)	$2,282	($1,942)	($3,532)
Cash Flow	($157)	($921)	$2,759
Beginning Cash	$6,437	$6,280	$5,359
Ending Cash	$6,280	$5,359	$8,118
Cash Flow Increase (Decrease)	($157)	($921)	$2,759

The next day the accountant called Barbara to inform her that she would be receiving a refund of approximately $6,482 from her taxes. Bruce and Sharon both went ballistic. They charged over to Barbara's house and threatened to disown her and the family. "You have no right looking into our personal financial situation. You are trying to steal the bar away from us! You are taking away my kids' education money."

The following day Bruce and Sharon showed up unannounced at Barbara's house with an unsigned contract (see Exhibit 7). Under duress, they took Barbara to see their attorney and placed pressure on her to sign the contract. After this, they quickly went to see Barbara's attorney, Bobby Free. There was a sense of urgency on the part of the Bruce and Sharon to get the contract signed immediately. Free could tell by the look on Barbara's face that she was under duress. Danny showed up at Free's office and they stated that they needed time to examine the contract before they would allow her to sign anything.

Exhibit 7: Contract Proposed by Bruce

AGREEMENT

This agreement made and entered into this 11th day of November, 2000, by and between Barbara A. Johnston, hereinafter referred to as Seller and Bruce S. Johnston, hereinafter referred to as Buyer:

WITNESSETH:

WHEREAS, Seller is the owner of a majority of the Stock in The Crown Inn, Inc.; and WHEREAS, Buyer desires to buy the Seller's stock, and to purchase all of the Seller's interest in the real and personal property where The Crowne Inn conducts business; and WHEREAS, the parties had previously agreed to a monthly payment for the purchase of Seller's stock which agreement the parties wish to codify herein.

NOW THEREFORE, in consideration of the mutual promises and covenants contained herein, the parties agree as follows:

1. That seller shall sell to Buyer, and the Buyer shall buy from Seller, the real and personal property where The Crowne Inn, Inc. conducts its business. The parties agree that subsequent to this Agreement, all of the documents will be prepared, to effectuate said transfer, including a deed to the real property and bill of sale to all personal property and both parties shall execute such necessary documents. The consideration for this transfer shall be the sum of $50,000.00, which the Buyer shall pay forthwith even though the transfer documents shall not be prepared until after the date of this Agreement.

2. That Buyer shall continue to pay to Seller, the sum of $500.00 per month, for the remainder of her life, said payment being the consideration for the present transfer of all of the Seller's stock in The Crowne Inn, Inc. Seller shall, immediately upon receipt of said funds, execute any and all documents necessary to transfer all of Seller's interest in the stock in The Crowne Inn to Buyer.

IN WITNESS WHEREOF, the parties hereto have entered in this Agreement the day and date first above written.

_____

Barbara A. Johnston, Seller

_____

Bruce S. Johnston, Buyer

State of Missouri   :

                          : SS.

County of Jackson   :

On this _____ day of _____, 2000, before me, the undersigned, a notary public, duly commissioned and qualified for said state, personally came Barbara A. Johnston, to me known to be the identical person whose name is subscribed to the foregoing instrument, and acknowledged the execution thereof to be her voluntary act and deed.

WITNESS my hand and notarial seal the day and year last above written.

_____
Notary Public

State of Missouri   :
                        : SS.
County of Jackson   :

On this _____ day of _____, 2000, before me, the undersigned, a notary public, duly commissioned and qualified for said state, personally came Bruce S. Johnston, to me known to be the identical person whose name is subscribed to the foregoing instrument, and acknowledged the execution thereof to be her voluntary act and deed.

WITNESS my hand and notarial seal the day and year last above written.

_____
Notary Public

Everyone left, but the turmoil continued. Danny updated the brothers and they determined that something had to be done about the situation. This had gone on for too long.

THE BAR INDUSTRY IN 2001

In 2001, the bar industry was in its mature stage of the industry life cycle. The sales of alcoholic beverages in the U.S. had increased from $90.5 billion in 1998 to $96.1 billion in 1999. Packaged alcohol consumption increased from $44.7 to $48.7 billion while alcoholic drinks increased from $45.8 to $47.4 billion during the same time period. A recent survey of 434 colleges polled by the Higher Education Research Institute found that beer drinking in 2000 had decreased from the previous year by a half percentage point (Dees, 2001).

Over the past few years the industry has seen numerous changes. One of the more popular trends was the increasing amount of import liquors and import beer from all over the world. Another trend was the increase in sales of micro brewed beer. Many bars have also increased the number of movies/videos, video games, and billiards available to customers.

Technology was also having an effect on the bar industry. Leisure time has been down 25% over the past 10 years due to the introduction of the Internet, digital television, and game consoles. Sixty percent of the bars in the U.S. currently have access to the Internet. Finally, there was the increasing liability associated with owning a bar due to the implementation of the .08 alcohol intoxication limit in most states.

LOCAL ENVIRONMENT & COMPETITION IN 2001

Kansas City was the home of pro baseball's Kansas City Royals and pro football's Kansas City Chiefs. The city was split in two by the Missouri River. There was a Kansas City, Kansas and a Kansas City, Missouri. Two million people currently live in the metropolitan Kansas City area.

The cost of living index for Kansas City was 98.6 on a U.S. scale = 100. This was significantly lower than other high cost areas like San Francisco, which had an index of 179.8. Wages for most occupations were close to the national average in the U.S. Furthermore, out of 180 metropolitan areas surveyed by the National Association of Home Builders, Kansas City ranked fourteenth in housing affordability during the fourth quarter of 2000.

The Crowne Inn was located on the northeast side of Kansas City (Clay County) about five miles from downtown. The surrounding area was a combination of both residential and commercial properties.

The total number of households in the surrounding area with the same zip code was 12,800 with a population of 31,500. The median age, household income, and household size was 43, $37,786, and 2.3. Most of the people owned their house while only 30% of the households had children.

The primary competitive advantage for The Crowne Inn was its location. Several businesses, two major universities, a medical school, and two major hospitals were located within a five-mile radius. In addition to the local residential market, this added an additional 30,000 people.

There were five competitors located within a one-mile radius. However, the Crowne Inn had its niche. Its reputation was a homey place where you could relax, get good food and drinks, and have quiet conversations.

THE DECISION

Barbara and her sons had to determine a final resolution with Bruce. It was quite evident that Bruce was unable to meet his oral obligations. Their attorney came up with three alternatives. First, they could sell the bar outright to Bruce and receive a lump sum. This would allow Bruce to pay off all of his future financial obligations to his mother in one lump sum. Second, they could have Bruce pay a smaller sum and continue with payments of $500 per month. Or third, they could sell the bar to a third party. Karl and Bruce discussed an appropriate way to deal with the problem. Karl communicated to his family that Bruce wanted to pay a lump sum of not more than $60,000. Furthermore, it became increasingly evident that Karl was now on Bruce's side. He was not looking at the situation from an objective viewpoint. Karl insinuated that Bruce had done nothing wrong. Bruce stated to Karl, "I am not willing to go above $60,000. If you want me to pay more than that I will go into business with the owner of Pappa's Pizza. We have been talking about opening a new pizza/bar in one of the fastest growing segments of the city, the East. This area is dangerous. We have been robbed three times in the last three years. If we move, this would put The Crown Inn out of business."

The family, excluding Karl, Bruce, and Sharon, met over Christmas and discussed their next move. They were unsure whether or not the $60,000 was a fair offer. They were also uncertain as to how they would determine a fair lump sum. Bruce had previously sent Karl a letter outlining all of the money that he had spent on his parents over the years. In the letter he stated that he had given his parents $98,275 over the past five years. He insinuated that he had already paid for the bar.

Exhibit 8: Money Bruce Spent on his Parents Since 1995

Type of Payment	Amount ($)
5 years at 500 month	$30,000
Mortgage on House	23,500
Extra Money given at X-Mas for 5 years	4,000
Cost of Insurance	30,000
Lawn & Snow Care at House	3,000
Repair Bills Paid	2,000
New Furnace and Air Conditioner	4,800
Personal Tax CPA Costs	975
TOTALS	$98,275

Danny asserted that $60,000 was a ridiculously low offer. In 1999, the bar had sales of $346,000 and Bruce and Sharon made $84,000 plus the profits from the bar. Danny stated that they should pay $175,000. Danny also had a great idea, We need to determine the average life expectancy for a person in Barbara's age group. Once we do this we can determine a fair offer.

Exhibit 9: Life Expectancy Table for Females

AGE	LIFE EXPECTANCY (Years)
10	68.6
20	59.8
30	50.2
40	40.6
50	31.4
60	22.9
65	19.0
66	18.2
67	17.5
68	16.8
69	16.0
70	15.4
80	9.1
90	4.7
100	2.5
110	1.3
120	0.6

Source: Health Care Financing Administration (HCFA), State Medical Manual 1999, # 3258.9 (HCFA Transmittal No. 64).

According to the tables she had a life expectancy of 17.5 years, however, due to her past health problems (e.g., heart condition), her life expectancy was 14.5 years. As the holidays came to an end, Karl, Cal, Tyler, and Danny had a number of questions. Was the lump sum method the best way to handle the problem? If so, was the $60,000 offer fair? If this was not a fair offer, what was fair? Furthermore, would Bruce be willing and/ or able to pay a higher lump sum? He had earlier told Karl that he was unwilling to pay $75,000. As they sat around pondering the situation, their mother was thinking, I do not want to lose my son and grandchildren over this bar. It is not worth it. However, Bruce made an oral agreement to take care of me.

DISCUSSION QUESTIONS

1. Describe the history of The Crowne Inn? What has made the business successful?

2. What mistakes did Harvey make during the succession process? As a result of having no written succession plan, what happened?

3. Why were the brothers so mad? Were they justified?

4. Bruce attempted to get his mother to sign a contract under duress (see Case Exhibit Do you think this was a fair contract? If not, what was wrong with the contract?

5. Bruce gave the brothers a detailed analysis of all of the money that he had given to their mother since 1995. What role should this play in determining your final recommendation to the family?

6. Based on the financial information in the case, place a value on the business using the following methodologies: Balance Sheet, Income Statement, and Discounted Cash Flow Methods.

7. Based on the financial and statistical information in the case, what would you recommend to the Johnston family? Why?

8. How do you think the culture of the family will change in the future?

"BEANOS ICE CREAM SHOPPE"

Todd A. Finkle, Gonzaga University

ABSTRACT

Terry Smith has spent the last six months preparing to purchase a Beano's Ice Cream franchise. Because his personal assets were limited, Smith needed a partner who could finance the purchase. After Smith found a prospective partner, Barney Harris, they negotiated a purchase price with Beanos. Then, Harris gave Smith a partnership proposal. As the case opens, Smith is evaluating the partnership proposal. His three choices are: to accept Barney Harris' partnership proposal, or to make a counter proposal, or to try to find a new partner.

INTRODUCTION

Two months ago, Terry Smith had been so confident that he would soon own his own Beanos Ice Cream franchise, that he had put an "I LOVE BEANOS ICE CREAM" bumper sticker on his Honda. As he looked at it now, he noticed how faded it had become in such a short time. He wondered if in fact it had been a short time -- or a lifetime.

Until recently, Smith had rarely second-guessed himself. After carefully researching an issue, he would base his decision on the facts and then proceed -- without looking back.

Now, however, he knew he had to put all of the momentum from the past six months to one side. He had to forget about the months spent investigating franchises, selecting Beanos, writing his business plan, and looking for financing. He had to forget about the fact that he had found only one prospective partner who could finance the deal, Barney Harris, and that he and his partner had spent several more months negotiating to purchase the franchise. He had to push away his own emotional investment in the deal now and make one more critical decision: should he go into partnership with Barney Harris?

If he signed the partnership proposal that Barney Harris had given him, Smith would get his franchise. If he did not sign the agreement, he may or may not ever see his dream come to life. It depended on whether he decided to make a counter offer, to look for a new partner, or to walk away from the deal altogether. It was that simple: sign it and get all the marbles, or risk everything for the chance to get something better.

Now, as Smith looked at his faded bumper sticker, he realized that he had to evaluate the proposal in the context of the whole franchise deal. The question was not just, "Is this a good partnership proposal?" The real question was, "Given the potential of this particular franchise, and given my financial and managerial needs, will this proposal help me reach my goals?"

SMITH'S BACKGROUND

In the fall of 1995, Terry Smith, a 36-year-old marketing representative for a Fortune 500 telecommunications firm in Cleveland, was among the thousands of employees who were downsized.

At first, he investigated the possibility of working for other major corporations in Cleveland. His education (a B.S. in biology and an MBA) and experience made him very marketable. During the seven years he had spent with the telecommunications firm, he had developed a solid reputation in his field. In a relatively short time, he received several job offers for about $60,000 per year.

And yet...Smith felt reluctant to jump back into a large corporation. He realized that as a new employee, he would be among the first to be cut, if his employer experienced a downturn. Did he want to go through that again?

Smith had had a positive experience as an entrepreneur during the years he was in college getting his degrees. He had started a successful mobile music company. While it had not made him a millionaire, it had paid for his education and living expenses, even though he had worked only when he could take time away from his studies.

One day, he found himself captivated by an article in Entrepreneur magazine. It pointed out that the number of downsized executives who were turning to entrepreneurship had doubled over the past two years. In 1993, between six and eight percent started their own businesses; in 1995, over 12 percent did so.

Smith decided that he needed to explore his options as an entrepreneur. He knew the down sides of owning a business: the long hours, the stress, problems with employees, paperwork, and a lack of benefits. However, he felt that these could be outweighed by the opportunity to make all of the important decisions himself.

After several months of research, he decided to seriously explore the purchase of an ice cream franchise in Gainesville, Florida called Beanos Ice Cream Shoppe, which cost $275,000 (see Exhibits 1-3 for the estimated costs and financial statements for a Beanos franchise). Smith had a net worth of $50,000 and a liquidity of $20,000, which meant that he had to obtain financing.

EXHIBIT 1: INVESTMENT BREAK DOWN OF A BEANOS ICE CREAM SHOPPE FRANCHISE

Expenditure	Dollars
Franchise Fee	$ 30,000
Design & Architecture Fees	15,000
Real Estate & Improvements	80,000
Professional Fees	2,000
Equipment	40,000
Signage & Graphics	15,000
Miscellaneous Opening Costs	7,000
Initial Inventory	11,000
Working Capital	75,000
Total:	**$ 275,000**

BEANOS ICE CREAM SHOPPE, INC.'S BACKGROUND

Beanos was founded by Bill Hogan, Jeff Pricer, and Annie Aubey, three former executives who had grown weary of the corporate world. In 1968, they founded Beanos based on a secret ice cream recipe.

Since opening its first ice cream shop, Beanos has become one of the most respected ice cream companies in the U.S., selling superpremium ice cream, low fat and non fat frozen yogurt, and ice cream novelties. Sales and net income for Beanos have been increasing in recent years. Net sales have increased from $48 million in 1989 to $120 million 1993. Net income has increased from $1.5 million to $6.7 million over the same time period. In the last quarter of 1994, net sales totaled $27,193,000, up two percent from $26,532,000. Overall, 1994 net sales went up from $120,328,000 to $128,802,000, an increase of seven percent.

The company used the finest, high quality, all natural ingredients. They have differentiated themselves from the competition with: (1) superior ingredients, (2) new product development, (3) new market development, and (4) environmentally conscious behavior. These strategies have allowed Beanos several competitive advantages over the competition in the frozen dessert industry. Beanos has held the number three market position in sales within the U.S.'s superpremium ice cream market for the past few years behind Haagen Dazs and Ben and Jerry's. The company has two primary growth strategies: (1) international expansion and (2) increased domestic penetration.

Beanos had 300 franchises located all over the world, with the majority located in the United States. Five percent of the franchises were company-owned and 75 percent of the franchises were located in the Washington D.C. Boston corridor and Southern California. More recently, the company has targeted warmer climates such as Florida, Texas, and Georgia.

The company has not had a franchise failure since 1991. Overall, only five percent of their franchises have failed. The average franchise had $350,000 in sales a year. However, in more successful markets, average sales were closer to $500,000. The company's domestic franchise agreements were generally for a ten-year term with an option for renewal. The agreements grant the franchisee an exclusive area to sell bulk ice cream and frozen yogurt, which the franchisee was required to purchase directly from the company.

Beanos provided the following to their franchisees: (1) a seven-day training seminar, (2) on-going operational support, which included access to a territory franchise consultant, (4) phone support, and (5) help with real estate and site selection. An input committee, comprised of five of the most successful franchisees, was developed to assist existing franchisees. There was also an annual franchisees' meeting, which included workshops. Finally, Beans sent field consultants to visit each franchisee four times a year.

Exhibit 2

Pro Forma Income Statement/Cash Flow Summary
For the Years 1997 - 2001 Expected Scenario
(in 000's)

	1997 $	1997 %Sales	1998 $	1998 %Sales	1999 $	1999 %Sales	2000 $	2000 %Sales	2001 $	2001 %Sales
Sales	$300.0	100.0%	$400.0	100.0%	$450.0	100.0%	$490.0	100.0%	$500.0	100.0%
Cost of Sales	105.0	35.0%	140.0	35.0%	157.5	35.0%	171.5	35.0%	175.0	35.0%
Gross Profit	195.0	65.0%	260.0	65.0%	292.5	65.0%	318.5	65.0%	325.0	65.0%
Operational Expenses										
Employee Wages	21.0	7.0%	28.0	7.0%	31.5	7.0%	34.3	7.0%	35.0	7.0%
Management Wages	30.0	10.0%	31.5	7.9%	33.1	7.4%	34.8	7.1%	36.5	7.3%
Health Insurance	3.0	1.0%	3.3	0.8%	3.6	0.8%	3.9	0.8%	4.2	0.8%
Rent	37.5	12.5%	39.3	9.8%	41.4	9.2%	43.5	8.9%	45.6	9.1%
Utilities	5.3	1.8%	5.4	1.3%	5.6	1.2%	6.2	1.3%	6.5	1.3%
Prop/Liability Insurance	4.5	1.5%	5.2	1.3%	5.1	1.1%	5.5	1.1%	5.9	1.2%
Marketing	13.6	4.5%	15.4	3.9%	17.4	3.9%	19.6	4.0%	20.0	4.0%
Accounting/Legal	2.0	0.7%	2.4	0.6%	2.6	0.6%	2.8	0.6%	2.9	0.6%
Supplies	4.2	1.4%	0.7	0.2%	1.0	0.2%	1.0	0.2%	1.2	0.2%
Repairs/Maintenance	1.4	0.5%	1.8	0.5%	2.1	0.5%	2.4	0.5%	2.8	0.6%
Telephone	1.8	0.6%	2.1	0.5%	2.4	0.5%	2.7	0.6%	2.7	0.5%
Bank Charges	0.3	0.1%	0.3	0.1%	0.6	0.1%	0.7	0.1%	0.8	0.2%
Association/Chamber Dues	0.5	0.2%	0.5	0.1%	0.5	0.1%	0.5	0.1%	0.5	0.1%
Auto	-	0.0%	4.5	1.1%	4.5	1.0%	5.0	1.0%	5.0	1.0%
Depreciation	12.0	4.0%	12.0	3.0%	12.0	2.7%	12.0	2.4%	12.0	2.4%
Miscellaneous Expenses	8.0	2.7%	3.0	0.8%	4.8	1.1%	5.0	1.0%	5.5	1.1%
Total Operating Expenses	145.0	48.3%	157.3	39.3%	168.2	37.4%	179.8	36.7%	186.6	37.3%
EBIT	50.0	16.7%	102.7	25.7%	124.7	27.7%	138.7	28.3%	138.4	27.7%
Interest Income	0.6	0.2%	1.2	0.3%	1.2	0.3%	2.0	0.4%	2.0	0.4%
Interest Expense	$15.0	5.0%	$12.1	3.0%	$9.1	2.0%	$5.7	1.2%	$2.1	0.4%
Earnings before Taxes	34.4	11.5%	91.8	23.0%	116.8	26.0%	135.7	27.7%	138.3	27.7%
Add: Depreciation Expense	12.0	4.0%	12.0	3.0%	12.0	3.0%	12.0	2.4%	12.0	2.4%
Cash From Operations	46.4	15.5%	103.8	26.0%	128.8	28.6%	147.7	30.1%	150.3	30.1%
Debt Service	0	0.0%	31.7	7.9%	34.7	7.7%	38.1	7.8%	41.7	8.3%
DISTRIBUTIONS	$46.4	15.5%	$72.1	18.0%	$94.1	20.9%	$109.6	22.4%	$108.6	21.7%

Exhibit 3

Pro Forma Financial Statement Assumptions
1997-2001

General: Projections are made on one store location in Gainesville, Florida. The projections do not include additional store openings projected in the business plan. It appears that cash flow from first store operation is adequate for additional store(s) after Year 3. The timing of first store opening would affect the timing of the projections but would not adversely affect the revenues and expenses used in the forecast, only the timing.

Depreciation: Equipment purchased of $40,000 is depreciated over a five year life. Real Estate improvements and expenditures of $80,000 are depreciated over 31.5 years consistent with IRS tax depreciation laws.

Advertising: Four Percent of sales after sales tax.

EBIT: Earnings Before Interest and Taxes

Interest Expense: Estimated at 9.25% applied to average outstanding debt balance.

Fixed Assets: Recorded at Historical Cost.

Debt Service: Initial borrowings of $275,000 at assumed rate of 9.25%. Payoff of debt service assumed to be made from internally generated funds and is forecasted to conclude in 2002. Extra funds will be used to pay off debt early.

INDUSTRY ENVIRONMENT

In 1995, the U.S. Frozen Dairy Dessert Industry was in its mature stage of the industry life cycle with the market segmented into the retail (dipping store franchises) sector and the supermarket (take home) sector. Estimated sales for 1998 were $12.8 billion, an increase of about 20 percent over 1993 sales. Two contrasting trends had developed in recent years: a movement towards full fat products (which appeal to indulgent consumers) and a movement towards fat free products (which appeal to health-conscious consumers). Brands, such as Healthy Choice, which were able to offer both rich taste and low-fat content, prospered.

Some of the consumer trends were: the fastest growing age group was the 45-54 year-olds, more two-income families, the U.S. annual population growth rate was expected to average 0.9 percent per year through the remainder of the decade, aging population, enhanced disclosure requirements for food labeling, more single occupant and single parent households, and health-conscious eating.

Ice cream has historically been one of the most popular dessert items. However, increased competitive pressures from entrants into supermarkets (Starbucks, Colombo, TCBY, and Swensen's) and new product development (novelty items like Haagen Dazs' frozen yogurt bars) made the industry fiercely competitive.

Due to the fierce competitive environment, Baskin Robbins, International Dairy Queen, Haagen Dazs, and TCBY have increased their advertising. Finally, there has been a movement towards locating stores in non traditional locations like airports, grocery stores, and in other franchises (such as Baskin Robbins and Dunkin' Donuts).

LOCAL ENVIRONMENT

Gainesville is located in north-central Florida. The city was ranked as Money Magazine's "Best Place to Live" in the U.S. for 1995. It had been ranked among Florida's most livable cities since 1991.

Employment growth in the 1990s had averaged 6.2 percent, which was nearly double the national average. Gainesville also had a low cost of living component compared to other cities of similar size in the U.S. In 1994, the unemployment rate was 2.8 percent, while the national average was 5.9 percent. In the past three years, Florida's economy has surpassed the national average. Florida was also one of nine states without a state income tax. Some of the statistics of Gainesville can be seen in Exhibit 4.

EXHIBIT 4: STATISTICS FOR GAINESVILLE, FLORIDA

Gainesville (excluding students):	91,000
Area Population (Alachua County):	191,000
Total Labor Force:	114,346
Cost of a Three Bedroom House:	$82,000
Property Tax:	$1,618
Retail Sales Tax (excluding food and medicine):	6%
State Personal Income Tax:	0%
Franchise and Inventory Tax:	0%
Unemployment:	2.8%
Robberies/100,000	301
Annual Sunny Days:	242
Mean Temperature (degrees F):	70.1
Average Sunshine/Day (hrs):	7.8
Annual Rainfall (inches):	49.9
Percent of population over 65:	9.3%

Source: *Gainesville/Alachua County Community Overview 1994* , *produced by The Council for Economic Outreach, Gainesville, Florida*

Prior marketing research efforts in Gainesville showed wide acceptance for Beano's products. Beano's had two promotional events in Gainesville, where ice cream was given to consumers. The feedback about the quality of the products was very positive, and the company had experienced success at selling products in local supermarkets.

Additionally, research showed that franchises located in college towns had sales averages that were surpassed only by resort areas. This made Gainesville very appealing, because the largest university in the South was located there. The University of Florida had an enrollment of 38,000 students and employed 15,500 people. Other institutions of higher education in Gainesville had a total enrollment of 20,000 students.

The population for Gainesville and Alachua County has increased 26 percent since 1980, an average increase of two percent a year (see Exhibit 5).

EXHIBIT 5: AREA POPULATION TRENDS

Year	Gainesville	Alachua County
1970	64,510	107,764
1980	81,370	151,369
1990	84,770	181,596
1995	91,000	191,000
2000	NA	208,900
2005	NA	221,600
2010	NA	233,900
2015	NA	245,200
2020	NA	256,200

Source: *Gainesville/Alachua County Demographics 1994*, *produced by The Council for Economic Outreach, Gainesville, Florida*

Exhibit 6 shows the Median Household Effective Buying Income Groups for Gainesville and Alachua County. The total effective buying income for Gainesville has risen from $627,766,000 in 1981 to $1,041,191,000 in 1992, an average increase of six percent a year. The average household income for Gainesville was $29,073.

EFFECTIVE BUYING INCOME GROUPS

Group	Gainesville	Alachua County	Florida
Under $10,000	21.80%	20.70%	12.60%
$10,000-19,999	20.6	19.7	18
$20,000-34,999	22.1	22.7	25.4
$35,000-49,999	14.2	15.1	18.8
$50,000-Over	21.3	21.8	25.2

Source: *Gainesville/Alachua County Demographics 1994*, *produced by The Council for Economic Outreach, Gainesville, Florida*

LOCAL COMPETITION

Fifteen local dipping store competitors are listed in Exhibit 7, which includes information about each store's age, number of employees, and estimated sales. It should be noted that of these fifteen, three stores have sales of $500 thousand to one million.

EXHIBIT 7: DIPPING STORE COMPETITORS IN GAINESVILLE

Store	Age	Employees	Sales
Dairy Queen	5 yrs	10-19	$500-1M
Dairy Queen	1	Unknown	Unknown
Baskin-Robbins	Pre 85	10-19	Less $500K
Baskin-Robbins	7	Unknown	Unknown
TCBY	10	5-9	$500-1M
TCBY	9	5-9	$500-1M
TCBY	5	5-9	Less $500K
Bresler's	5	5-9	Less $500K
Doug's Dairy Twirl	5	5-9	Less $500K
Fast Eddie's	7	1-4	Less $500K
Lauries Cafe	3	10-19	Less $500K
Lauries Cafe	2 months	Unknown	Unknown
Gator Ice Cream	1	5-9	Less $500K
Ice Cream Club	1	5-9	Less $500K
Real Italian Ice	Unknown	Unknown	Unknown

In addition to these dipping stores, the local market also included supermarkets, convenience stores, restaurants, and an ice cream truck that parked near campus. Of these sources, three were seasonal. The ice cream truck, the campus food court, and a campus Freshen's Yogurt all operated only during the school year.

Four features were missing from the local competition. First, there were no national competitors of superpremium desserts in Gainesville. Second, no competitor had a place for customers to sit outside. Third, no competitor had a policy of "giving back to the community." Fourth, there were no Haagen-Dazs stores. This was significant because Haagen-Dazs had been one of the first and strongest competitors, with sales peaking at $560 thousand at one location. A decline in sales prompted their withdrawal from the market.

A discussion of the four largest players in the local market follows.

Lauries Cafe

Lauries Cafe was a locally owned competitor that served superpremium ice cream, low fat frozen yogurt, bagels, gourmet coffee, sandwiches, and salads. They had two stores and offered delivery services. The first store was located directly across from the University and had been there for three years. The second store was new and larger than the first.

TCBY

The city had three TCBY stores. Two of the franchises had sales between $500,000 and $1,000,000. These were located in the upper-income areas of Gainesville. The other store was younger (five years old) and located near campus. The stores sold soft serve frozen yogurt and superpremium ice cream products along with novelty items. Currently, TCBY was marketing their "Treats" program heavily. Their Treats program featured candy mixed into their ice cream and frozen yogurt.

International Dairy Queen

Two successful Dairy Queen franchises were located in Gainesville. Dairy Queen sold hamburgers, hot dogs, barbecue, fish and chicken sandwiches, french fried potatoes, and onion rings. Their desserts consisted of cones, shakes, malts, sundaes and sodas, hard-packed products, and frozen ice cream cakes and logs.

Baskin-Robbins

Baskin Robbins had two stores in Gainesville. One was located directly across from the main campus. It had standing room only. They recently remodeled this store and signed a ten-year lease. The other store was located one mile west of the University. Baskin Robbins was known for their variety of flavors. They served both frozen yogurt and other ice cream products.

SMITH'S GOALS AND FINANCIAL OBJECTIVES

Smith saw an opportunity to obtain a franchise that had brand-name recognition and a history of success. Florida already had four Beanos franchises in Miami, Fort Lauderdale, Jacksonville, and Orlando. However, there were ample opportunities to open other stores in Florida.

Smith's goals were:

* Phase I: Open one franchise in the Gainesville area in the fall of 1996. For the first two years of operation, the focus would be on the success of that store;

* Phase II: Open a second store in Tallahassee in early 1998;

* Phase III: open a third, fourth, and fifth store in consecutive years (1999, 2000, and 2001) in Orlando.

The financial objectives were:

Objective 1: Pay off any loans to each store by the sixth year.

Objective 2: Maintain an average return on investment of 20 percent for each store.
Objective 3: Maintain a positive cash flow starting in year one for each store.

Objective 4: Have sales of 2.5 million at the end of ten years.

THE SEARCH FOR INVESTORS

Because Smith had already founded one company, he knew how difficult raising capital could be. He developed a list of people to talk with, and then proceeded as follows:

SBA Consultant

The Small Business Administration (SBA) consultant, Tom Hughes, was impressed with Smith's education, work experience, and detailed business plan. He stated that Smith would have no problem getting a loan of $175,000 as long as he had one third of the loan amount in liquid assets. For example, if Smith wanted a loan of $175,000, he would need approximately $58,000 in liquid assets. However, Smith's liquidity had dropped to $7,000 over the past few months, due to living expenses. Consequently, he needed an investor(s).

Mr. Hughes also asserted that if Smith got an investor who owned 20 percent or more of the company, the SBA required that person to sign on the note. Smith realized that this could pose a problem because the investor(s) would be at risk for the entire investment of $275,000 if they put up $100,000. That could decrease their desire to invest in the venture. Mr. Hughes also explained that Smith could not receive an SBA loan in the state of Ohio. He would have to go through an SBA branch office located in Florida.

Banker

Smith's banker was Mike Tork, a casual friend. Tork was also impressed with Smith's credentials and affirmed that he should not have a problem getting an SBA loan for $175,000 if he got an investor(s) to put in $100,000. Tork stated the bank preferred to see the following before granting a loan: (1) quality management team, (2) likelihood of success, and (3) financial projections. Tork also stated that obtaining a loan would be easier due to Beanos' successful track record.

The bank required Smith to submit his business plan, tax returns for the past three years, and a current copy of his personal financial statement. Tork sent a copy of the business plan to the branch manager in Orlando, Florida, Don Pelham. Pelham told Smith that he might be willing to give him a conventional loan, which would exclude the SBA. Pelham stated, "We want you to be successful, and we will do whatever it takes. The more successful you become, the more successful we become." Pelham gave Smith two scenarios from which to choose.

The first scenario was an SBA loan guaranteed by the federal government. This would involve a lot of paperwork. Pelham estimated the interest rate to be around 9.25-9.5% or one to one-and-one-half percent above prime, plus a closing cost of $3,300. The terms of the loan would be worked out later, but Smith figured he would pay off the loan over a six or seven year period of time.

The second scenario would be a conventional loan from the bank. The time frame to obtain this loan was similar to the SBA's. However, the terms of this loan would be much more conducive to the needs of Smith's company. The loan would be broken down into operating and reducing lines of credit (both using variable interest rates). The exact interest rate percentages were not discussed. However, Smith learned through friends that these loans were usually structured at five points above prime.

The operating line of credit would be oriented towards short-term operations (working capital, inventory, and payroll). Pelham told Smith that they were very flexible on the terms. For instance, they would allow Smith to pay interest only during the first year. Pelham also said that he was willing to let Smith pay interest only for up to 36 months. However, the loan would have to be paid off over six-to-eight years.

The reducing line of credit would be used for equipment, renovation, and other fixed asset allocation. For this line, Pelham also stated that he would allow Smith to pay interest-only for up to two or three years, and Smith would have to pay off the note at the end of six-to-seven years.

SCORE Counselor

Smith's last meeting was with the local Service Corps of Retired Executives (SCORE) counselor, George Willis. Willis had worked for Dupont for 30 years in various marketing positions and had owned his own executive search franchise for 14 years. Willis had also consulted with several franchisees in the frozen dessert industry.

Willis told Smith to obtain two partners with an equity interest of 20 percent or less because having one partner with a 33 or 40 percent interest would put you at the mercy of that partner. What if that partner decided not to do the deal? What if something happened to that partner? Also, that partner would have too much control because he or she has the money. If you have two partners, you would have much more control.

If one partner drops out, then you could get another. Smith stored this information and began his search for capital.

Family, Friends and Savings

Remembering his days in graduate school, Smith sought out the number one source of financing for most startups: friends, family, and savings. He failed at finding resources there.

Business Professionals

Smith's next step was networking through his database of business professionals in the Cleveland area. The first person he contacted was an acquaintance, Barney Harris, whom he had met a year earlier through a friend. Harris was a very successful restaurateur. Smith called Harris to arrange a meeting. Harris agreed, but wanted a copy of the business plan a week in advance. Smith dropped off a copy of the plan and a confidentiality agreement contract the next day.

A week later, Smith and Harris met. Harris stated, "You know Terry, most of the people who come to see me with business deals just talk. They do not have a business plan, and they expect me to invest hundreds of thousands of dollars with them. Your business plan is excellent. I like how you examined the business from broad and narrow perspectives. This is exactly what I like to see." Harris was also impressed with Smith's intensity and ambition. Harris stated that he knew Smith had what it takes to become successful -- "a fire in the belly." Harris told Smith that he was interested in becoming a potential partner, not an investor, and would be willing to put up $100,000.

After four months of hard work, Smith was excited at the opportunity of obtaining a partner. In his excitement, Smith stated that he was willing to give up 33 percent of the company in exchange for an investment infusion of $100,000. No further business professionals were contacted.

BEANOS SELECTION PROCESS

The selection process at Beanos required the potential franchisee(s) to send in an application form, psychological questionnaire, and personal financial statement. The next step was an independent phone interview that lasted one hour, followed by another half-hour for questions from the applicant. After this stage, there was a personal interview at Beanos' corporate headquarters in Phoenix, Arizona. The interview focused on the specifics of running a small business.

This process lasted approximately six weeks. After Smith and Harris passed, they received a letter that had a password in it that allowed them to contact any franchisee.

Beanos also sent the potential franchisee a copy of their Uniform Franchise Offering Circular (UFOC), a legal document containing information on the company's history, management, finances, operations, and franchisees.

Smith quickly took advantage of this opportunity to gather more information by making a list of questions. He contacted ten franchisees and learned about sales, profitability, successful and unsuccessful marketing strategies, employees, and horror stories of partnership agreements. One of the franchisees from Tucson, Arizona was kind enough to send Smith a copy of his financial statements from the previous year. After examining the differences between the franchisee's numbers and his projected proformas, Smith made some changes (see Exhibit 8 for revised expected scenario).

One of the most significant changes that Smith noticed was the cost of the franchise. Early on in the negotiation process, Smith estimated the cost of a franchise at $275,000. After talking with several franchisees in similar college towns, he estimated the cost of starting a franchise in Gainesville at $220,000, including working capital.

Smith also noticed that he initially overestimated the profitability of the business. In his original financial statements, Smith estimated the expected net income of the business at: $34,400, $91,800, $116,800, $135,700, and $138,300 for the years 1997-2001. He revised his figures to be: $29,000, $49,000, $67,600, $87,100, and $87,800. There was a significant difference, primarily due to his failure to include employee wages in the financial statements. This was a gross oversight.

Smith realized that he needed to get the partnership agreement out of the way as soon as possible. After all, they had been negotiating with Beanos for over five months now. Beanos had given Smith and Harris the green light. Now it was time for them to fulfill their side of the deal, to produce a partnership agreement and then to move forward with the construction of the franchise.

Exhibit 8

Revised Pro Forma Income Statement/Cash Flow Summary
For the Years 1997 - 2001 Expected Scenario
(in 000's)

	1997		1998		1999		2000		2001	
	$	%Sales	$	%Sales	$	%Sales	$	%Sales	$	%Sales
Sales	$340.0	100.0%	$385.0	100.0%	$435.0	100.0%	$490.0	100.0%	$500.0	100.0%
Cost of Sales	119.0	35.0%	134.8	35.0%	152.3	35.0%	171.5	35.0%	175.0	35.0%
Gross Profit	221.0	65.0%	250.3	65.0%	282.8	65.0%	318.5	65.0%	325.0	65.0%
Operational Expenses										
Employee Wages	46.9	13.8%	52.0	13.5%	57.6	13.3%	64.9	13.3%	66.8	13.4%
Management Wages	30.0	8.8%	31.5	8.2%	33.1	7.6%	34.8	7.1%	36.5	7.3%
Payroll Taxes	10.0	2.9%	11.2	2.9%	12.4	2.9%	14.0	2.9%	14.3	2.9%
Worker's Compensation	1.2	0.4%	1.5	0.4%	1.5	0.4%	1.7	0.4%	1.8	0.4%
Health Insurance	3.0	0.9%	3.3	0.9%	3.6	0.8%	3.9	0.8%	4.2	0.8%
Rent	37.5	11.0%	39.3	10.2%	41.4	9.5%	43.5	8.9%	45.6	9.1%
Utilities	5.3	1.6%	5.4	1.4%	5.6	1.3%	6.2	1.3%	6.5	1.3%
Prop/Liability Insurance	4.5	1.3%	5.2	1.4%	5.1	1.2%	5.5	1.1%	5.9	1.2%
Marketing	13.6	4.0%	15.4	4.0%	17.4	4.0%	19.6	4.0%	20.0	4.0%
Accounting/Legal	2.0	0.6%	2.4	0.6%	2.6	0.6%	2.8	0.6%	2.9	0.6%
Supplies	4.2	1.2%	0.7	0.2%	1.0	0.2%	1.0	0.2%	1.2	0.2%
Repairs/Maintenance	1.4	0.4%	1.8	0.5%	2.1	0.5%	2.4	0.5%	2.8	0.6%
Telephone	1.8	0.5%	2.1	0.5%	2.4	0.6%	2.7	0.6%	2.7	0.5%
Bank Charges	0.3	0.1%	0.3	0.1%	0.6	0.1%	0.7	0.1%	0.8	0.2%
Association/Chamber Dues	0.5	0.1%	0.5	0.1%	0.5	0.1%	0.5	0.1%	0.5	0.1%
Auto	-	0.0%	4.5	1.2%	4.5	1.0%	5.0	1.0%	5.0	1.0%
Depreciation	12.0	3.5%	12.0	3.1%	12.0	2.8%	12.0	2.4%	12.0	2.4%
Miscellaneous Expenses	8.0	2.4%	3.0	0.8%	4.8	1.1%	5.0	1.0%	5.5	1.1%
Total Operating Expenses	181.5	53.4%	192.9	50.1%	217.7	50.0%	226.6	46.2%	234.3	46.9%
EBIT	39.5	11.6%	57.4	14.9%	74.6	17.1%	91.8	18.7%	90.7	18.1%
Interest Income	0.6	0.2%	1.2	0.3%	1.2	0.3%	2.0	0.4%	2.0	0.4%
Interest Expense	$10.9	3.2%	$9.6	2.5%	$8.2	1.9%	$6.7	1.4%	$5.0	1.0%
Earnings Before Taxes	29.0	8.5%	49.0	12.7%	67.6	15.5%	87.1	17.8%	87.8	17.6%
Add: Depreciation Expense	12.0	3.5%	12.0	3.1%	12.0	2.8%	12.0	2.4%	12.0	2.4%
Cash From Operations	41.0	12.1%	61.0	15.8%	79.6	18.3%	99.1	20.2%	99.8	20.0%
Debt Service	0	0.0%	12.7	3.3%	13.9	3.2%	15.3	3.1%	16.8	3.4%
DISTRIBUTIONS	$41.0	12.1%	$48.3	12.5%	$65.7	15.1%	$83.8	17.1%	$83.0	16.6%

169

HARRIS' PARTNERSHIP PROPOSAL

Smith went to Harris and told him that it was time for them to draw up a partnership agreement. They had previously talked about a partnership proposal where Harris' percentage of the business would be 33 percent for an investment infusion of $100,000. Smith offered to write up the proposal. However, Harris insisted that he would write up the initial proposal. Two weeks later, Smith received it (see Exhibit 9) in the mail.

Smith found three surprises in this proposal. First, Harris changed the structure of the deal. Secondly, Harris charged him for accounting services, when Smith could do the book work himself. Third, the buyout clause proposed three times the cash flow of the business, averaged over the number of years they were in business, divided by the ownership percentage. Cash flow was not defined.

Smith was stunned. Quickly, he sketched out the proposal that he had expected to receive, so that he could compare them side by side (see Exhibit 10).

CONCLUSION

Terry Smith winced as he turned away from his "I LOVE BEANOS ICE CREAM" bumper sticker. He knew he had three choices: take what Harris had offered in the proposal, even though it was not the proposal Smith had expected; give Harris a counter proposal that included the three changes Smith wanted, knowing that there was a chance that Harris would back away from the deal altogether; or, start looking for a new partner. Smith started to walk across the parking lot, knowing it was time to make his next move.

EXHIBIT 9: BARNEY HARRIS' PARTNERSHIP PROPOSAL

Short term goal: 1 Store by fall 1996

Long term goal: 5 Stores

Incorporation: Limited Liability Corporation

My Investment: $100,000 with $5,000 going to equity in the company and $95,000 as a loan to the company. The loan would be repaid off in the next five years. I would receive quarterly interest at the prime rate for the loan. Also I would like to increase my equity position to 49% of the company.

Scoop Shop Operations: Terry Smith agrees to spend 100% of his time operating the store.

Book Work: I would like to have my accountant do all of the book work. Her fees are as follows: $2,000 to set up the books and $600/month thereafter, not including franchise reports, budgets, and forecasts.

Buy Out Arrangement: I would like to propose three times the cash flow of the business, averaged over the number of years we are in business. This figure would then be divided by our ownership percentages. For example, if our partnership developed cash flows of $100,000/year and you wanted to purchase my interest, we would multiply the $100,000 times three for $300,000 times my ownership percentage of .49, meaning the purchase price would be $147,000.

EXHIBIT 10: EXPECTED PROPOSAL FROM HARRIS

Short term goal: 1 Store by fall 1996

Long term goal: 5 Stores

Incorporation: Limited Liability Corporation

Your Investment: Harris' investment would be $100,000, with $100,000 going towards a 33% equity position. The other $120,000 will be obtained through an SBA loan. All debt service must be current prior to distributions paid out to partners. The expansion of future stores will occur at a later date.

Scoop Shop Operations: All day-to-day operations will be performed by Smith.

Bookwork: Smith will do the bookwork and have a payroll service do the taxes.

Buy Out Arrangement: Two formulas will be used to estimate the value of the company:

    Price-to-Sales

    Discounted Cash Flow

Purchase price will be repaid over a five year period while the seller holds the note to the debt. The loan will be repaid on a quarterly basis at the current prime rate for that quarter (as quoted in the Wall Street Journal). I also propose that we each have a first right of refusal of our stock and neither party has the right to sell until after three years.

DISCUSSION QUESTIONS

1. What were the internal strengths and external opportunities that Smith's franchise would face? What were the internal weaknesses and external threats?

2. Should Smith and Harris go for an SBA loan or a conventional loan? Why? What problems will this cause for Smith?

3. Harris states that he wants 49 percent of the company for a $90,000 95,000 loan at prime to be repaid over a five-year period of time. Does this seem like a fair deal for Smith?

4. For the buy out arrangement, Harris wants three times the cash flow from the business averaged over the number of years the business has been open. This figure would then be divided by the ownership percentage of the person who is being bought out. Based on the financial material in the case, does this seem like a fair buy out clause? Why or why not? If not, how would you devise a fair buy out clause based on the financial projections in this case?

5. After the franchiser approved Harris and Smith as partners, Smith began to work on the agreement. Is this the correct time to do this? Why or why not? Is there anything Smith should have done to protect himself?

6. Smith states that one of the primary reasons he wants to go into business for himself was the financial rewards. Based on the figures in the case study, do you think that Smith has made the correct decision to forgo his corporate job at $60,000 a year in exchange for a Beano's franchise?

7. Overall, do you think it would be wise for Smith to become a partner with Harris in this venture? Why or why not?

REFERENCES

1. Answers to Frequently Asked Questions about Franchising. *Franchising in the Economy.* International Franchise Association (IFA), 1995

2. Hill, T. and Jacobs, M. (1995). "Franchise Turnover Ratio Below Nine Percent." Frandata Corp. for the International Franchise Association's Education Foundation.

3. Top 50 Franchisers Ranked by System Wide Sales. *Restaurant Business,* November 1, 1995.

4. Vaughn, B. (1976). The International Expansion of U.S. Franchise Systems: Status and Strategics. *Journal of International Business,* Spring, pp. 65 72.

WEST POINT MARKET: MANAGING A CHALLENGE FROM THE EEOC

Todd A. Finkle, Gonzaga University
Robert A. Figler, The University of Akron
Kenneth A. Dunning, The University of Akron

ABSTRACT

Russell Vernon, a second-generation owner and manager of West Point Market in Akron, Ohio must decide whether to settle, go to court or reconcile (mutually agreeable solution) with the Equal Employment Opportunity Commission on an allegation of racial discrimination. He firmly believes that he is innocent. If he chooses to reconcile or settle the case out of court, he could be construed as a racist. If he chooses to go to court and loses, he may lose his family business. This emotionally charged situation is presented as a management decision that must be based on an analysis of the facts. The case is especially interesting due to the perceptions that students have on "the role of governmental agencies" and "the use of racial-based quotas in the workforce."

INTRODUCTION

It all started with a letter from the Equal Employment Opportunity Commission (EEOC) on March 29, 1994 to Russell Vernon, the owner of West Point Market. The one-page letter stated that the federal government had "probable cause" to believe that two dozen minority job applicants were unlawfully turned away without being fairly considered for employment.

With this brief document, a drama began to unfold. The EEOC believed that they had a strong case because less than ten percent of West Point Market's employees were African-American, compared to 33 percent in the city of Akron. Vernon believed that he had a strong case because his staffing reflected the fact that there were very few blacks with the appropriate job skills in the surrounding areas for his grocery store. The EEOC and West Point Market both felt passionately that they would win if their case if they went to court.

Determining Russell Vernon's guilt or innocence in this legal matter is outside of the scope of this case. Vernon faced one of the biggest challenges of his life. How should he manage this legal challenge? What should he do about it? How should he invest his time and money in defending himself? Should he reconcile? Settle quickly out of court? Take the EEOC to court? Vernon thought that it was very possible that this incident could break his business.

RUSSELL VERNON AND HIS COMPANY

Russell Vernon was a tall, slim, energetic native of Akron, Ohio. Friends described him as intellectual and sincere. Born in 1942, he was married and had two sons, Rick and Mike. At the age of 36 he had become the president and sole stockholder of West Point Market, an upscale food store founded in 1936 by his father and two partners.

Almost immediately upon taking control, Russell began to feature fine wines, cheeses, and candy in the store. Within a few years West Point Market established a reputation as Akron's best store for wines and cheeses. The store also began to feature specialty breads and prepared foods, such as lasagna and chicken. Customers responded positively to these items and West Point Market's profits increased dramatically with the higher margins that gourmet items customarily carry (Wilkinson and Frank, 1995).

West Point Market's target market was two-income families and professionals who sought upscale items and superior service. In 1995 the store dominated the gourmet retail business in the Akron metropolitan area, where 22 percent of the 250,000 households earned $50,000 or more per year.

In order to expand the store to its current size of 25,000 square feet, West Point

Market had borrowed $2 million in the late 1980s. In 1991 its sales reached $8.1 million. From 1992 to 1994 sales increased 3 percent or 4 percent a year while net profits increased from $159,000 to $169,300. Exhibit 1 provides financial results for 1992 through 1996. In 1994 West Point Market had 83 full-time and 54 part-time employees, up from 64 and 44 in 1991.

Under Russell Vernon's leadership the store gained a national reputation for its customer service. His accomplishments won attention in the popular press as well as trade publications, academic articles, and textbooks. Dr. Leonard Berry, director of the Center for Retailing Studies at Texas A&M University, named West Point Market as one of the top ten service companies in the United States. His textbook on retailing described the store as "a master's thesis on food retailing" because it offered a unique food-shopping experience (Berry, 1995). Writing in a special edition of Arthur Andersen's national retailing newsletter, Russell Vernon described his business this way:

We are an entertainment center, a stage for the products we sell. Our ceiling heights, lighting and color create a theatrical shopping environment. Our signature products include Killer Brownies, Chocolate Raspberry Suicides, Peanut Butter Krazies...We offer more than 100 mustards, 25 olive oils, and as many vinegars. Our music is classical; our restrooms feature turn-of-the-century art, residential fixtures, indirect lighting, and fresh flowers (Vernon, 1996).

Exhibit 1: Pro Forma Income Statement/Cash Flow Summary for West Point Market for the Years 1992-1996 (in 000s)

	1992		1993		1994		1995		1996	
	$	%Sales	$	%Sales	$	%Sales	$	%Sales	$	%Sales
Sales	$8,340	100.0%	$8,680	100.0%	$8,934	100.0%	$9,254	100.0%	$9,550	100.0%
Cost of Sales	5,001	60.0%	5,251	60.5%	5,451	61.0%	5,601	60.5%	5,801	60.7%
Gross Profit	3,339	40.0%	3,429	39.5%	3,483	39.0%	3,653	39.5%	3,749	39.3%
Operational Expenses										
Employee Wages, Taxes & Benefits	1,731	20.8%	1,799	20.7%	1,835	20.5%	1,960	21.2%	2,020	21.2%
Management Wages, Taxes & Benefits	300	3.6%	305	3.5%	315	3.5%	325	3.5%	335	3.5%
General and Administrative Expenses	651	7.8%	660	7.6%	660	7.4%	680	7.3%	697	7.3%
Depreciation	80	1.0%	80	0.9%	80	0.9%	80	0.9%	80	0.8%
Other Miscellaneous Expenses	150	1.8%	155	1.8%	160	1.8%	170	1.8%	180	2.1%
Total Operating Expenses	2,912	33.5%	2,999	34.6%	3,050	34.1%	3,215	34.7%	3,312	34.7%
Earnings Before Income Taxes (EBIT)	427	5.1%	430	5.0%	433	4.9%	438	4.7%	437	4.6%
Interest Income	12	0.1%	13	0.1%	14	0.2%	14	0.2%	15	0.2%
Interest Expense	198	2.4%	195	2.2%	190	2.1%	186	2.0%	181	1.9%
Earnings Before Taxes	241	2.9%	249	2.9%	257	2.9%	267	2.9%	271	2.8%
Taxes	82	1.0%	85	1.0%	37	1.0%	91	1.0%	92	1.1%
Net Income	$159	1.9%	$164	2.0%	$169	1.9%	$176	1.9%	$179	2.1%
Add: Depreciation Expense	80	1.0%	80	0.9%	80	0.9%	80	0.9%	80	0.8%
Cash From Operations	239	2.9%	244	2.8%	249	2.8%	256	2.8%	259	2.7%
Debt Service	37	0.4%	40	0.5%	45	0.5%	49	0.5%	55	0.6%
FREE CASH FLOW	$202	2.4%	$204	2.3%	$205	2.3%	$207	2.2%	$205	2.1%

* 1995 & 1996 are estimated

HUMAN RESOURCES MANAGEMENT AT WEST POINT MARKET

In addition to its products, atmosphere, and store design, writers often reported on West Point Market's hiring practices. The company's employee turnover was one-third of the industry average. As he explained to the case writers,

> We have achieved our success through our employees. We do that by empowering our employees to satisfy the customer. We expect employees to be enthusiastic, have excellent communication skills, and be friendly and supportive. Hiring decisions are based on the interviewee's demeanor, enthusiasm, hygiene and grooming, appreciation for West Point Market's commitment to great service, availability for work and desired level of pay. We hire a unique type of employee. We do not just hire clerks, but associates that have an investment in the company. They take care of our business in a very personal and individual way.

Hiring knowledgeable, service-oriented employees was an essential goal of West Point Market. The company hired Vernon's son, Mike, in January 1992 as its first full-time director of human resources. Vernon wanted his son in the position because Make had 15 years of experience in a variety of positions within the company and Russell trusted him. Until then the store's general manager had taken care of all matters related to employees. Mike Vernon served as director of human resources until January 1993, when Debra Leidy took over the job. At that point, the company had no formalized policies for recruitment or hiring. According to Mike Vernon, "We tried putting the procedure in writing at one point, but it was just an extra step." Leidy described West Point Market's recruiting process in 1993:

> When we recruit for applicants for job openings we do some advertising, but not a lot. We primarily rely on people who come to the store looking for work and word of mouth referrals. Twenty-five percent of our applicants come from word-of-mouth advertising from present employees. If they are hired, the employee receives a $25 referral fee. When advertising is done, the ads are placed primarily in the Akron Beacon Journal, and sometimes in the Cleveland Plain Dealer, Senior Focus (a local paper for senior citizens), and The West Side Leader.

> In general, we advertise for skilled job vacancies, such as Chefs, Bakers, and Meat Cutters. There is generally no need to advertise for retail employees, as there is a steady flow of walk-in applicants for these positions. If a person comes in looking for work, he/she will generally be brought into my office and given an application. I look over the application and if they meet the basic job qualifications, I contact their references. If the applicant makes it past this stage, the Department Head and I decide whether or not to personally interview the applicant.

The Department Head and myself conduct the interviews. The interviews are not in a specific protocol and generally last ½ to 1 hour. No notes are taken, and no records are kept. We both have equal authority in the hiring process. After the process is over, the applications are kept on an "active file" for 60 days and an "inactive file" for one year. During this time frame, the applicants are still available for job openings.

West Point had 10 to 15 department heads. Examples of departments included seafood, meats, cheeses, wine, bakery, candy, and fresh produce. Directly underneath the department heads were associates. In many cases, employees needed specific job knowledge or educational experience. For instance, a sales associate in the cheese department would be expected to have knowledge of 350 different cheeses from around the world and 26 signature cheese spreads made by West Point Market. Wine sales associates were also expected to have knowledge on the variety of wines from all over the world. Furthermore, it was not uncommon for employees to travel to Europe to find new brands to sell in the store.

Entry-level positions fell into five categories: cook, cashier, miscellaneous food preparation, office, and sales. For a listing of the job groups, their titles and the number of people hired from July 1991-March 1994 see Exhibit 2.

Exhibit 2

Job Group	Job Titles	Employees Hired	African-Americans Hired
Cook	Snack Baker, Kitchen Associate, Produce Trimmer, Produce Prep, Floral Designer	26	4
Cashier	Cashiers	13	1
Misc. Food Prep.	Bakers Helper or Gopher (I.e., dishwasher), Kitchen Maintenance Associate, Store Driver.	6	0
Office	Office Cashier, Store Receptionist	5	0
Sales	Courtesy Clerk, Bakery Sales Associate, Deli Sales Associate, Catering Associate, Cheese Associate, Produce Associate, Dairy/Frozen Stocker, Specialty & Grocery Stock Associate, Beer Pop & Water Stocker, Seafood Sales Associate, Meat Sales Associate, Wine Sales Associate, Gift Sales Associate, Specialty Non-foods Associate.	169	19
TOTALS		**219**	**24**

THE CENTRAL EVENTS

On March 31, 1991, three years before the EEOC contacted Russell Vernon, a memorable scene occurred in the store. This is how Vernon recalled it: James Ford, a local African-American civil rights attorney, entered West Point, walked over to an African-American courtesy clerk and grabbed her by her arm. He asked her why she was not a cashier. Without waiting for an answer, Attorney Ford shouted, "I want to see all the African-Americans who work here right now!" Vernon quickly greeted Ford and attempted to talk with him. Vernon remembers "defusing" the situation, but coming away with the feeling that the scene had created a strongly negative impression on everyone present.

Several weeks later, the local chapter of the National Association for the Advancement of Colored People (NAACP) stated the following in a letter to Vernon, "We would like to meet with you to discuss the steps that West Point Market can take to include more African-Americans on your staff." Russell Vernon and his son Mike both attended the meeting; James Ford (the civil rights attorney) did not. The meeting resulted in a list of ideas to increase the number of African-Americans in the store, and a commitment to the following in 1992:

• Establish a new human resources department that is geared to the care and success of current and future employees.

• Place the Equal Opportunity Employment (EOE) label on all future job ads.

• Establish working relations with the NAACP and other affiliated groups that will work to provide West Point Market with qualified black applicants.

Russell Vernon sent a letter with the statement of commitment and a list of specific ideas to the address that the NAACP representative had given to him. The post office returned the letter to him with a notice that the address was unknown. Vernon attempted to verify the address, but the post office employee stated that he had no record of address for the NAACP. Vernon assumed that the NAACP would contact him, and so he placed the returned correspondence in a file and waited to be contacted. No such contact was made.

Vernon did, however, carry out his commitments. First, a new Human Resources Department was established, with his son as its director. Second, the placement of the Equal Opportunity Employer (EOE) was inserted on each job advertisement. Finally, West Point established working relationships with a variety of organizations including the NAACP, Akron Public Schools, and the U.S. Department of Labor Bureau of Apprenticeship and Training. Nothing happened for the next three years.

COMMISSIONER'S CHARGE

On March 29, 1994 Vernon received a letter from the EEOC that stated the federal government had "probable cause" to believe that two dozen minority job applicants were unlawfully turned away without being fairly considered for employment. The commissioner's charge from the EEOC (see Exhibit 3) stated that West Point Market failed to and/or refused to hire African-Americans for all positions because of their race. The EEOC stated that their charges were based on information from witnesses, the company's reputation in the business community, and a comparison of the company's workforce profile to availability estimates in the relevant labor market areas.

Exhibit 3: Request for Information Charge No. 220941271

For all West Point Market, Inc. facilities during the period March 29, 1991 to the present, please submit the following;

1. List the name, address, phone number, and number of employees for each facility.

2. a. Provide description and copy of the recruitment and selection policies. Provide a copy of all related documents such as employment applications, test, interview forms, applicant logs, etc.

   b. If not stipulated in the policies requested above, describe the recruitment and selection process (how are applications/resumes accepted, and how are they organized, how long are they considered active, how long are they retained, the screening process, etc.) for all positions, including management positions. Specify any differences in policies or procedures for different job groups, if appropriate.

   c. State the name, race, and title of the persons involved in each stage of the recruitment and selection process referred to in 2 (b).

   d. State the name and title of the person(s) who is the custodian of the records designated in this request for information, and the physical location of these records.

3. List all the recruitment efforts, including but not limited to school placements, outside organizations, and employment agencies utilized for all retail positions.

4. Copies of all job ads for positions which were published during the period March 29, 1991 to the present. Indicate for each job ad, the name of the publication, the dates of publication, and the contact person.

5. Copies of all employee handbooks in effect during the relevant period.

6. Copies of all union agreements covering retail employees which were in effect during the relevant period.

7. Copies of all job descriptions for all positions and the minimum qualifications for each job.

8. Copies of all applicant logs for the relevant period.

9. Provide list (separately by each facility) of all retail vacancies filled from March 29, 1991 to the present, by name, person hired, race, date of hire, job title, EEO-1 category (sales worker, clerical, etc.), job status (full or part-time) and date of termination if applicable.

10. Grouped separately by each store, and within each store by job sought, provide a copy of all employment applications submitted during the period March 29, 1991 to the present. Attach all interview notes and any other screening documents to the original employment application.

Additionally, separate for each store the application of those hired from those not hired.

The EEOC stated that this did not constitute a finding of a violation, and the commission planned to investigate the matter with "minimal interference" to West Point Market's operations. The letter also asked Vernon to provide specific information within two weeks. The charges against West Point Market were called a "pattern of practice," meaning that the EEOC had used complex statistical analysis to compare thousands of hiring decisions. A defense of his pattern of practice would require its own statistical analyses.

Vernon had suspicions of who might have triggered the commission's charges. Because no employees had complained and no private parties had filed charges, his suspicions remained unconfirmable. The deputy director of the EEOC's Cleveland office, Walter Champ, said that his office had been following Vernon's actions for years. Champ pointed out that the commissioner in Washington would not have signed the complaint if the case did not appear to be strong.

Vernon turned for advice to his regular law firm. At an hourly rate of $225 the firm assigned a new attorney who was inexperienced in employment law. The attorney agreed that the charges were outrageous and that Vernon should not be forced to spend thousands of dollars to defend himself. The attorney recommended that Vernon ignore the charges. Vernon decided not to respond to the charges or to request any additional information.

There the matter rested for the next nine months.

WEST POINTS'S WORKFORCE

From July 1, 1991 through March 24, 1994, West Point Market ran approximately 32 classified advertisements in the Akron Beacon Journal, the West Side Leader, Bakery Marketing and Production, the Canton Repository and the Cleveland Plain Dealer for 240 openings. West Point Market received 1287 applications during this period; 1043 (81 percent) of the applicants were white and 244 (19 percent) were African-American. West Point hired 26 cooks, 13 cashiers, six food preparation specialists, five office personnel and 169 sales associates. Twenty-four African-Americans were hired during the allegation period: one cashier, four cooks and 19 sales associates.

THE COMMISSIONER'S DECISION

On January 16, 1995, Commissioner Barry Hoberman issued the following decision, "We believe that West Point Market discriminated against African-Americans in recruiting and hiring." The decision specifically stated that West Point Market engaged in recruitment practices that discriminated against African-Americans; failed to hire African-Americans into entry-level positions; and failed to maintain proper records on its employment process in accordance with EEOC regulations.

To settle the charge, the EEOC demanded that West Point Market place a full-page classified advertisement aimed exclusively at African-Americans; achieve a 33 percent African-American work force within five years; pay nearly $100,000 to 24 African-American applicants who the EEOC believed had been victims of discrimination during West Point's hiring process; hire African-American applicants to the exclusion of others; and report to the EEOC on its job applicants, including their race, for the next five years.

The letter stated that the EEOC was interested in providing justice to potential victims of discrimination. For an overview of the EEOC and how it proves discrimination see Appendices 1 and 2.

APPENDIX 1: THE EEOC in 1996

The Equal Employment Opportunity Commission is the federal agency that enforces the Age Discrimination Employment Act of 1967, Title VII of the Civil Rights Act of 1964 (as amended), the Equal Pay Act of 1963, the Americans with Disabilities Act of 1990, and the Civil Rights Act of 1991. These acts prohibit employment discrimination based on race, sex, religion, national origin, age, or handicap status. The agency's job is to receive complaints, gather information, and take the appropriate action.

The process begins when a complaint is filed. Approximately 80 percent of the charges are considered local because they are filed by employees who believe that they have been discriminated against. They contact a local EEOC and may file a charge within 180 days of the allegedly discriminatory act.

The remaining 20 percent of the charges (Commissioner's Charges) are not considered to be local charges because they are not initiated by an employee. Rather, they are filed by one of the agency's five commissioners who oversee the EEOC's activities in Washington, DC. Typically, this charge is used against giant corporations who operate in many locations across the country. It is rare that a small business such as West Point Market should face a commissioner's charge, but it is in fact what happened. When a commissioner initiates a charge, the EEOC contacts the employer directly with the charge that stated the allegation. The EEOC is not required by law to identify the names of the people who requested the investigation.

Once an allegation has been made, the EEOC will send a copy of the charge to the employer. If there is probable cause to investigate, the EEOC will ask the employer to provide certain types of information. The EEOC then performs an investigation.

If the EEOC finds reasonable cause to believe that discrimination has occurred, it must seek to conciliate the charge to reach a voluntary resolution between the charging party and the respondent. If the conciliation is not successful, then the EEOC or the charging party may litigate the case.

From the fiscal year 1991 to fiscal year 1994 the number of discrimination charges increased dramatically. This was due to the passage of the 1990 Americans with Disabilities Act (ADA) and the 1991 Civil Rights Act, which increased the allowable damage awards and was followed by a surge in allegations of sexual harassment. Annual charge receipts increased from 62,135 in fiscal year 1990 to 91,189 in fiscal year 1994. In the same period, due to budget restrictions, available investigators decreased from 762 to 732. As a result the average caseload per investigator grew from 51.3 in 1990 to 122 in fiscal year 1994. The investigators could not keep pace with the escalating charge receipts. Furthermore, there was a projected year-end backlog of 120,000 charges by the end of 1995.

APPENDIX 2: HOW DOES the EEOC PROVE DISCRIMINATION?

To determine if discrimination in staffing has occurred within an organization, the EEOC can follow two different paths: disparate treatment or disparate impact. To prove discrimination the EEOC needs evidence and proof, particularly as these charges pertain to the staffing system itself and its specific characteristics in practice.

When an organization is accused of disparate treatment, the plaintiff claims that they intentionally discriminated against people on the basis of specific characteristics such as race or sex. For example, not hiring women with young children while hiring men without children or hiring minorities to become janitors while Whites are made waiters. The effect of such decisions, even though they may be prompted by the employer's idea of good business practice, is to subject a specific group to negative treatment because of a personal characteristic (Gatewood and Feild, 1999, page 43).

If a disparate treatment case goes to court, a sequence of events occurs. First, to prove whether or not disparate treatment exists within an organization, a plaintiff must show that the following four conditions exist:

- The person belongs to a protected class.

- The person applied for, and was qualified for, a job the employer was trying to fill.

- The person was rejected despite being qualified.

- The position remained open and the employer continued to seek applicants as qualified as the person rejected (Heneman, Judge, and Heneman, 2000).

If this is done successfully, the plaintiff is said to have established a prima facie case of discrimination. If this is not done, the case should be dismissed.

If the plaintiff is successful in proving that a prima facie case exists, the defendant must present a clear and specific job-based explanation for its actions in order to defend itself. The defendant must provide a legitimate, nondiscriminatory reason for rejecting the plaintiff. This is relatively easy to do. For example, previous defendants have successfully argued that the qualifications of the individual were inferior to those selected. If the argument is clear and specific, the defendant meets its burden of proof. The defendant does not have to persuade the judge that it actually used this as the basis for rejecting the plaintiff. It is up to the plaintiff to prove that the employer did not use it. The argument is usually more acceptable when the defendant's reasons include some objective data. The argument is less acceptable, if the reasons are based solely on subjective judgments, especially if these are made without clear definition and procedures.

If the organization is successful in defending itself, then the plaintiff must prove that the organization's defense is a pretext and the true reason for rejection was prejudice. Previous court cases have accepted racial slurs made by company managers, records that the company's treatment of the plaintiff were inconsistent with other individuals of other demographic groups, and statistics showing the demographic group of the plaintiff were underrepresented in the company's workforce. If the data are not acceptable, the plaintiff is unsuccessful in countering the defense of the organization (Gatewood and Field,1998).

Disparate impact, also known as adverse impact focuses on the motive or intent underlying them. In this form organizational selection standards are applied uniformly to all groups of applicants, but the net result of these standards is to produce differences in the selection of various groups. Two classic examples of such discrimination are the requirement of a high school diploma, which had been used extensively for entry-level positions, and of height minimums, for example 5'6", which may have been used for police and some manual positions. The problem is that such standards disqualify a much larger percentage of groups. For instance, more Whites have high schools diplomas than most minority groups. A number of frequently used and seemingly valid selection requirements has been the subject of disparate impact discrimination charges, including arrest records, type of military discharge, various educational degrees, scores on some tests and interviews, years of previous work experience, and financial history. The use of each of these has been linked to the disqualification of a high percentage of at least one demographic group of applicants (Gatewood and Field, 1998).

Statistics are used in cases of both forms of discrimination. In disparate treatment cases, statistics are mainly used to assist the plaintiff in rebutting the defendant's explanation of the selection practice under question. In disparate impact cases, statistics are most often used by the plaintiff in demonstrating that a pattern of adverse effect has occurred. The two main types of statistics that have been used are applicant stock (relevant labor market approach) and applicant flow statistics (selection ratio approach).

Applicant stock statistics require the calculation of the percentage of the targeted minorities employed in the organization versus the percentage of available minorities employed in the population. To determine if discrimination exists, the EEOC compares the relevant labor market (RLM) data with the targeted population within the organization.

Data on the RLM usually comes from the U.S. Census, chamber of commerce, industry and other reports. The RLM has two components: the geographical location and skill level. In general, geographical units are explained in terms of the nation, state, or Standard Metropolitan Statistical Area (SMSA), which is the region surrounding a central city or town. Appropriate skill level is reported in terms of the numbers reported as holding or qualified to hold specific jobs.

The following is an example of how the EEOC would use the RLM approach:

$$\frac{\text{Number of African-American managers in the organization}}{\text{Total number of managers in the organization}} \quad \text{vs.} \quad \frac{\text{Number of appropriately skilled African-American managers in the labor force}}{\text{Total number of appropriately skilled managers in the labor force}}$$

This example requires the calculation of the percentages of African-Americans that are employed in the organization as managers and the available number of African-American managers available in the labor force or RLM.

The percentages are then compared to search for disparities. If the percentage of African-American managers in the organization's workforce is significantly smaller than the percentage in the comparison group then there is the possibility that racial discrimination has occurred in the selection process. This process is referred to as "utilization analysis."

The other statistical technique used by the EEOC is applicant flow statistics. Applicant flow statistics compare proportions taken at two time frames, before and after the selection has taken place.

Number of minority applicants selected		Number of nonminority applicants selected
--	vs.	--
Number of minority applicants		Number of nonminority applicants

If the percentage difference for the minority group is significantly smaller than the percentage for the non-minority group, evidence of discrimination is present. The courts have used two statistical tests to assist in their decisions using this method: the Four-Fifths Rule and the Standard Deviation Rule. The Four-Fifths Rule is said to indicate discrimination if the hiring of minorities is less than 80 percent of the rate of hiring for non-minorities. For example, assume that West Point Market hired 90 percent of their white applicants, but only 60 percent of their African-American applicants. Since, 60 percent is less than four-fifths of 90 percent, statistical evidence of discrimination is present. The 80 percent rule is only a guideline and provides for exceptions based on sample size considerations and practical significance of difference in selection rates.

The Standard Deviation Rule provides a rule of thumb to judge whether or not the number of African-Americans actually hired is roughly representative of their population in the applicant pool. This method requires the calculation of the standard deviation. The general rule is that the number selected should be within a range defined by the standard deviation units from the expected number selected.

To determine the standard deviation you must multiply the following and then take the square root of the final product:

$$\frac{\text{Total minority applicants}}{\text{Total applicants}} \quad X \quad \frac{\text{Total non-minority applicants}}{\text{Total applicants}} \quad X \quad \begin{array}{c}\text{Total} \\ \text{Persons} \\ \text{Selected}\end{array}$$

For example, assume that 200 individuals selected from an applicant pool of 500 applicants were African-American and 300 were White. Inserting these numbers into the equation would yield a standard deviation of 6.93. Two standard deviations would be approximately 14. If African-Americans were selected in the same proportion as they were represented in the applicant pool, you would expect that 80 African-Americans would have been selected (200 X .40 of applicants). In this case, the acceptable selection range would be 80 plus or minus 14, or the range from 66 to 94 African-Americans selected. According to this type of analysis, a firm that hires less than 66 African-Americans, or greater than 94, could be accused of racial discrimination.

VERNON'S NEW DEFENSE TEAM

At this point Vernon decided that his attorney had erred badly in recommending that he ignore the EEOC's demands. Concluding that he needed someone with experience in employment law, Vernon dropped his law firm and hired a specialist, Neil Klingshirin, to advise him. The new attorney summarized the EEOC's charges, then told Vernon, "We need to determine the best strategy to provide a clear and specific job-based explanation for your actions." Klingshirin analyzed the case against WPM:

The EEOC used applicant stock statistics (Labor Market Comparison Approach) to determine that discrimination occurred at your store. They want you to have a 33 percent African-American work force in place within five years, however they never stated where the percentage came from. This is not the SMSA for Akron, however my research indicates that this is the approximate percentage of African-Americans that are employed by the Akron fire and police departments. It appears that the EEOC is using the percentage of African-Americans in the city of Akron as their relevant labor market. And since you have less than 10 percent African-Americans on your workforce, they are assuming that you are discriminating against African-Americans.

Even so, thought Klingshirin, "there is good news." The definition of the labor market used in statistical comparisons frequently was the subject of intense argument during court cases. The proportion of a given demographic group in the labor market could change radically depending on the combination of geography and skill level that was chosen. Furthermore, the law did not specify how large a difference in percentages was tolerated before a court would conclude that an employer had discriminated. He told Vernon that several court cases "could help our case. "

Klingshirin proposed the following course of action:

"The EEOC assumed that Akron's African-American workforce had the appropriate qualifications for your entry-level job openings. On the contrary, we need to prove that you need people with specific job qualifications. We need to perform our own formal utilization analysis and examine the percentage of available workers in each job category (Cooks, Cashiers, Misc. Food Preparation, and Office and Sales). I have done some research on your applicant pool and noticed that 20 percent of your applications came from outside the city of Akron. Therefore, I recommend that we use the numbers for Summit County. This includes the city of Akron and the surrounding communities. I have already retrieved the numbers for Summit County (see Exhibit 4)."

EXHIBIT 4: 1990 U.S. CENSUS JOB CLASSIFICATIONS DETAILED BY RACE AND SEX FOR SUMMIT COUNTY, OHIO

		MALES			FEMALES		
	OVERALL TOTALS	TOTAL MALES	WHITE	BLACK	TOTAL FEMALES	WHITE	BLACK
Cooks	4,583	2,145	1,779	289	2,438	1,954	427
Cashiers	6,224	1,092	946	120	5,132	4,250	811
Misc. Food Prep. Occupations	1,856	930	643	276	926	753	163
Office	761	244	216	28	517	441	69
Sales Workers	4,148	1,348	1,261	87	2,800	2,583	206

Vernon and his new lawyer created a three-stage defensive strategy. First, they would defend their hiring records with statistical information that the EEOC would understand. Second, they would try to respond positively to the settlement demands. Third, they would build support from friends – including the African-American community – to place political pressure on the EEOC to resolve the crisis.

To combat these changes, Vernon hired Dr. Gerald Barrett, a University of Akron Professor with a Ph.D. in Industrial/Organizational Psychology and a law degree. Dr. Barrett performed a utilization analysis to examine the percentage of available African-American workers in Summit County, which included the city of Akron, for each job category: Cooks, Cashiers, Misc. Food Preparation, Office and Sales.

Stage two of the defense strategy was to respond positively to the settlement demands. Vernon agreed in principle that a greater effort could be made to attract a more diverse workforce. He hired a new Director of Human Resources, Terrie Freiman, who increased West Point's networking with the African-American community. Although she did not have a college degree, she did have experience in Human Resources Management. Relationships were built with the Arlington St. Baptist-Urban League, the local chapter of the NAACP, the Summit County Department of Human Service, and the city's African-American activities such as "Hands Across the Bridge," a celebration of Akron's diversity.

Vernon proposed alternatives to the cash payments for back pay and damages to the victims of discrimination identified by the EEOC. He proposed that West Point Market invite new applications from the 24 African-Americans who had not been hired. Any of them who were hired and remained with West Point for one year then would receive free tuition to a local college while continuing to work at West Point Market.

The final stage of Vernon's strategy was to build support from friends. He aimed to create political pressure on the EEOC to resolve the crisis. Vernon put all his marketing skills into the campaign. He mailed background information to U.S. senators and the local U.S. representative and solicited their letters of support. He also wrote to the Office of Advocacy in the Small Business Administration. Vernon also began a "grass roots" movement at home. The president of the state grocers association regularly updated state legislators on West Point's situation.

West Point Market was also a member of several national organizations including the Society of Human Resource Management (SHRM) and the Food Marketing Institute. Their lobbyists supported Vernon and introduced him to key people in Washington. Prominent African-American leaders in Akron circulated petitions of support. The Akron chapter of the NAACP, now under new leadership, wrote to the EEOC's Cleveland office in support of West Point. According to the chapter, "We have never seen or heard of any unfair practices at West Point. We will stand by them all the way."

The chairman of the EEOC in Washington D.C. also received many letters. One was from Ohio's governor, James Voinovich:

> Recently a situation was brought to my attention that is very confusing to me. There is a small, family-owned retail business in Akron called the West Point Market. They have enjoyed a stellar reputation as being a good citizen in the Akron area. The Akron NAACP has confirmed this company's high level of support in providing jobs to African-Americans and in financially supporting NAACP programs over the years. I do not understand why or how a charge can be levied when there has been no specific complaint filed. I find this incredulous; it is incomprehensible to me how this could be happening. Furthermore, there has never been one race-discrimination complaint filed against West Point with the Ohio Civil Rights Commission, the state agency that often works with the EEOC in investigation complaints.

As word spread throughout Akron about the EEOC's charges, support for West Point grew. Loyal customers started a $6,000 defense fund, and the local newspaper backed the company.

THE REVERSAL

On April 25, 1995 it appeared that Vernon's three-stage strategy had succeeded. The EEOC announced that it was willing to drop its demand for a workforce comprising 33 percent African-Americans and to explore creative alternatives to back pay for the affected class members. During the initial stages of negotiations, the Small Business News, an Akron-Cleveland publication, ran an explosive article on the event. The reporter already had interviewed the civil rights attorney when he approached Vernon. "By the time he interviewed me," Vernon reflected, 'no comment' was not an option."

The article was largely sympathetic to West Point, portraying the company as a victim who was confident of winning its case and the EEOC as tool of organized labor. The article alleged that the United Food & Commercial Workers Union had initiated the complaint. (A forerunner to this union had been ousted by West Point's employees in a 1957 decertification note case that was so notable that the Wall Street Journal had covered the story.) The union's chief organizer, Lou Maholic, was asked if his union had played any role in the complaint. He replied, "I may have given the (EEOC's) phone number to some people who called to complain."

Four months later, the EEOC's Cleveland office notified Vernon that it would no longer honor its proposed terms nor the previously accepted portions of the settlement, and that it wanted to triple to $210,000 the back pay due from West Point. The EEOC gave no reason for its latest action. At the same time, Congress amended the Equal Access to Justice Act (EAJA) to include a special provision for small businesses. The EAJA allows defendants to recover legal fees (up to $125 per hour) and other expenses (e.g., expert witnesses, reasonable cost of any study, analysis, or a project that is found necessary for the preparation of the party's case). This would allow West Point Market to recover their legal fees if the court decided that the EEOC had demanded a settlement that was "unreasonable" when compared to the trial court's ultimate award.

THE DECISION

Russell Vernon thought that his decision might make or break his company. He saw three options available to West Point Market.

• Bring his case to court, filing under the Equal Access to Justice Act to recover West Point's legal fees of $100,000. A loss would mean paying West Point's legal fees as well as the EEOC's proposed penalties, for a total of $310,000.

• Settle out of court, paying the $210,000 sought by the EEOC. Combined with the $67,000 already spent on West Point's legal defense, this would bring the total loss to $277,000. Could Vernon afford to do this?

• Reconcile with the EEOC out of court. If Vernon chose this option, West Point could not recover any of the money already spent on its defense.

Vernon also had to consider that a victory in court would afford an opportunity to clear his reputation. If he settled out of court or reconciled, he might be perceived as a racist. This could be detrimental to the store's future.

Placing a bag of Chocolate Raspberry Suicides into a customer's shopping bag, Russell Vernon pondered all that he had learned over the past few months about discrimination cases. He was sure that this decision would be among the most important he had ever made.

DISCUSSION QUESTIONS

1. Like virtually all-independent retailers with 100 employees, West Point Market does not employ a professional human resources manager who has a legal background. What were the costs and benefits of this decision? What alternatives are available to resource-constrained small businesses?

2. Why did the EEOC use the relative labor market approach (RLM)? Calculate the Four-Fifth's Rule for the Selection Ratio Approach. Did the EEOC have statistical evidence against West Point Market that indicated disparate treatment?

3. Determine the statistical evidence the EEOC would have had against West Point Market if they used applicant flow statistics and the Standard Deviation Rule?

4. Vernon's defense team used the labor market comparison approach and applied the Standard Deviation Rule to stock statistics to defend Vernon's selection of employees. Calculate these percentages. Do they support Vernon's position?.

5. Based on Vernon's human resource practices, finances, statistical evidence and other pertinent information, what would you recommend to Vernon? What is the likelihood that Vernon will prevail in court?

6. What mistakes did Russell Vernon make and what should he have done differently?

7. Discuss Vernon's feelings towards the government. Did his feelings have an affect on the outcome of the case?

8. Discuss legally defensible recruiting and hiring practices so small businesses can reduce the probability of being targeted for racial discrimination.

REFERENCES

1. Berry, L. (1995). On Great Service. *New York: Free Press.*

2. Castenda v. Partida, 430 U.S. 482, 497 n. 17 (1977). *Supreme Court Reporter.* p. 1272-1283. St. Paul: West Publishing Company.

3. Equal Employment Opportunity Commission Budget for Fiscal Year 1999, *United States Budget for 1999.* Washington DC.

4. Ettore, J. (1995). "Vernon to the Defense," *Small Business News.* November, p. 10-15.

5. Fisher, C., Schoenfeldt, L., and Shaw, J. (1996). *Human Resources Management.* Houghton Mifflin Company: Boston.

6. Gatewood, R., and Field, H. (1998). *Human Resource Selection.* Dryden Press: Orlando, FL.

7. Hazelwood School District v. United States, 433 U.S. 299,307 (1977). *Supreme Court Reporter.* p. 2736- 2744. St. Paul: West Publishing Company.

8. Heneman, H., Judge, T.and Heneman R. (2000): *Staffing Organizations 3rd Edition.* Irwin/McGraw-Hill: Boston, MA.

9. International Brotherhood of Teamsters v. United States, 431 U.S. 324, 229 n. 20 (1977). *Supreme Court Reporter.* p. 1843-1858. St. Paul: West Publishing Company.

10. Vernon, R. (1996). "Fighting Back—A Small Retailer Takes on the EEOC," *Arthur Andersen Retailing Issues Letter.* 8:6, p.3.

11. Wilkinson, J. and Frank, G. (1995). "West Point Market: Baking Specialty Breads," *Case Research Journal.* 15:3, p. 57-70.

"SHOULD I BUY THE JERRYS FAMOUS FROZEN DESSERTS CHAIN?"

Todd A. Finkle, Gonzaga University
Phil Greenwood, University of Wisconsin at Madison

ABSTRACT

The purpose of the case study is to acquaint the reader with the flow of events that occur during the initial stages of a small business acquisition. Phil Hogan had become frustrated with corporate America and decided that he wanted to purchase his own small business. Through an old friend, Phil came upon an excellent opportunity to purchase a very successful frozen dessert retail chain. Phil contacted the owner of Jerry's Famous Frozen Desserts, Robert Hicks. Hicks asserted that he wanted to see a financial statement from Phil indicating that he had a minimum net worth of $2 million and a letter of introduction from his banker. Phil obtained the financial statements from an entrepreneur who was interested in investing in the venture and obtained a letter from his banker. Two weeks later, Phil received the audited financial statements for the past four years from Jerry's. After reading the financials, Phil realized that this was a great opportunity to make a great sum of money. Jerry's had annual sales of $2.023 million and a net profit of $423,000. He talked with his potential investor about the deal, but the investor backed out. Phil now had to line up financing on his own. He also had to figure out how to structure the deal and determine if the asking price of $2 million was too high.

INTRODUCTION

As Phil Hogan lifted the final pages of his business plan out of his printer, he looked at the clock. It was almost midnight, which meant that he had about seven hours to get ready for another day at work.

But the idea of going to his job was not what was keeping him awake at this hour. No, it was the idea of owning his own business that invigorated him this night, as it had many nights, for many years.

It had started with a newspaper route—and the wish to be independent, make some money, and call the shots. At age 12, he had sketched out a time line that included business ownership at age 30.

That didn't happen, of course. But now, at age 36, he was a CPA with a lot of valuable experience behind him, and he was ready. For the last five years, he had been a senior financial analyst, and now, a marketing representative for Pfizer Laboratories. Before that he had been a senior internal auditor for McDonald's, and had worked for an accounting firm.

Lately, he had begun to think that if he was ever going to pull himself out of the corporate world, it would have to be now.

Now, stepping over the stacks of Inc. and Entrepreneur magazines on the floor by his desk, Phil took a moment to think about how the last year had gone:

January, 2010: Contacted friends, business associates and acquaintances to tell them he was interested in purchasing a small business that:

- Had a net income of $50,000/year for the last five years,
- Was located in the South,
- Was a retail business,
- Had an owner who was selling because of retirement, illness, or death.

March, 2010: A former college roommate called to tell him about Jerry's Famous Frozen Desserts, three upscale frozen dessert stores that meet his criteria. Called the owner, Robert Hicks, to request more information. Received a letter from Mr. Hicks' accountant stating that before he shared this information, he wanted to see financial statements that verified Phil's financial capacity to purchase the company.

April, 2010: Contacted friends to ask if this was the proper procedure. They said it was. Began to look for a potential investor. Started to work on a business plan.

June, 2010: A friend arranged a lunch with a potential investor, Terry Dunleavy, who currently owned 12 businesses, one of which invested in small businesses. After reading Phil's (unfinished) business plan, Mr. Dunleavy expressed an interest in investing, and agreed to provide a copy of his financial statements to send to Robert Hicks.

July, 2010: Received the past four years of Jerry's financial statements.

Now Phil picked up those statements to look at them again. (See Exhibits 1 and 2). Because they looked so good, Phil had visited the company and completed his research for his business plan.

With the plan in hand, he knew his next step would be to ask some experts to read the plan, and tell him what they thought of this investment opportunity.

EXHIBIT 1

Jerry's Famous Frozen Desserts Consolidated Income Statement
For the Years Ended 2006-2009 (in 000's)

	2006	%Sales	2007	%Sales	2008	%Sales	2009	%Sales
Sales	$ 2,100.0	100.0%	$ 2331	100.0%	$ 2611	100.0%	$ 2023	100.0%
Cost of Goods Sold								
Food and Supplies	336.0	16.0%	396.0	17.0%	444.0	17.0%	445.0	22.0%
Direct Labor	179.0	8.5%	186.0	8.0%	183.0	7.0%	142.0	7.0%
Spoilage	11.0	0.5%	12.0	0.5%	13.0	0.5%	70.0	3.5%
Overhead	357.0	17.0%	373.0	16.0%	418.0	16.0%	324.0	16.0%
Total Cost of Goods Sold	883.0	42.0%	967.0	41.5%	1,057.0	40.5%	980.0	48.4%
Gross Profit	**1,217.0**	**58.0%**	**1,364.0**	**58.5%**	**1,553.0**	**59.5%**	**1,043.0**	**51.6%**
Operational Expenses								
Depreciation	63.0	3.0%	70.0	3.0%	78.0	3.0%	61.0	3.0%
Administrative Expenses	147.0	7.0%	186.0	8.0%	209.0	8.0%	162.0	8.0%
Advertising	74.0	3.5%	140.0	6.0%	131.0	5.0%	101.0	5.0%
General	63.0	3.0%	70.0	3.0%	104.0	4.0%	61.0	3.0%
Total Operating Expenses	**347.0**	**16.5%**	**466.0**	**20.0%**	**522.0**	**20.0%**	**385.0**	**19.0%**
Income Before Taxes	870.0	41.4%	897.0	38.5%	1,031.0	39.5%	658.0	32.5%
Taxes	261.0	12.4%	269.0	11.5%	309.0	11.8%	236.0	11.7%
Net Income	**609.0**	**29.0%**	**628.0**	**26.9%**	**722.0**	**27.7%**	**423.0**	**20.9%**

EXHIBIT 2

Jerry's Famous Frozen Desserts Consolidated Balance Statement
For the Years Ended 2006-2009 (in 000's)

Assets	2006 $	%Assets	2007 $	%Assets	2008 $	%Assets	2009 $	%Assets
Cash	$125.0	8.9%	$200.0	11.1%	$240.0	11.9%	$125.0	5.4%
Inventory	40.0	2.9%	45	2.5%	50.0	2.5%	120.0	5.2%
Property and Equipment	1,200.0	85.7%	1,450.0	80.8%	1,600.0	79.4%	1,925.0	83.9%
Other	35.0	2.5%	100.0	5.6%	125.0	6.2%	125.0	5.4%
Total Assets	**1,400.0**	**100.0%**	**1,795.0**	**100.0%**	**2,015.0**	**100.0%**	**2,295.0**	**100.0%**
Liabilities and Net Worth								
Accounts Payable	35.0	2.5%	45.0	2.5%	50.0	2.5%	90.0	3.9%
Long-Term Debt	225.0	16.1%	350.0	19.5%	225.0	11.2%	250.0	10.9%
Letter-of-Credit	125.0	8.9%	100.0	5.6%	85.0	4.2%	75.0	3.3%
Deferred Taxes	20.0	1.4%	50.0	2.8%	50.0	2.5%	20.0	0.9%
Total Liabilities	**405.0**	**28.9%**	**545.0**	**30.4%**	**410.0**	**20.3%**	**435.0**	**19.0%**
Net Worth	**995.0**	**71.1%**	**1,250.0**	**69.6%**	**1,605.0**	**79.7%**	**1,860.0**	**81.0%**
Liabilities & Net Worth	**1,400.0**	**100.0%**	**1,795.0**	**100.0%**	**2,015.0**	**100.0%**	**2,295.0**	**100.0%**

201

THE BUSINESS PLAN

Robert Hicks and John Roberts, the founders of Jerry's Famous Frozen Desserts, did 18 months of research before starting their first frozen dessert store. Their initial location was an old deserted gas station in Austin, Texas. They financed their first store with $35,000 in savings, a Small Business Administration--backed loan of $55,000 from Texas Savings and Loan, and capital from their credit cards. In August, 2001, the pair had transformed the gas station into Jerry's Famous Frozen Desserts. Having been successful from the beginning, they attributed their profitability to high quality products, giving back to the community, and various forms of advertising such as word of mouth, radio stations, newspaper ads, and free press from business publications. As their stores increased in popularity, they expanded to three locations in the Austin area.

Jerry's sells high quality superpremium, regular, and low-fat ice cream. Their upscale products include sundaes, malts, shakes, cones, and soft-serve. They also sell a limited number of products (e.g. pints of ice cream) for the take-home market. The best selling products are soft-serve French silk and chocolate chip cookie dough. Jerry's products tend to have a more chocolate versus a fruit base. Their marketing research indicates the typical customer is between the ages of 24-45 years of age.

Several factors have contributed to Jerry's success. Establishing itself as the first upscale frozen dessert store in the Austin market in 2001 has given Jerry's the advantage of brand name recognition and first to market. People recognize the name Jerry's Famous Frozen Desserts. Others have tried to overtake their lead in the market but they have failed. Haagen-Dazs opened a store on University Boulevard two years ago, only to have it fail. Another regional chain out of Dallas, called Candee's Frozen Specialties also failed after one year.

Competitive pressures from other upscale, retail frozen dessert companies are also limited. The only other national chains which compete with Jerry's are Haagen-Dazs and Ben & Jerry's Homemade. Currently, Ben & Jerry's and Haagen-Dazs are currently not located in the Austin area.

A major contributing factor to the success of Jerry's is their superior products. Ingredients in their products are very high quality. The smooth (soft-serve) nature of Jerry's products is conducive to the needs of the fastest growing age segment in the U.S., 45-54 year olds. In addition, one of the owners, Robert Hicks, devotes 90 percent of his time to developing new types of products. Finally, Jerry's has developed an excellent reputation in Austin for its involvement with the community.

The following publicity and awards testify to the success of Jerry's Famous Frozen Desserts:

- Voted "Best in Business" for the month of June, 2009 by In Business magazine.

- Voted best in places for dessert (ice cream/frozen yogurt) in Austin, TX for 2007-2008, 2008-2009 by the Annual Guide to Austin.

- Voted "Best Ice Cream in Texas" by Texas Trails magazine, The Magazine of Life in Texas in 2009.

- Appeared in a 2009 feature article in the Austin Chronicle. Austin's daily newspaper.

AUSTIN DEMOGRAPHICS

Jerry's Famous Frozen Desserts is situated in beautiful Austin, Texas. The Austin area has consistently been ranked by Money magazine as one of the "Best Places to Live" in the United States. It is the capital of Texas and home to one of the largest and finest universities in the world, the University of Texas at Austin. Austin is located in Wilson County. The 2010 estimated population for Wilson County is 454,699 and for the city of Austin is 292,013 respectively. Projected increases in population are shown in Table 1. The median estimate for household income in 2010 was $50,000 for Wilson County and $45,000 for the city of Austin.

TABLE 1: PROJECTED POPULATION GROWTH FOR AUSTIN, TEXAS

Projection	Wilson County	% Increase	Austin	% Increase
1980	323,545		170,616	
1990	367,085	13%	190,766	12%
2000	416,088	13%	209,523	10%
2010	454,699	9%	292,013	39%
2020	488,515	7%	NA	

Source: Wilson County Regional Planning Commission and 2010 Census; figures include University of Texas at Austin Students.

THE U.S. FROZEN DESSERT INDUSTRY

Total sales for the frozen dessert industry in 2010 was over $15 billion. Growth of the industry will be in two areas: (1) full-fat products that appeal to indulgent consumers and (2) fat-free products that appeal to consumers' health and diet concerns.

Currently, 90 percent of U.S. households purchase ice cream with consumption peaking in the summer. Ice cream is traditionally one of the most popular and profitable desserts in the United States. A survey by Restaurants and Institutions in 2010 showed that 40 percent of operators' menus have hard ice cream, 30 percent offer sundaes, and more than 25 percent offer ice cream specialties.

Industry Structure and Products

The U.S. Frozen Dairy Dessert Industry is currently in its mature stage of the industry life-cycle. The market is segmented into the retail (dipping store) sector and the supermarket (take-home) sector. Recent attention has been emphasized on the supermarket sector where the likes of Colombo, TCBY, and Swensen's have entered the market. Profits are becoming harder to sustain in the supermarket sector due to the added competitive pressures from new firms entering the market.

Classification of various types of ice cream products is based on the percentage of butterfat and overrun (air content) content. Typically, higher quality ice creams contain fresh whole products, less air, and as much as 20 percent butterfat. The product segments are:

• Superpremium Ice Cream 16-20 percent butterfat and less than 40 percent overrun. A four ounce scoop had 260 calories. Examples: Jerry's Famous Frozen Desserts, Haagen-Dazs, Ben & Jerry's Homemade, and Frusen Gladje.

• Premium Ice Cream 12-16 percent butterfat and 40-60 percent overrun. A four-ounce scoop had 180 calories. Examples: Breyer's, Edy's, and Sealtest.

• Luxury Ice Cream Specialty brands that are the most expensive, like Godiva.

• Low Calorie/Low Fat Contains only 2-7 percent milk fat. Example: ice milk.

• Frozen Yogurt Only about 1.7 percent milk fat at 120-125 calories per cup. Examples: TCBY and I Can't Believe It's Yogurt.

• Novelty Products Bars, sticks, cones, sandwiches, parfaits. Account for 20-25 percent of total ice cream sales. Examples: Milky Way, Snickers, 3 Musketeers, Butterfingers, Nestle's Crunch, Bon Bons, and Dove Bar.

• Soft-Serve Ice Cream Typically this is ice milk (3-10 percent butterfat). Children comprise 50 percent of sales in this segment.

• Frozen Custard A form of ice cream that has a very high fat content, but not the highest. Example: Various frozen custard stores.

Industry Threats & Trends

The Census Bureau estimates the total U.S. population annual growth rate will slow down to a mere 0.9 percent/year in the future and the fastest growing age group will be the 45-54 year olds. The changing demographics of the U.S. could have a negative effect on the frozen dessert industry. As people increase in age, their taste preferences change, this could drastically affect the sales of frozen dessert companies unless they adapt to the older generation's needs. Older people still buy dessert items, but they tend to shy away from products full of nuts and candy. To combat this trend, Ben & Jerry's Homemade, has introduced a new line of "smoothie" ice cream. Therefore, Ben and Jerry's has appeased the taste buds of the older generation.

Currently, 30 percent of all family households are run by a single parent, of which 80 percent of those are women. The growing number of single-occupant and single-parent households combined with more working women and increased travel is fueling a shift in demand towards the away-from-home market for consumer food and beverage spending. This is a promising sign for the frozen dessert industry.

One of the biggest competitive pressures in the immediate future for the dipping store sector will be from supermarkets selling frozen dessert items. As more and more competitors enter supermarkets, consumers will have a larger base of products to choose from. Furthermore, buying desserts at the store will be more economical. As Bob Vranek, a family man from Charlotte, North Carolina states, "Why would I want to take my four kids to a TCBY store and spend $20 when I can go to the supermarket and buy a half gallon of frozen yogurt for $5.00? What would you do?"

During the 2000s, the U.S. frozen dessert industry has seen a redirection towards the health conscious consumer with the introduction of several new products (e.g. low fat and fat-free products). NutraSweet® was introduced as a substitute to replace sugar. In addition, frozen yogurt, which contained little butterfat, sugar, or cholesterol has become very popular in the 1990s and 2000s.

The current trend is the "split personality" in consumer taste preferences. Consumers want to eat healthy, but they want it to taste rich and creamy. There is an increasing demand for very rich and light products. This has left a shrinking demand for mid-range products. The current trend is towards richer, mix-in ingredient packed premium products and lighter, health-and diet-oriented products.

In high demand are low-fat ice creams, with no more than three grams of fat per serving. ConAgra, a major corporation that competes in the grocery segment in the frozen dessert industry reports there are 978 brands of regular and light ice cream, yogurt, and sherbert in the U.S. marketplace. Their Healthy Choice Premium Low-Fat Ice Cream ranks eighth in dollar sales. Their strategy is the continual development of new healthy products such as low-fat flavors like Malt Caramel Cone, Cappuccino Chunk, and Black Forest. According to Ken Colnar, director of marketing and sales for ConAgra, "The key to success is you need to give consumers what they want--an ice cream so rich and creamy that they forget its low in fat."

Further evidence of the trend away from ice cream is the frozen yogurt market, which is growing at a 12 percent annual rate (see Exhibit 3). New products are constantly being developed in the frozen yogurt market. Everything from fat-free fruit flavors to brands with chunks of nuts, brownies, and candy are being developed. Firms are developing two versions of frozen yogurt: one light line and another oriented towards indulgence.

EXHIBIT 3: FROZEN YOGURT SALES SOAR

Brand	Manufacturer	($millions)	% Change from Prior Year	Market Share
Private Label	----	$94.0	-4.2%	16.8%
Dreyer's/Edy's	Dreyer's	$74.5	34.9%	12.5%
Kemps	BolsWessanen	$61.7	13.1%	10.4%
Ben & Jerry's	B & J Homemade	$44.1	30.4%	7.4%
Breyers	Unilever	$36.3	6.4%	6.1%
Colombo	General Mills	$27.4	6.9%	4.6%
Haagen-Daz	Grand Metropolitan	$27.0	17.4%	4.6%

Due to the passage of the Nutrition Labeling and Education Act of 1990, which took effect in May, 1993, supermarket consumers will increasingly choose healthier products in the future. All products are required to list the calories and fat content on their labels. While the trend in supermarkets is changing, the effect of the Nutrition Labeling and Education Act on the dipping store segment is unknown at this time.

Competition in the U.S. Frozen Dessert Industry

Jerry's faces tough competition from two sectors, supermarkets and dipping stores.

Supermarkets:

Grand Metropolitan: Pet, Haagen-Dazs, and Baskin-Robbins.

Integrated Resources: Steve's Homemade Ice Cream, Swensen's, and Heidi's

Kraft General Foods: Sealtest, Breyer's, Borden, Colombo, Frusen Gladje, and TCBY.

Other competitors: Ben & Jerry's Homemade, Gelare, Breyer's, Friendly's, Dreyer's/Edy's, Mayfield's, Bassett's, Honey Hill Farms, Larrys, private local grocery brands, and other companies putting out novelty products (Bon Bons, Butterfinger, Dove, Eskimo, Milky Way, Nestle's Crunch, 3 Musketeers, Snickers).

Dipping Stores:

National Competitors: Ben & Jerry's Homemade, Haagen-Dazs, TCBY, Baskin Robbins, Colombo, Frusen Gladje, I Can't Believe It's Yogurt, and International Dairy Queen.

Regional Competitors: Honey Hill Farms, Swensen's, Friendly's, Steve's Homemade Ice Cream, Breyer's, and some other chains.

Competition of Dipping Stores in Austin, Texas:

Jerry's competition from national chains is limited in the Austin area. There are six International Dairy Queens and three TCBYs. There is a larger number of local competitors. Currently there are five Chocolate Ice Cream & Candy Stores, one Van Jordan's Ice Cream Co., two Mimi's Ice Cream Parlors, one Jamie's Chocolate Shoppe, and a variety of restaurants serving dessert items.

International Dairy Queen

Dairy Queen was founded in 1940 in Illinois and expanded through granting territory franchise rights for specific geographical areas. The company's current name, International Dairy Queen, was formed in 1962. The firm develops and services a system of quick-service restaurants, which are franchised by the company to offer hard and soft-serve ice cream, limited menu items, and beverages under Dairy Queen, Brazier, and other trademarks. The Brazier product line features hamburgers, hotdogs, barbecue, fish and chicken sandwiches, french fried potatoes, and onion rings. The Dairy Queen dairy dessert product lines include cones of various sizes as well as shakes, malts, sundaes and sodas, hardpacked products for home consumption, and specialty frozen confections (frozen ice cream cakes and logs). The products are prepared in the store from the company's specialty formulated ingredients.

The company currently has 5,790 franchised Dairy Queen units in the U.S., Canada, Japan, and several other countries. System-wide sales were over $2.1 billion. Dairy Queen has also diversified into the fast-food industry by acquiring the franchise rights to the following chains: Golden Skillet in 1981; Orange Julius in 1987; and Karmelkorn Shoppes, Inc. which sell popcorn, candy, and other treat items in 1986.

International Dairy Queen has implemented the "Treat Center" concept. This franchising concept combines Dairy Queen treat items, together with either or both Orange Julius and Karmelkorn menu items under one storefront within a shopping mall. The concept is based on the economies of leasing and improved sales volumes of the combined products. Currently, there are over 100 Treat Centers units, of which 87 were in the U.S. and 18 in Canada. The company franchised all the Treat Centers.

TCBY

TCBY® is the leading operator and franchisor of soft-serve frozen yogurt stores. Currently there are over 800 TCBY outlets. One-fourth of these are in non-traditional locations (e.g. airports, roadside travel plazas, hospitals, schools, and other non-commercial food service locations). TCBY's revenues come from the sale of frozen yogurt and yogurt products, company-owned yogurt shops, equipment sales, and franchise royalties and sales.

Ben & Jerry's Homemade: A Potential Entrant

Ben & Jerry's currently is not in the Austin area, however, the threat of entry remains very possible over the several years as Ben and Jerry's expands their franchising areas. If this were to occur, they would be a main competitor of Jerry's Famous Frozen Desserts.

Ben & Jerry's Homemade was founded in 1978 after Bennett R. Cohen, a college dropout, and friend Jerry Greenfield, took a $5.00 correspondence class on how to make ice cream. Since opening their first ice cream shop in an old empty gas station, Ben and Jerry's, Homemade Inc. has become a leading producer of superpremium ice cream, ice cream novelties, and both low-fat and non-fat frozen yogurt. Ben & Jerry's current strategies are:

- Differentiation: Utilizing the finest, high quality, all natural ingredients, they develop ice cream and yogurt products with large chunks of mix-ins. They differentiate themselves from the competition by having superior ingredients and a larger amount of mix-ins.
- Product Development: They have developed several original flavors such as Rainforest Crunch, Chocolate Chip Cookie Dough, Praline Pecan, Chunky Monkey, Wavy Gravy, and Cherry Garcia. They are continually developing new innovative products.
- Market Development: Since their inception, Ben & Jerry's has targeted two focus groups: (1) a frozen yogurt line oriented towards the health conscious customer and (2) a "Smooth, No Chunks" line oriented towards the 35-54 age group. A Ben & Jerry's spokesperson states that their most popular frozen yogurt flavors are versions of their rich ice cream flavors. Their new smooth no chunks line is oriented towards older customers who don't tend to like large pieces of mix-ins in their ice cream.
- Social Causes: Another primary cause for their success is their belief in giving back to society. Ben & Jerry's founded an organization entitled Ben & Jerry's Foundation, Inc., which gives 7.5 percent of their pre-tax profit to charities. The money assists causes like AIDS, homelessness, immigrant rights, environment, and sexual harassment.

- Geographical Expansion: They currently have over 100 franchises located all over the world. In addition, they sell their products in grocery stores all over the U.S. To cease the problem of competing with their franchises, Ben & Jerry's sells a limited variety of their products at the same price of franchisees. Ben & Jerry's was recently purchased by Unilever for $326 million. This is bound to have a negative effect on their corporate culture. Currently, Ben and Jerry's holds the number two market position with 43% of the superpremium ice-cream market compared with 54% for Haagen-Dazs.

JERRY'S WEAKNESSES, OPPORTUNITIES, AND THREATS

Weaknesses

One of the major weaknesses of Jerry's Famous Frozen Desserts is their current management. John Roberts, the business oriented partner, died in 2009. The remaining partner, Robert Hicks, is the creative part of the company. As a result of Robert's inexperience, within the last year, turnover at Jerry's has increased. This is thought to be the primary reason why Robert Hick's wants to sell the chain. The final weakness is the lack of products with different types of fruit in them. The menu is limited primarily to chocolate-based products.

Opportunities

Several opportunities exist for Jerry's. The most obvious is the huge potential for growth. Jerry's has a proven successful concept and product base. They have the potential to grow by opening new corporate stores and/or franchising. Jerry's also has the potential to grow through non-traditional forms (e.g. kiosk stands, carts, sell desserts at ballgames, concerts, and other entertainment venues). Home delivery also offers growth opportunities. Currently, no firm delivers upscale frozen dessert products in the Austin area.

Product development offers another avenue for growth. Jerry's needs to continually develop new products to differentiate itself from the competition. The potential to take some of these products and sell them in other markets (e.g. supermarkets and restaurants) is enormous.

Another opportunity for Jerry's is the rising population base of the Austin area. Austin is expected to increase its population by 4 percent per year from 2000 to 2010. The increase in the number of single-occupant and single-parent households will continue to fuel the trend toward away-from-home meals. In addition, the increasing number of two income families will allow higher income people the luxury of going out for desserts.

Since the fastest growth age group is the 45-54 year olds, Jerry's has the opportunity to take advantage of the growth in this population segment by emphasizing the "smooth" aspect of their ice cream products.

Threats

The major threat to Jerry's is the mature stage of the industry life-cycle with intense competition (from both supermarkets and dipping stores). Other threats are the increasing health consciousness of consumers, the aging population base which will bring a change in people's eating habits, the slowed population growth in the U.S., and the passage of the Nutrition Labeling and Education Act of 1990.

MANAGEMENT TEAM

Phil has gathered the following key people to be part of his management team following the acquisition. They have the experience and education to grow Jerry's into a national chain of frozen dessert stores.

Mr. Phil Hogan, CEO/President and Board Member

Mr. Hogan, age 36, holds both a B.S. (Accounting) and M.B.A. (Finance) from the University of Texas at Austin. Mr. Hogan is also a CPA. Mr. Hogan brings a wealth of industry experience to Jerry's. He spent three years as a certified public accountant with Peat, Marwick, Mitchell, & Company in Dallas. This was followed by two years at McDonald's Corporation where he was a senior internal auditor responsible for operational and financial audits of franchise restaurants. The audits focused on sales reporting, cash receipts, inventory controls, cash receipt and disbursement controls, and fraud reviews. After McDonald's, Mr. Hogan spent five years at Pfizer Laboratories in various positions like senior operations auditor, senior financial analyst, and marketing representative for their alternate site production sales force. Mr. Hogan currently lives in the Houston area.

Mr. George Harris, Consultant and Board Member

Mr. Harris, age 38, has both a B.S. and M.B.A. in Business Administration specializing in entrepreneurship and small business management from Babson College. Mr. Harris has been a successful entrepreneur for the past 15 years. His entrepreneurial background began by working in his family's restaurant, and followed with 10 years of other work experience in the restaurant industry. Currently, Mr. Harris owns two very successful restaurants in the Kansas City, Missouri area.

Dr. John Frank, Consultant and Board Member

Dr. Frank, age 55, holds both a B.S. and an M.B.A. in Accounting from San Diego State University. He also has a Ph.D. in Business Administration from the University of Wisconsin-Madison and is a CPA. Dr. Frank is both an entrepreneur and an educator. He has started and grown two successful companies. Dr. Frank is world renowned in the area of entrepreneurship and small business management. His current title is professor of management at the University of Texas at Austin Graduate School of Business.

Professional Advisors and Services

Accounting: The accounting firm that will be utilized in the acquisition process is the Austin Accounting Group. They will continue to be the accounting firm utilized following the acquisition.

Banking & Legal: Mr. Hogan has obtained the services of Doug Brady, an attorney in Austin to assist with the acquisition process. Legal advice is also being obtained from friends of Mr. Hogan's, Mr. Kevin Sizemore and Mr. Gordon Goldstrom. Banking services have also been retained from Mike Jones, a branch manager at SouthtWest Bank in Austin.

SUMMARY OF THE COMPANY

The company had a successful track record for the past eight years. The owner wanted out due to the death of his partner. Furthermore, even though the U.S. frozen dessert industry was in its mature stage, Jerry's had created a very profitable niche. One of the major players, Haagen-Daz, failed against Jerry's. Jerry's had sustained a strong brand name within Austin. Additionally, Austin was a great part of the country to be in. Warm weather, lakes, pretty country and apparently unlimited opportunity to grow the chain.

FIELD NOTES

These are the notes made by the consultants who Phil Hogan turned to first. This case is based on an actual business and these notes reflect the first step in a real consulting relationship.

Knowing of our background in this area, Phil Hogan called us when he began to write his business plan. We provided some guidance to him during the writing of the plan, and we helped him sketch plans for action: (See Exhibits 4 and 5).

EXHIBIT 4: Action Plan: Acquisition Process
- Continue the negotiation process and obtain financial statements from the company. Line up potential investor(s).
- Have accountant analyze financial statements for irregularities and place an estimated value on the company.
- Discuss negotiations and financials with attorney.
- Visit Jerry's: meet with owner; tour operations; interview customers, suppliers, and employees.
- Place a value on the company through financial and non-financial issues.

- Structure the deal.
- Write letter of intent.
- Negotiate the price of the business.
- Perform due diligence, write purchase agreement, and close the deal.
- Manage the acquisition.

EXHIBIT 5: Action Plan: Post-Acquisition Process

- Meet with employees and inform them of new management. Make them feel open enough to discuss problems, opportunities, threats, and weaknesses of the business. Let them know that the open communication is encouraged. I will have a cellular phone and the managers can contact me if an important issue arises.
- Obtaining information from employees, customers (satisfaction surveys), and suppliers will be critical in the success of the venture. These activities will be done within the first month after the acquisition.
- The following managerial techniques will be implemented after the acquisition: empowerment, decentralization, pay-for-performance, and manage by walking around (MBWA)--similar style to Sam Walton of Wal-Mart.
- Management will emphasize the design of a person's job: feedback from their job, skill variety, job identity, significance, and variety.
- A mission statement, objectives, and a new policy manual will be developed. Everyone in the company will have knowledge of the overall mission and objectives. Incentives will also be implemented for employees. The policy manual will be comprised of: expectations, compensation, employee rights, sexual harassment, health, safety issues, and other issues.
- A strong effort will be made to retain employees due to the high costs of turnover. Selection, recruitment, and retention will have special areas of focus for management.
- Lower-level employees will have incentives. These have not been determined, however some examples are: arriving for work every day on time will result in a 10 percent bonus at the end of the month; employees will be required to write one recommendation every week to assist the business (a prize for the best response will be given every month).
- A positive supportive culture will be instituted. The culture will emphasize profitability, concern for employees, the environment, and ethical conduct.

The next areas for discussion were financing and valuation. We explained to Phil that there are several ways to value companies and structure deals. Robert Hicks had previously stated that he needed at least $175,000/year after taxes. He stated that he would need at least $2 million in cash in order for this to occur. We shared the following general guidelines on financing with Phil:

FINANCING ALTERNATIVES FOR SMALL BUSINESS ACQUISITIONS

Small business acquisitions can be structured through debt, equity, or a combination of both. The following briefly reviews some of these options.

Debt Financing

These are loans obtained for the purchase of a small business. The most popular forms of debt financing are:

- **Savings, Friends, Family and Credit Cards:** Capital is obtained from savings, friends, family or credit cards.

- **Seller Financing:** A portion of the selling price of the business is financed through the seller. Seller financing is sometimes partially structured through a consulting contract, whereby the seller will continue to work for the company and receive a yearly salary.

- **Government Programs:** Federal, state, and local government loan programs (e.g. Small Business Administration and local economic development programs) have money available for small business acquisitions. These interest rates are usually cheaper than bank rates.

- **Commercial Banks:** Loans that are available from commercial banks. The problem with this source of money is that banks usually require collateral before they will allow you to borrow funds.

- **Mezzanine Financing:** This form of financing allows a bank to provide a term loan over an intermediate time period (e.g. usually 7 10 years) with an option to convert a balloon payment at the end into some equity ownership.

- **Asset Based Lenders (ABLs):** These are companies that lend money based on a percentage of an existing company's equipment, accounts receivable, cash flow, inventory, or other assets. They can be found in finance companies or departments of commercial banks.

Equity Financing

Equity capital is money in exchange for a percentage of ownership in a business. Some of the more popular forms of equity financing are:

- **Private Investors:** Comprised of family, friends, suppliers, accountants, customers, business associates, business professionals, or attorneys.

- **Venture Capital:** Money which can be obtained from private venture capital firms, Small Business Investment Companies (SBICs) and Minority Enterprise Small Business Investment Companies (MESBICs), venture capital subsidiaries of large financial institutions, and industrial corporations. The cost of capital is very high (30-50 percent/year).

- **SBICs:** Small Business Investment Companies (SBICs) are privately owned venture capital companies sponsored by the federal government. They provide straight debt or equity financing or a combination of both.

At our next meeting, we plan to discuss financing alternatives in more detail, and we plan to begin to explore the topic of valuation. We agreed to work with Phil on the topics of financing and valuation. In addition, we suggested that he contact his friends and business acquaintances for advice.

DISCUSSION QUESTIONS

1. What oddities existed in the financial statements for the company?

2. What are the forms of debt and equity financing available to Phil Hogan?

3. Structure a creative financial package on how you might finance the purchase of the chain.

4. How would you value the firm?

5. Would you purchase the chain? Why or why not?

Made in the USA
San Bernardino, CA
12 January 2018